The Recalcitrant *Imago Dei*

The Veritas Series

Belief and Metaphysics
Edited by Conor Cunningham and Peter M. Candler, Jr

Christ, History and Apocalyptic: The Politics of Christian Mission
Nathan R. Kerr

The Recalcitrant Imago Dei*: Human Persons and the Failure of Naturalism*
J. P. Moreland

Tayloring Reformed Epistemology: Charles Taylor, Alvin Plantinga and the de jure *Challenge to Christian Belief*
Deane-Peter Baker

Theology, Psychoanalysis, Trauma
Marcus Pound

Transcendence and Phenomenology
Edited by Conor Cunningham and Peter M. Candler, Jr

VERITAS

The Recalcitrant *Imago Dei*

Human Persons and the Failure of Naturalism

J. P. Moreland

scm press

in association with

The Centre of Theology and Philosophy
University of Nottingham

Published in 2009 by SCM Press
Editorial office
13–17 Long Lane,
London, EC1A 9PN, UK

SCM Press is an imprint of Hymns Ancient and Modern Ltd
(a registered charity)
St Mary's Works, St Mary's Plain,
Norwich, NR3 3BH, UK

www.scm-canterburypress.co.uk

British Library Cataloguing in Publication data

A catalogue record for this book is available from the British Library

978 0 334 04215 0

Typeset by Regent Typesetting, London
Printed and bound in Great Britain by
CPI Antony Rowe, Chippenham, Wiltshire

To Francis Beckwith
Sturdy lover of the *Imago Dei*

Contents

Centre of Theology and Philosophy

www.theologyphilosophycentre.co.uk

Every doctrine which does not reach the one thing necessary, every separated philosophy, will remain deceived by false appearances. It will be a doctrine, it will not be Philosophy.
Maurice Blondel, 1861–1949

This book series is the product of the work carried out at the Centre of Theology and Philosophy, at the University of Nottingham.

The COTP is a research-led institution organized at the interstices of theology and philosophy. It is founded on the conviction that these two disciplines cannot be adequately understood or further developed, save with reference to each other. This is true in historical terms, since we cannot comprehend our Western cultural legacy unless we acknowledge the interaction of the Hebraic and Hellenic traditions. It is also true conceptually, since reasoning is not fully separable from faith and hope, or conceptual reflection from revelatory disclosure. The reverse also holds, in either case.

The Centre is concerned with:

- The historical interaction between theology and philosophy.
- The current relation between the two disciplines.
- Attempts to overcome the analytic/Continental divide in philosophy.
- The question of the status of 'metaphysics'. Is the term used equivocally? Is it now at an end? Or have twentieth-century attempts to have a post-metaphysical philosophy themselves come to an end?
- The construction of a rich Catholic humanism.

I am very glad to be associated with the endeavours of this extremely important Centre that helps to further work of enormous importance. Among its concerns is the question whether modernity is more an interim than a completion – an interim between a pre-modernity in which the porosity between theology and philosophy was granted, perhaps taken for granted, and a postmodernity where their porosity must be unclogged and enacted anew. Through the work of leading theologians of international stature and philosophers whose writings bear on this porosity, the Centre offers an exciting forum to advance in diverse ways this challenging and entirely needful, and cutting-edge work.

Professor William Desmond (Leuven)

VERITAS

Series Introduction

'. . . the truth will set you free.' (John 8.32)

Pontius Pilate said to Christ, 'What is truth?' And He remained silent. In much contemporary discourse, Pilate's question has been taken to mark the absolute boundary of human thought. Beyond this boundary, it is often suggested, is an intellectual hinterland into which we must not venture. This terrain is an agnosticism of thought: because truth cannot be possessed, it must not be spoken. Thus, it is argued that the defenders of 'truth' in our day are often traffickers in ideology, merchants of counterfeits, or anti-liberal. They are, because it is somewhat taken for granted that Nietzsche's word is final: truth is the domain of tyranny.

Is this indeed the case, or might another vision of truth offer itself? The ancient Greeks named the love of wisdom as philia, or friendship. The one who would become wise, they argued, would be a 'friend of truth'. For both philosophy and theology might be conceived as schools in the friendship of truth, as a kind of relation. For like friendship, truth is as much discovered as it is made. If truth is then so elusive, if its domain is terra incognita, perhaps this is because it arrives to us – unannounced – as gift, as a person, and not some thing.

The aim of the Veritas book series is to publish incisive and original current scholarly work that inhabits 'the between' and 'the beyond' of theology and philosophy. These volumes will all share a common aspiration to transcend the institutional divorce in which these two disciplines often find themselves, and to engage questions of pressing concern to both philosophers and theologians in such a way as to reinvigorate both disciplines with a kind of interdisciplinary desire, often so absent in contemporary academe. In a word, these volumes represent collective efforts in the befriending of truth, doing so beyond the simulacra of pretend tolerance, the violent, yet insipid reasoning of liberalism that asks with Pilate,

What is truth? – expecting a consensus of non-commitment; one that encourages the commodification of the mind, now sedated by the civil service of career, ministered by the frightened patrons of position.

The series will therefore consist of two 'wings': 1, original monographs; and 2, essay collections on a range of topics in theology and philosophy. The latter will principally be the products of the annual conferences of the Centre of Theology and Philosophy (www.theologyphilosophycentre.co.uk)

Conor Cunningham
Peter Candler
Series editors

Acknowledgements

Several people have been instrumental in the publication of this work. Gratitude goes to Conor Cunningham for his enthusiastic support for the project. I am thankful to Joseph Gorra for his editorial work in preparing the manuscript for publication along with his helpful indexing. I am indebted to several people for their feedback or their published ideas each of which exerted a major influence on my own thinking about the issues addressed in the pages to follow: Francis Beckwith, Garry DeWeese, Stewart Goetz, David Horner, Mark Linville, Scott Rae, Victor Reppert, Scott Smith, Richard Swinburne, Charles Taliaferro.

I

Naturalism, Theism and Human Persons: Identifying the Central Crisis of Our Age

Storm clouds have cast an ominous, growing shadow on Western culture for some time now. The result is a crisis of epic proportions. The seeds for the crisis were sown in America by 1930, but it took until the 1960s for those seeds to leaven the public square. When the musical group Kansas released their song 'Dust in the Wind' in 1977, the words of the chorus gave expression to a growing suspicion, an existential, even if largely suppressed, angst: 'Dust in the wind, all we are is dust in the wind.' By contrast with the East, in which it is turtles all the way down, apparently, something in the twentieth-century water supply caused Westerners to believe it is air, earth, fire and water all the way down, at least under the sun (cf. Ecclesiastes 1).

The crisis cuts at the very heart of what it means to be and to live as a human person. Christian thinkers have not been unaware of the problem. In his seminal exposure of the issue in 1968, Protestant thinker Francis Schaeffer warned that with the emergence of the hard sciences as the only or vastly superior source of knowledge of reality, the 'mannishness of man' becomes lost, and the essence of human persons, their activities (significance, love) and their faculties (freedom, rationality), are forever placed in a non-rational, even irrational upper storey, forever lost to rational investigation.[1] On the Catholic side, Pope John Paul II's encyclical letter *Veritatis Splendor* proclaims that the emergence of naturalism and physicalism has effaced the Church's teaching that by the natural light of reason (supplemented with Holy Scripture) general revelation provides knowledge of important facts about the nature of human persons, rationality, freedom and moral action.[2]

Secular thinkers are wise to the crisis as well. Berkeley philosopher John Searle recently noted:

> There is exactly one overriding question in contemporary philosophy . . . How do we fit in? . . . How can we square this self-conception of ourselves as mindful, meaning-creating, free, rational, etc., agents with a universe that consists entirely of mindless, meaningless, unfree, nonrational, brute physical particles?[3]

Along similar lines, the former dean of Yale Law School, Anthony T. Kronman, not long ago argued that the rise of an exclusivist empirical, third-person approach to knowledge certified the hegemony of the hard sciences. The social sciences followed suit with the result that the humanities lost respect, and crucial questions about human persons, especially regarding the meaning of life, are now considered otiose and beyond rational investigation.[4]

Would that the impact of this crisis were limited to intellectuals, but such is not the case. It has affected Western culture generally. In 1941, Harvard sociologist Pitirim A. Sorokin wrote a book entitled *The Crisis of Our Age*. Sorokin divided cultures into two major types: *sensate* and *ideational*. A *sensate* culture is one in which people only believe in the reality of the physical universe capable of being experienced with the five senses. A sensate culture is secular, naturalistic, scientistic, this worldly, and empirical.

By contrast, an *ideational* culture embraces the sensory world, but goes on to accept the notion that an extra-empirical, immaterial reality can be known as well, a reality consisting of God, the soul, immaterial beings, values, purposes, and various abstract objects like numbers and propositions. Sorokin warned that a sensate culture eventually disintegrates because it lacks the intellectual resources necessary to sustain a public and private life conducive of corporate and individual human flourishing. After all, if we can't know anything about values, life after death, God, and so forth, how can we receive solid guidance to lead a life of wisdom and character?

Sorokin's warning has turned into a prophetic fulfilment. To cite one indicator of this, in 1979 Christopher Lasch's bestseller *The Culture of Narcissism* appeared on the scene. It remains one of the most insightful analyses of American culture I have ever read. Lasch analysed cultural patterns during the previous 21 years, and the book's subtitle was grim: *American Life in an Age of Diminished Expectations*. According to Lasch, beginning around 1958 therapists began to face an escalation of patients who did not suffer from any specific problem. Instead, they suffered from vague, ill-defined anxiety/depression that seemed 'to signify an underlying change in the organization of personality, from what has been called inner-direction to narcissism'.[5]

Here is Lasch's concluding description of the narcissistic personality ubiquitous in our culture: 'The ideology of [narcissistic] personal growth, superficial optimism, radiates a profound despair and resignation. It is the faith of those without faith.'[6] In referring to 'those without faith', Lasch is talking about the rise of scientific naturalism as our certified view of reality, and of secularism, along with religious scepticism, cynicism and indifference that goes with it. And secularism is responsible for the 'profound despair and resignation' that lies in the subconscious bosom of Western mankind.

Why the Crisis is to be Expected

One of the roles of a worldview is to provide an explanation of facts, of reality the way it actually is. Indeed, it is incumbent on a worldview that it explain what does and does not exist in ways that follow naturally from the core explanatory commitments of that worldview.

In this sense, we call a worldview an explanatory hypothesis. From worldview explanations of facts to scientific theorizing to explaining little things in everyday life (for example, why my daughter's room is messy), we all quite appropriately engage in 'if–then' reasoning or what philosophers call the Hypothetico-Deductive Method: If the moon were in such and such a place, then the tide would be thus and so. But the tide isn't thus and so, so the moon must not be in that place. If my daughter did not come straight home from school, she would not have had time to clean her room, the room is messy, so it is likely she did not come straight home from school. And so on.

Now, the dictionary defines 'recalcitrant' as 'being obstinately unco-operative, hard to handle or deal with'. A recalcitrant fact is one that is obstinately unco-operative in light of attempts to handle it by some theory. A theory may explain some facts quite nicely. But a recalcitrant fact doggedly resists explanation by a theory. No matter what a theory's advocate does, the recalcitrant fact just sits there and is not easily incorporated into the theory. In this case, the recalcitrant fact provides falsifying evidence for the theory.

One way to 'handle' recalcitrant facts is to deny them. Another is to proffer an ad hoc adjustment to one's theory. An ad hoc adjustment of a theory is an irrational, intellectually unacceptable adjustment of a theory whose sole rationale is to save it from falsifying evidence. As such, an ad hoc adjustment has no other independent reasons that can be offered on its behalf.

The Bible teaches that human beings are made in the image of God. This implies that there are things about our make-up that are like God is. At the beginning of his *Institutes of the Christian Religion*, John Calvin observed: 'No man can survey himself without forthwith turning his thoughts towards the God in whom he lives and moves; because it is perfectly obvious, that the endowments which we possess cannot possibly be from ourselves . . . '[7]

As image-bearers, human beings have all those endowments necessary to re-present and be representative of God, and to accomplish the tasks placed before them and exhibit the relationality into which they were meant to live, such as endowments of reason, self-determination, moral action, personality and relational formation. In this sense, the image of God is straightforwardly ontological. Even if we functionalize the image or treat it in largely relational terms, something that I am loath to do, it is still true that a thing's functional abilities or relational aptitudes are determined by its kindedness. Thus, even the functional, relational aspects of the image of God have ontological implications. There are two ways to accomplish such functionalization.[8] First, the image of God can be taken in the *representative* sense according to which humankind was made to represent God in his activity of ruling on the earth on God's behalf. Second, the image can be taken in the *relational* sense according to which it is constituted by certain important interpersonal relationships with God and other persons. It should be obvious that either approach presupposes the ontological understanding. Something can represent God in the way just specified only if it has certain powers and attributes apt for carrying out the appropriate representational activities. And an entity can stand in certain relations and not others depending on the kind of thing that entity is, and an entity flourishes in certain relations and not others depending on the sort of thing it is.

Given the ontological nature of the image of God, among other things, this implies that the makeup of human beings should provide a set of recalcitrant facts for other worldviews. The reasoning behind this claim goes like this: If Christianity is true, then certain features should characterize human beings. Those features do, in fact, characterize human beings. Thus, these features provide a degree of confirmation for Christianity. They characterize God and, moreover, come from Him. He made us to have them. The Christian offers a challenge to other worldviews – particularly, naturalism: Show that you have a better explanation for these features than Christianity does (with its doctrine of the image of God), or show that these features are not actually real, even though they seem to be.

Important examples of such features, and thus of such recalcitrant facts, are consciousness, free will, rationality, the self, intrinsic value and equal rights/dignity, the reality and nature of human meaning and flourishing. These features have stubbornly resisted reduction or elimination, or so I shall argue. Thus, they provide confirmation for biblical theism and evidence against scientific naturalism.

The Nature of Scientific Naturalism

At this point, it may be wise to look briefly at the nature of naturalism as a worldview to gain further insight into why these alleged recalcitrant facts are such a problem for naturalists. Naturalism usually includes

1 Different aspects of a naturalist epistemic attitude (for example, a rejection of so-called 'first philosophy' along with an acceptance of either weak or strong scientism).
2 A Grand Story which amounts to an aetiological account of how all entities whatsoever have come to be, told in terms of an

event causal story described in natural scientific terms with a central role given to the atomic theory of matter and evolutionary biology.

3 A general ontology in which the only entities allowed are those that either (a) bear a relevant similarity to those thought to characterize a completed form of physics or (b) are dependent on and determined by the entities of physics and can be explained according to the causal necessitation requirement (given a 'suitable' arrangement of matter, the emergent entity *must* arise) in terms of the Grand Story and the naturalist epistemic attitude.

For most naturalists, the ordering of these three ingredients is important. The naturalist epistemic attitude serves as justification for the naturalist aetiology, which, in turn, helps to justify the naturalist's ontological commitment. Moreover, naturalism seems to require coherence among the postulates of these three different areas of the naturalistic turn. David Papineau claims that we should set philosophy within science, in that philosophical investigation should be conducted within the framework of our best empirical theories. It follows that 'the task of the philosophers is to bring coherence and order to the set of assumptions we use to explain the empirical world'.[9] For example, there should be coherence among third-person scientific ways of knowing; a physical, evolutionary account of how our sensory and cognitive processes came to be; and an ontological analysis of those processes themselves. Any entities that are taken to exist should bear a relevant similarity to entities that characterize our best physical theories; their coming-to-be should be intelligible in light of the naturalist causal story; and they should be knowable by scientific means.

Scientism constitutes the core of the naturalist epistemology. Wilfrid Sellars said that 'in the dimension of describing and explaining the world, science is the measure of all things, of what is that it is, and of what is not that it is not.'[10] Contemporary naturalists embrace either weak or strong scientism. According to the former, nonscientific fields are not worthless nor do they offer no intellectual results, but they are vastly inferior to science in their epistemic standing and do not merit full credence. According to the latter, unqualified cognitive value resides in science and in nothing else. Either way, naturalists are extremely sceptical of any claims

rp C
rp C
rp C
C
p C
p C
p C
rp C
rp C
rp C
p C
p C
rp C

J.P. Mooreland

"Recalcitrant Imago Dei"

Andy

outoftheashe@gmail

(414) 322-1306

about reality that are not justified by scientific methodology in the hard sciences.

For example, that methodology is a third-person one that sanctions only entities capable of exhaustive description from a third-person perspective. Scepticism prevails for entities that require the first-person perspective as their basic mode of epistemic access. For such naturalists, the exhaustive or elevated nature of scientific knowledge entails that either the only explanations that count, or the ones with superior, unqualified acceptance, are those employed in the hard sciences.[11] At least two philosophical theses elaborate the naturalistic epistemic and methodological constraints for philosophy. First, there is no such thing as first philosophy (a subject matter with respect to which philosophy is autonomous from and authoritative in comparison to science); rather, there is continuity between philosophy and natural science. Second, scientific theories that are paradigm cases of epistemic/explanatory success, such as the atomic theory of matter, or evolutionary biology, employ combinatorial modes of explanation. Thus any process that constitutes the Grand Story and any entity in the naturalist ontology should exhibit an ontological structure analysable in terms that are isomorphic with such modes of explanation. Colin McGinn has defended this idea along with what he takes it to entail, namely the inability of naturalism to explain genuinely unique emergent properties:

> Can we gain any deeper insight into what makes the problem of consciousness run against the grain of our thinking? Are our modes of theorizing about the world of the wrong shape to extend to the nature of mind? I think we can discern a characteristic structure possessed by successful scientific theories, a structure that is unsuitable for explaining consciousness . . . Is there a 'grammar' to science that fits the physical world but becomes shaky when applied to the mental world?
>
> Perhaps the most basic aspect of thought is the operation of *combination*. This is the way in which we think of complex entities as resulting from the arrangement of simpler parts. There are three aspects to this basic idea: the atoms we start with, the laws we use to combine them, and the resulting complexes . . . I think it is clear that this mode of understanding is central to

> what we think of as scientific theory; our scientific faculty involves representing the world in this combinatorial style.[12]

In sum, the naturalist epistemic attitude countenances, and only countenances:

1. the hard sciences along with mathematical empiricism as the paradigm of knowledge;
2. a certification of third-person ways of knowing while eschewing the first-person;
3. an employment of combinatorial modes of explanation for the nature, coming-to-be and perishing of all macro-wholes above the basic level of micro-physical particles (waves, wavicles, strings, or whatever; hereafter, simply 'particles'); and
4. a rejection of first philosophy.

Let us call the naturalist creation account the 'Grand Story': all of reality – space, time, and matter – came from the Big Bang, and various heavenly bodies developed as the universe expanded. On at least the earth, some sort of pre-biotic soup scenario explains how living things came into being from non-living chemicals. And the processes of evolution, understood in either neo-Darwinian or punctuated equilibrium terms, gave rise to all the life forms we see including human beings. Thus, all organisms and their parts exist and are what they are because they contributed to (or at least did not hinder) the struggle for reproductive advantage, more specifically, because they contributed to the tasks of feeding, fighting, fleeing, and reproducing.

The Grand Story has three key features. First, at its core are two theories that result from combinatorial modes of explanation: the atomic theory of matter and evolutionary theory. If we take John Searle to be representative of naturalists here, this means that causal explanations, specifically bottom-up but not top-down causal explanations, are central to the (alleged) explanatory superiority of the Grand Story.[13]

Second, it expresses a scientistic philosophical monism according to which everything that exists or happens in the world is susceptible to explanations by natural scientific methods. Prima facie, the most consistent way to understand naturalism in this regard is to see it as entailing some version of strong physicalism: everything that exists is fundamentally matter, most likely, elementary 'particles' (whether taken as points of potentiality, centres of mass/energy, units of spatially extended stuff/waves or reduced to/eliminated in favour of fields), organized in various ways according to the laws of nature. By keeping track of these particles and their physical traits we are keeping track of everything that exists. No non-physical entities exist, including emergent ones. When naturalists venture away from strong physicalism, however, they still argue that additions to a strong physicalist ontology must be depicted as rooted in, emergent from, dependent upon the physical states and events of the Grand Story.

Third, the Grand Story is constituted by event causality and eschews both irreducible teleology and agent causation in which the first relatum of the causal relation is in the category of substance and not event. In this sense, at the fundamental level of analysis, the only sort of causality permitted is mechanical and efficient-causal. And the Grand Story is deterministic in two senses: diachronically such that the state of the universe at any time t coupled with the laws of nature determine or fix the chances for the state of the universe at subsequent times; synchronically such that the features of and changes regarding macro-wholes are dependent on and determined by micro-phenomena.

Finally, it is important to say a bit more about naturalist ontological commitments. A good place to start is with what Frank Jackson calls the location problem.[14] According to Jackson, given that naturalists are committed to a fairly widely accepted physical story about how things came to be and what they are, the location problem is the task of locating or finding a place for some entity (for example, semantic contents, mind, agency) in that story. As an illustration, Jackson shows how the solidity of macro-objects can be located within a naturalist worldview. If solidity is taken as impenetrability, then given the lattice structure of atoms composing, say, a table and chair, it becomes obvious why they cannot penetrate each other. Given the naturalist micro-story, the macro-world could not have been different: the table could not penetrate the chair. Location is necessitation.

So, again, we see three constraints for developing a naturalist ontology and locating entities within it:

1 Entities should conform to the naturalist epistemology.
2 Entities should conform to the naturalist Grand Story.
3 Entities should bear a relevant similarity to those found in chemistry and physics or be shown to depend (with metaphysical or nomological necessity) on entities in chemistry and physics.

Regarding the naturalist epistemology, all entities should be knowable by third-person scientific means. Regarding the Grand Story, one should be able to show how any entity had to appear in light of the naturalist event causal story according to which the history of the cosmos amounts to a series of events governed by natural law in which micro-parts come together to form various aggregates with increasingly complex physical structures.

We are now in a position to comment about naturalism and various forms of emergence. An emergent property is a completely unique, new kind of property different from those that characterize its subvenient base. Accordingly, emergent supervenience is the view that the supervenient property is a simple, intrinsically characterizable, novel property different from and not composed of the parts, properties, relations and events at the subvenient level. We may characterize 'novel' as follows:

> Property P is a *novel* emergent property of some particular x at level l_n just in case P is an emergent property, x exemplifies P, and there are no determinates P′ of the same determinable D as P such that some particular at level $l_{i = 1-(n-1)}$ exemplifies P or P′.[15]

A structural property is one that is constituted by the parts, properties, relations and events at the subvenient level. A structural property is identical to a configurational pattern among the subvenient entities. It is not *sui generis*.

The most consistent form of naturalism is strong physicalism according to which all particulars, laws, properties and relations are physical. This is because the various constraints on the naturalist ontology strongly suggest that these and only these sorts of entities will exist. But some naturalists have ventured into various forms of emergentism. In the category of individual, if we reject an eliminativist strategy, then all wholes 'above' the microphysical level are structural, relational entities constituted by the parts, properties and external relations at the micro-physical level. Such wholes stand in a constituent/whole relation to these micro-physical entities and are actually wider entities at the basic level. Regarding the category of property, consider the following:

Emergence$_0$: New features that can be deduced from base (e.g., fractals).

Emergence$_1$: Ordinary structural properties (e.g., being water, solidity).

Emergence$_{2a}$: *Sui generis*, simple, intrinsically characterizable, new kinds of properties relative to base that are also epiphenomenal (e.g., being painful construed epiphenomenally).

Emergence$_{2b}$: *Sui generis*, simple, intrinsically characterizable, new kinds of properties relative to base with new causal powers construed as passive liabilities (e.g., being painful understood as having top-down causal liabilities).

Emergence$_{2c}$: *Sui generis*, simple, intrinsically characterizable, new kinds of properties with conscious active power and rationality.

Emergence$_3$: An emergent, suitably unified mental ego with conscious active power and rationality.

Emergence$_4$: An emergent, suitable unified mental ego with conscious active power and rationality, capable of moral action and exhibiting high, equal value/rights as other such egos.

Clearly, emergence$_0$ and emergence$_1$ fit nicely in the naturalist mereological hierarchy and conform to the naturalist epistemology (e.g., combinatorial explanation) and Grand Story. But emergence$_{2a}$ through emergence$_4$ should be disallowed for reasons we have already mentioned. It would seem that all a naturalist could do with them is simply to label them as contingent brute facts and assert that they are not a problem for the naturalist. In my view, we have reasons to be highly suspicious of a naturalist view that accepts one or more of these sorts of properties and also claims that naturalism is explanatorily and epistemically superior to alternative worldviews. These properties defy naturalist explanation and they provide confirmation for biblical theism construed as a rival to naturalism.

Moreover, there is an increasingly heavy burden of proof on a naturalist ontology as one moves from emergence$_{2a}$ to emergence$_4$. All types of emergence fall prey to previous arguments against emergent entities (e.g., you cannot generate a new kind of simple property from combinatorial processes involving entities bereft of these properties and which merely rearrange according to external relations). Emergence$_{2a}$ requires less justification than stronger forms of emergence because it does not require a rejection of closure. Emergence$_{2b}$ is subject to these arguments and additional difficulties with top-down causation and causal closure. But relative to emergence$_{2c}$ and emergence$_3$ it has the advantage of exhibiting the same sort of causal power – passive liability subject to law – that characterizes causal particulars at the micro-physical level.

Emergence$_{2c}$ has all the problems exemplified by emergence$_{2b}$ and it also suffers from having a unique sort of active causal power different from causal powers of the naturalist ontology besides agent causal events. Emergence$_3$ shares difficulties with emergence$_{2c}$ and it also suffers from two further facts not easily accommodated in the naturalist ontology if they are taken as irreducible and uneliminable facts about the world: the indexical fact associated with 'I' and difficulties with explaining how one can get a sort of primitive, substantial unity in which its various inseparable parts/faculties are internally related to the substantial subject from a mereological aggregate constituted by a structural arrangement of separable parts that stand in external relations to each other and their mereological whole. Emergence$_4$ adds the whole problem of the existence and instantiation of intrinsic value, the problem of grounding high, equal value/rights, and the need for faculties apt for moral knowledge and action.

Prospectus

In light of what we have seen, it should be clear that there is a problem. It is generated by the hegemony of naturalism and it is focused on what to do with human persons in light of this culturally certified framework. To cite one more figure, Crispin Wright notes:

> A central dilemma in contemporary metaphysics is to find a place for certain anthropocentric subject-matters – for instance, semantic, moral, and psychological – in a world as conceived by modern naturalism: a stance which inflates the concepts and categories deployed by (finished) physical science into a metaphysics of the kind of thing the real world essentially and exhaustively is. On one horn, if we embrace this naturalism, it seems we are committed either to reductionism: that is, to a construal of the reference of, for example, semantic, moral and psychological vocabulary as somehow being within the physical domain – or to disputing that the discourses in question involve reference to what is real at all. On the other horn, if we reject this naturalism, then we accept that there is more to the world than can be embraced within a physicalist ontology – and so take on a commitment, it can seem, to a kind of eerie supernaturalism.[16]

As is often said, there it is. Postmodernism is not the way forward and here's why. According to postmodernism, the self is a social construction, a creation of language, a reification of the first person pronoun 'I' and, as such, the self is a culturally relative, historically conditioned construct. As Philip Cushman asserts, 'there is no universal, transhistorical self, only local selves; no universal theory about the self, only local theories'.[17]

Besides the fact that this is hardly a robust view of human persons and it is wildly at odds with Scripture, a problem for those of us working in a biblical tradition, two things follow from this. First, there is no unity to the self and no enduring ego.[18] Rather the self is a bundle of social roles and relations that are expressions of the arbitrary flux of the group. This has disastrous implications for helping people separate and individuate in any objective sense. If postmodernism is true, all that can happen is for a struggling person to disown one arbitrary socially constructed self while standing in another one. One wonders if such a trip is worth the effort. Further, on this view there is no point in owning one's pathologies, since it is always open to a patient simply to distance from an arbitrary, fleeting constructed self in which the pathology is embedded.

Second, as postmodern critic Terry Eagleton points out, since the self is a passive social construction, 'there are no subjects sufficiently coherent to undertake . . . actions'.[19] Active agency and free action disappear under the postmodern cloud of constructivism. Thus, postmodern thought is on a collision course with important developments in psychological theory during the last ten years that have emphasized the self as an active, free agent. Moreover, as Immanuel Kant wisely noted, the goal of the moral life and, presumably, of therapy, is the production of a good will, of a person who freely and rationally chooses to live a virtuous life that honours the moral law. If this goal is removed from the table, as it must be for postmodernists, it becomes opaque as to just exactly what people are trying to accomplish when they (falsely) take themselves to be choosing to grow as people.

In my opinion, the way forward is to embrace theistic realism and show that it is not the sort of 'eerie supernaturalist' caricature that Wright and other naturalists falsely paint. By 'theistic realism' I have in mind Tom Morris's description:

> [T]he Judeo-Christian religious tradition, is not just a domain of poetry, imagery, mystical transport, moral directive, and noncognitive, existential self-understanding. Interacting especially with the philosophically developed tradition of Christian theology, [I] join the vast majority of other leading contributors to contemporary philosophical theology in taking for granted *theological realism*, the cognitive stance presupposed by the classical theistic concern to direct our thoughts as well as our lives aright. It has been the intent of theologians throughout most of the history of the Christian faith to describe correctly, within our limits, certain important facts about God, human beings, and the rest of creation given in revelation and fundamental to the articulation of any distinctively Christian world view. In particular, reflective Christians throughout the centuries have understood their faith as providing key insights into, and resources for, the construction of a comprehensive metaphysics.[20]

In the remainder of this book, we shall seek to apply a theological realist stance to the task of probing the tension between naturalism and human persons. I am eager to show that, in actual fact, several features of human persons are recalcitrant facts for naturalism and provide evidence for Judaeo-Christian monotheism. In this chapter we have examined limitations on a naturalist ontology that follow from naturalism itself taken as a worldview epistemically/explanatorially superior to its rivals. Let N stand for the truth of naturalism and $Emergence_{2a}$. In the terms of epistemic appraisal proffered by Chisholm, it seems that, ¬(N & $Emergence_{2a}$) is at least *epistemically in the clear* where a proposition is *epistemically in the clear* provided only that subject S is not more justified in withholding that proposition than in believing it. Alternatively, it is at least *reasonable to disbelieve* (N & $Emergence_{2a}$) (S is not more justified in withholding that proposition than in disbelieving it).[21] And one would be more justified in disbelieving the conjunction of N with deeper grades of emergence as listed above.

However, there are additional limits for a naturalist ontology when a plausible rival worldview is brought into the picture. As Timothy O'Connor points out, emergent properties, especially mental properties, must be shown to arise by way of causal necessitation from a micro-physical base if we are to 'render emergent phenomena naturalistically explicable'.[22] Among his reasons is the idea that if the link between micro-base and emergent properties is a contingent one, then the only explanation for the existence and constancy of the link is a theist explanation.[23] O'Connor's claim seems to me to be correct, and the presence of a rival hypothesis, in this case biblical theism, provides additional reasons for rejecting naturalism, given the various recalcitrant facts in view, because they not only provide disconfirming evidence against naturalism, they also provide confirming evidence for its rival.

In the terms of epistemic appraisal proffered by Chisholm, it seems that, given biblical theism and what we have seen about the naturalist ontology, ¬(N & $Emergence_{2a}$) is at least *beyond reasonable doubt* where a proposition being *beyond reasonable doubt* for a subject S means that S is more justified in believing that proposition than in withholding it. Alternatively, given biblical theism, (N & $Emergence_{2a}$) is at least *reasonable to disbelieve* (S is more justified in disbelieving that proposition than in withholding it).[24]

Let us begin in earnest, then, and see what we can learn about the cosmos from the fact of human (and animal) consciousness.

2

Naturalism, Consciousness and Human Persons

A major burden of the pages to follow is to present and defend an argument that the existence of God is the best explanation for finite examples of consciousness in creatures such as humans and various animals. Finite consciousness provides strong evidence that God exists. Part of my defence will involve showing that scientific naturalism is utterly incapable in principle of providing any explanation whatever for finite consciousness. The scientifically, indeed, the culturally authorized naturalist story of how all things came about revolves around the atomic theory of matter and evolutionary theory. As Phillip Johnson observes,

> The materialist story is the foundation of all education in all the departments in all the secular universities, but they do not spell it out. It is
>
> In the beginning were the particles and the impersonal laws of physics.
> And the particles somehow became complex living stuff;
> And the stuff imagined God;
> But then discovered evolution.[1]

According to the atomic theory of matter, all chemical change is the result of the rearrangement of tiny little parts – protons, neutrons and electrons. According to evolutionary theory, random mutations are largely responsible for providing an organism with a change in characteristics, some of which provide the organism with a survival advantage over other members of its species; as a result, the organism's new traits eventually become ubiquitous throughout the species.

To recall a point made in Chapter 1, this story is physically deterministic in two ways. First, the physical state of the universe (and everything in it, including you) at a particular time and the impersonal laws of nature are sufficient to determine or fix the chances of the next successive state. This is temporal determination. Second, the features and behaviour of ordinary-sized objects like glaciers, rocks, human beings and animals is fixed by the states of their atomic and subatomic parts. This is bottom-up or parts-to-whole determinism. If genuinely mental consciousness exists, it is a causally impotent epiphenomenon. Among other things, this means that a feeling of thirst never causes someone to get a drink; thoughts and beliefs play no role in directing or bringing about our behaviour. Many philosophers rightly think that if a view implies epiphenomenalism, the view must be rejected.

It is also a strictly physical story. And that is where a second, and most fundamental problem of consciousness enters the picture. If you begin with matter and simply rearrange it according to physical laws by means of strictly physical causes and processes, then you will end up with increasingly different arrangements of – you guessed it – matter. Start with matter and tweak it physically and all you will get is tweaked matter. This is especially true if the tweaking amounts to the rearrangement of the same entities into new external relations. There is no need or room for mind and consciousness to enter the picture. However, if you begin with the Logos, then Mind is the fundamental reality and its appearance in cosmic history is not an ontological problem as it is for the scientific naturalist. But we are getting ahead of ourselves.

The problem of the origin of consciousness has been around ever since the crowning of the mechanical, atomistic philosophy in the seventeenth century. A leader of that movement was chemist Robert Boyle, and there were several things Boyle believed could not be explained by matter and its various forms. And one of them was mind:

> I must profess to you that I make a great doubt whether there be not some phenomena in nature which the atomists cannot satisfactorily explain by any figuration, motion, or connection of material particles whatsoever: for some faculties and operations of the reasonable soul in man are of so peculiar and transcendent

> a kind that, as I have not yet found them solidly explicated by corporeal principles, so I expect not to see them in haste made out by such. And if a spiritual substance be admitted to enter the composition of a man and to act by and upon his body, . . . it will appear that an incorporeal and intelligent being may work upon matter: which would argue at least a possibility that there may be a spiritual Deity, and that he may intermeddle with and have an influence upon the operations of things corporeal.[2]

From a naturalist perspective, then, consciousness is among the most mystifying features of the cosmos. Geoffrey Madell opines that 'the emergence of consciousness, then is a mystery, and one to which materialism signally fails to provide an answer.'[3] Naturalist Colin McGinn claims that its arrival borders on sheer magic because there seems to be no naturalistic explanation for it:

> How can mere matter originate consciousness? How did evolution convert the water of biological tissue into the wine of consciousness? Consciousness seems like a radical novelty in the universe, not prefigured by the after-effects of the Big Bang; so how did it contrive to spring into being from what preceded it?[4]

Finally, naturalist William Lyons argues that

> [physicalism] seem[s] to be in tune with the scientific materialism of the twentieth century because it [is] a harmonic of the general theme that all there is in the universe is matter and energy and motion and that humans are a product of the evolution of species just as much as buffaloes and beavers are. Evolution is a seamless garment with no holes wherein souls might be inserted from above.[5]

Lyons's reference to souls being 'inserted from above' appears to be a veiled reference to the explanatory power of theism for consciousness. Some argue that, while finite mental entities may be inexplicable on a naturalist worldview, they may be explained by theism, thereby furnishing evidence for God's existence. In this chapter, I shall defend this argument from consciousness (hereafter, AC) by describing two relevant issues in scientific theory acceptance, presenting a summary of AC, characterizing naturalism and showing why mental entities are recalcitrant facts for naturalists and evaluating three explanations of consciousness that serve as rivals for AC.

While the origin of consciousness is at the centre of a storm, the nature of consciousness is pretty commonsensical. Suppose you are in the recovery room immediately after surgery. You are still deeply under anaesthesia. Suddenly and somewhat faintly, you begin to hear sounds. It is not long until you can distinguish two different voices. You begin to feel a dull throb in your ankle. The smell of rubbing alcohol wafts past your nose. You remember a childhood accident with the same smell. You feel an aversion towards it. You feel thirsty and desire a drink. As you open your eyes to see a white ceiling above, you begin to think about getting out of the hospital. What is going on? The answer is simple: You are regaining consciousness.

Note two things about this example. First, whereas any physical object (state, process, property, relation) can and only can be completely described from within a third-person perspective, descriptions of states of consciousness require an approach from within the first-person point of view. Second, states of consciousness are best defined ostensively: by citing, pointing to specific examples. Both of these observations are exactly what the dualist approach to consciousness would predict.

At least five kinds of conscious states exist. A *sensation* is a state of awareness or sentience, such as a conscious awareness of sound or pain. Some sensations are experiences of things outside me like a tree or the colour red. Others are awarenesses of states within me like pains. Emotions are a sub-class of sensations and, as such, they are forms of awareness of things. I can be aware of something in an angry way. A *thought* is a mental content that can be expressed in an entire sentence. Some thoughts logically imply other thoughts. For example, 'All dogs are mammals' entails 'This dog is a mammal'. If the former is true, the latter must be true. Some thoughts don't entail, but merely provide evidence for other thoughts. For example, certain thoughts about evidence in a court case provide grounds for the thought that a person is guilty. Thoughts are the sorts of things that can be true or false, reasonable or unreasonable. A *belief* is a person's view, accepted to varying degrees of strength, of how things really are. A *desire* is a certain felt inclination to do, have, or experience certain things or to avoid such. An *act of will* is a choice, an exercise of power, an endeavouring to act, usually for the sake of some purpose.

Are properties such as being a pain or being a thought, and the events composed of them (a specific occurrence of a pain or a particular thought) genuinely mental or are they physical? Property dualists argue that mental states are not physical since they possess five features not owned by physical states:

1. There is a raw qualitative feel or a 'what-it-is-like' to have a mental state such as a pain.
2. At least many mental states have intentionality – *ofness* or *aboutness* – directed towards an object.
3. Mental states are inner, private and immediate to the subject having them.
4. Mental states require a subjective ontology – namely, mental states are necessarily owned by the first-person sentient subjects who have them.
5. Mental states fail to have crucial features (e.g., spatial extension, location) that characterize physical states and, in general, cannot be described using physical language.

There is a very crucial observation to make about material substances, properties, processes, relations and events: *No material entity presupposes or requires reference to consciousness for it to exist or be characterized.* You will search in vain through a physics or chemistry textbook to find consciousness included in any description of matter. A completely physical description of the world would not include *any* terms that make reference to or characterize the existence and nature of consciousness.

Let's assume that matter is actually like what our chemistry and physics books tell us it is. Now imagine that there is no God and picture a universe in which no conscious, living beings came-to-be. In such an imaginary world, there would be no consciousness anywhere in the universe. However, in this imaginary world, matter would still exist and be what scientists tell us it is. Carbon atoms would still be carbon atoms; electrons would still have negative charge. An electron is still an electron regardless of whether or not conscious minds exist in the world. This is what we mean when we say that the existence and nature of matter are independent of the existence of consciousness. This should make us very sceptical when physicalists claim that our conscious mental life is nothing but a series of physical events in our brain and nervous system.

Given an accurate description of consciousness (see above), it becomes clear that mental properties/events are not identical to physical properties/events. Mental states are characterized by their intrinsic, subjective, inner, private, qualitative feel, made present to a subject by first-person introspection. For example, a pain is a certain felt hurtfulness. The true nature of mental states cannot be described by physical language, even if through study of the brain one can discover dependency relations between mental/brain states. In addition to the 1–4 above, mental states have some or all of the following features, none of which is a physical feature of anything. Thoughts can be true or false, but it makes no sense to say that a brain state, body movement or anything physical is true or false. Thoughts, beliefs, desires and sensations have intentionality – they are of or about objects – but physical states aren't about anything. They just are. Some sensations are vague, for example, a sensation of an object may be fuzzy or vague, but no physical state is vague. Some sensations are pleasurable or unpleasurable, but nothing physical has these properties. A cut in the knee is, strictly speaking, not unpleasurable. It is the pain event caused by the cut that is unpleasurable. Mental states can have the property of familiarity (such as when a desk looks familiar to someone), but familiarity is not a feature of a physical state. Since mental states have these features and physical states do not then mental states are not identical to physical states.

Necessitation and physical causal explanations in realist construals of natural science

Though some demur, at least five reasons have been proffered for the claim that causal explanations in the natural sciences exhibit a kind of causal necessity, that on a typical realist construal of natural science, physical causal explanations must show – usually by citing a mechanism – why an effect *must* follow given the relevant causal conditions:

1 Causal necessitation unpacks the deepest, core realist notion of causation, namely, causal production according to which a cause 'brings about' or 'produces' its effect.
2 Causal necessitation fits the paradigm cases of causal explanation (e.g., macro-solidity/impenetrability in terms of micro-lattice structures, repulsive forces; mass proportions in chemical reactions in terms of atomic models of atoms/molecules, bonding orbitals, energy stability, charge distribution) central to the core theories (e.g., the atomic theory of matter) that constitute a naturalist worldview and in terms of which it is purported to have explanatory superiority to rival worldviews.
3 Causal necessitation provides a way of distinguishing accidental generalizations from true causal laws.
4 Causal necessitation supports the derivation of counterfactuals (if that chunk of gold had been placed in aqua regia, then it would have dissolved) from causal laws (gold dissolves in aqua regia).
5 Causal necessitation clarifies the direction of causality and rules out the attempt to explain a cause by its effect.

The Argument from Consciousness

AC may be expressed in inductive or deductive form. As an inductive argument, AC may be construed as claiming that given theism and naturalism as the live options fixed by our background beliefs, theism provides a better explanation of consciousness than naturalism and, thus, receives some confirmation from the existence of consciousness.

AC may also be expressed in deductive form. Here is one deductive version of AC:

(1) Genuinely non-physical mental states exist.
(2) There is an explanation for the existence of mental states.
(3) Personal explanation is different from natural scientific explanation.
(4) The explanation for the existence of mental states is either a personal or natural scientific explanation.
(5) The explanation is not a natural scientific one.

(6) Therefore, the explanation is a personal one.
(7) If the explanation is personal, then it is theistic.
(8) Therefore, the explanation is theistic.

Theists such as Robert Adams[6] and Richard Swinburne[7] have advanced a slightly different version of AC which focuses on mental/physical correlations and not merely on the existence of mental states. Either way, AC may be construed as a deductive argument.

Premises (2), (4) and (5) are the ones most likely to come under attack. Before I address them, I should say a word about (3), which turns on the fact that personal explanation differs from event causal covering law explanations employed in natural science. Associated with *event* causation is a covering law model of explanation according to which some event (the *explanandum*) is explained by giving a correct deductive or inductive argument for that event. Such an argument contains two features in its *explanans*: a (universal or statistical) law of nature *and* initial causal conditions.

By contrast, a *personal* explanation (divine or otherwise) of some state of affairs brought about intentionally by a person will employ notions such as the intention of the agent and the relevant power of the agent that was exercised in causing the state of affairs. In general, a personal explanation of some basic result R brought about intentionally by person P where this bringing about of R is a basic action A will cite the intention I of P that R occur and the basic power B that P exercised to bring about R. P, I, and B provide a personal explanation of R: agent P brought about R by exercising power B in order to realize intention I as an irreducibly teleological goal.

To illustrate, suppose we are trying to explain why Wesson simply moved his finger (R). We could explain this by saying that Wesson (P) performed an act of endeavouring to move his finger (A) in that he exercised his ability to move (or will to move) his finger (B) intending to move the finger (I). If Wesson's moving his finger was an expression of an intent to move a finger to fire a gun to kill Smith, then we can explain the non-basic results (the firing of the gun and the killing of Smith) by saying that Wesson (P) performed an act of killing Smith (I_3) by endeavouring to move his finger (A) intentionally (I_1) by exercising his power to do so (B), intending thereby to fire the gun (I_2) in order to kill Smith. An explanation of the results of a non-basic action (like going to the store to get bread) will include a description of an action plan. A personal explanation does not consist in offering a mechanism, but rather in correctly citing the relevant person, his intentions, the basic power exercised and, in some cases, offering a description of the relevant action plan.[8]

Advocates of AC employ the difference between these two modes of explanation to justify premise (2). Briefly, the argument is that given a defence of premises (4) and (5), there is no natural scientific explanation of mental entities. Thus, the phenomena cited in (1) may not be taken as *sui generis* facts that can be explained naturalistically. Moreover, the appearance of mental entities and their regular correlation with physical entities are puzzling phenomena that cry out for explanation. Since personal explanation is something people use all the time, this distinctive form of explanation is available, and its employment regarding the phenomena cited in (1) removes our legitimate puzzlement regarding them.

Premise (4) will be examined in conjunction with two alternatives to AC that reject it: Colin McGinn's position and panpsychism.

That leaves (5). At least four reasons have been offered for why there is no natural scientific explanation for the existence of mental states (or their regular correlation with physical states):

1 ***The uniformity of nature.*** Prior to the emergence of consciousness, the universe contained nothing but aggregates of particles/waves standing in fields of forces relative to each other. The story of the development of the cosmos is told in terms of the rearrangement of micro-parts into increasingly more complex structures according to natural law. On a naturalist depiction of matter, it is brute mechanical, physical stuff. The emergence of consciousness seems to be a case of getting something from nothing. In general, physico-chemical reactions do not generate consciousness, not even one little bit, but they do in the brain, yet brains seem similar to other parts of organisms' bodies (e.g., both are collections of cells totally describable in physical terms). How can like causes produce radically different effects? The appearance of mind is utterly unpredictable and inexplicable. This radical discontinuity seems like heterogeneous rupture in the natural world. Similarly, physical states have spatial extension and location but mental states seem to lack spatial features. Space and consciousness sit oddly together. How did spatially arranged matter conspire to produce non-spatial mental states? From a naturalist point of view, this seems utterly inexplicable.

2 ***Contingency of the mind/body correlation.*** The regular correlation between types of mental states and physical states seems radically contingent. Why do pains instead of itches, thoughts or feelings of love get correlated with specific brain states? Based on strong conceivability, zombie and inverted qualia worlds are possible. No amount of knowledge of the brain state will help to answer this question. Given the requirement of causal necessitation for naturalistic causal explanations, there is *in principle* no naturalistic explanation for either the existence of mental states or their regular correlation with physical states. For the naturalist, the regularity of mind/body correlations must be taken as contingent brute facts. But these facts are inexplicable from a naturalistic standpoint, and they are radically *sui generis* compared to all other entities in the naturalist ontology. Thus, it begs the question simply to announce that mental states and their regular correlation with certain brain states is a natural fact. As naturalist Terence Horgan acknowledges, 'in any metaphysical framework that deserves labels like "materialism", "naturalism", or "physicalism", supervenient facts must be explainable rather than being *sui generis*'.[9] Since on most depictions, the theistic God possesses libertarian freedom, God is free to act or refrain from acting in various ways. Thus, the fact that the existence of consciousness and its precise correlation with matter is contingent fits well with a theistic personal explanation that takes God's creative action to have been a contingent one. God may be a necessary being, but God's choice to create conscious beings and to correlate certain types of mental states with certain types of physical states were contingent choices, and this fits nicely with the phenomena themselves.

3 ***Epiphenomenalism and causal closure.*** Most naturalists believe that their worldview requires that all entities whatever are either physical or depend on the physical for their existence and behaviour. One implication of this belief is commitment to the causal closure of the physical. On this principle, when one is

tracing the causal antecedents of any physical event, one will never have to leave the level of the physical. Physical effects have only physical causes. Rejection of the causal closure principle would imply a rejection of the possibility of a complete and comprehensive physical theory of all physical phenomena – something that no naturalist should reject. Thus, if mental phenomena are genuinely non-physical, then they must be epiphenomena – effects caused by the physical that do not themselves have causal powers. But epiphenomenalism is false. Mental causation seems undeniable and, thus, for the naturalist the mental can be allowed to have causal powers only if it is in some way or another identified with the physical. The admission of epiphenomenal non-physical mental entities may be taken as a refutation of naturalism. As naturalist D. M. Armstrong admits,

> I suppose that if the principles involved [in analysing and explaining the origin of or processes of change in things within the single all-embracing spatio-temporal system which is reality] were completely different from the current principles of physics, in particular if they involved appeal to mental entities, such as purposes, we might then count the analysis as a falsification of Naturalism.[10]

4 ***The inadequacy of evolutionary explanations.*** Naturalists are committed to the view that, in principle, evolutionary explanations can be proffered for the appearance of all organisms and their parts. It is not hard to see how an evolutionary account could be given for new and increasingly complex physical structures that constitute different organisms. However, organisms are black boxes as far as evolution is concerned. As long as an organism, when receiving certain inputs, generates the correct behavioural outputs under the demands of fighting, fleeing, reproducing and feeding, the organism will survive. What goes on inside the organism is irrelevant and only becomes significant for the processes of evolution when an output is produced. Strictly speaking, it is the output, not what caused it, that bears on the struggle for reproductive advantage. Moreover, the functions organisms carry out consciously *could just as well have been done unconsciously*. Thus, both the sheer existence of conscious states and the precise mental content that

constitutes them is outside the pale of evolutionary explanation. As Howard E. Gruber explains:

> the idea of either a Planful or an Intervening Providence taking part in the day-to-day operations of the universe was, in effect, a competing theory [to Darwin's version of evolution]. If one believed that there was a God who had originally designed the world exactly as it has come to be, the theory of evolution through natural selection could be seen as superfluous. Likewise, if one believed in a God who intervened from time to time to create some of the organisms, organs, or functions found in the living world, Darwin's theory could be seen as superfluous. Any introduction of intelligent planning or decision-making reduces natural selection from the position of a necessary and universal principle to a mere possibility.[11]

Gruber's concession is a serious one. It amounts to the recognition that *in principle* the evolutionary naturalist account can explain the origin of all organisms and their parts. If some aspect of living things such as their mental lives is in principle incapable of evolutionary explanation, this provides support for a theistic mode of explanation for this aspect of living things and, indeed, weakens the hegemony of evolutionary naturalistic explanation in those cases where the explanandum is in principle within its pale.

We have looked at four reasons why many scholars, including many naturalists, hold that naturalism requires the rejection of consciousness construed along dualist lines. Paul Churchland is representative of those who accept this implication of taking the naturalistic turn. Speaking of the conjunction of naturalism and evolution, Churchland asserts:

> The important point about the standard evolutionary story is that the human species and all of its features are the wholly physical outcome of a purely physical process . . . If this is the correct account of our origins, then there seems neither need, nor room, to fit any nonphysical substances or properties into our theoretical account of ourselves. We are creatures of matter. And we should learn to live with that fact.[12]

Alternatives to AC

Frank Jackson and the location of mental facts

Frank Jackson begins his attempt to develop a naturalistic account of the mental by contrasting two very different approaches to metaphysics. The first he calls serious metaphysics. Serious metaphysics is not content to draw up large pluralistic lists of *sui generis* entities. Rather, it is primarily explanatory metaphysics, advocates of which seek to account for all entities in terms of a limited number of basic notions. The second we may call a 'shopping list' approach whose primary goal is a careful description and categorical analysis of reality.

Possibly taking his cue from the methodology of physical science and its emphasis on theoretical simplicity, Jackson claims that the scientific naturalist will prefer serious metaphysics. Moreover, given that naturalists are committed to a fairly widely accepted physical story about how things came to be and what they are – the Grand Story – serious metaphysics presents the naturalist with a difficulty called the location problem: the task of locating or finding a place for some entity (for example, semantic contents, mind, agency) in that story.

For Jackson, the naturalist must either locate a problematic entity in the basic story or eliminate the entity. Roughly, an entity is located in the basic story just in case it is entailed by that story. Otherwise, the entity must be eliminated. Jackson provides three examples of location. First, just as density is a different property from mass and volume, it is not an additional feature of reality over and above mass and volume in at least this sense: an account of things in terms of mass and volume implicitly contains, i.e., entails, the account in terms of density. Second, Jones's being taller than Smith is not an additional feature of reality over and above Jones and Smith's heights because the relational fact is entailed, and in this sense located, by the latter.

More importantly, Jackson focuses on the location of macro-solidity. He acknowledges that prior to modern science there was a widely accepted commonsense notion of macro-solidity, namely being everywhere dense. However, due to modern science, this notion has been replaced with being impenetrable. So understood, macro-solidity may be located in the basic micro-story: given a description of two macro-objects in terms of their atomic parts, lattice structures, and sub-atomic forces of repulsion, this description entails that one macro-object is impenetrable with respect to the second.

Jackson believes there are four important sorts of troublesome entities that the naturalist must locate: mental properties/events, facts associated with the first-person indexical, secondary qualities, and moral properties. Focusing on mental properties/events, Jackson claims that the naturalist must argue that they globally supervene on the physical. He unpacks this claim with two clarifications. First, he defines a minimal physical duplicate of our world as

> a world that (a) is exactly like our world in every physical respect (instantiated property for instantiated property, law for law, relation for relation), and (b) contains nothing else in the sense of nothing more by way of kinds or particulars than it *must* to satisfy (a).[13]

Second, he advocates B*: Any world which is a minimal physical duplicate of our world is a psychological duplicate of our world.

Jackson concludes in this way:

> Let Φ be the story as told in purely physical terms, which is true at the actual world and all the minimal physical duplicates of the actual world, and false elsewhere; Φ is a hugely complex, purely physical account of our world. Let ψ be any true sentence which is about the psychological nature of our world in the sense that it can only come false by things being different psychologically from the way they actually are: every world at which ψ is false differs in some psychological way from our world. Intuitively, the idea is that ψ counts as being about the psychological nature of our world because making it false requires supposing a change in the distribution of psychological properties and relations . . . [E]very world at which Φ is true is a world at which ψ is true – that is, Φ entails ψ.[14]

Has Jackson succeeded in providing a naturalistic explanation of mental properties/events that provides a more reasonable alternative to AC? For at least two reasons, the answer is no: Jackson fails convincingly to locate mental properties in the Grand Story, and his employment of serious metaphysics begs the question against advocates of AC and requires distortion of the metaphysical facts concerning consciousness.

First, Jackson fails convincingly to locate mental properties in the Grand Story. Jackson selects solidity as a paradigm case of location to which he will assimilate other entities (for example, semantic contents). But Jackson does not really locate solidity, and even if he does, solidity and its location are a bad analogy with consciousness and its location such that the successful location of the former does not provide grounds for locating the latter. As Jackson acknowledges, the pre-scientific notion of solidity is being everywhere dense. But this notion is not located in the basic physical story – there are minimal physical duplicates of our world whose macro-objects do not exemplify being everywhere dense – so what actually happens is that being everywhere dense is eliminated in favour of being impenetrable.

However, even if we grant that solidity is being impenetrable, this paradigm case, along with the other two (density, being taller than) provide inadequate analogies for justifying the claim that mental properties may be located in accordance with B*. For one thing, solidity is part of the basic story – there is both macro- and micro-solidity – but granting the rejection of panpsychism and assuming with (1) of AC that mental properties are *sui generis* emergent and not structural properties, mental properties are not part of the basic story.

Second, it seems pretty clear that it is on the basis of strong conceivability – positive insight into the nature of the relevant properties and relations – that, given mass/volume, given particulars and their heights, and given lattice structure, atomic parts and forces of repulsion, it is simply inconceivable that there could be a possible world where the corresponding macro-objects failed to have a certain density or stand in a certain taller-than relation or be impenetrable with respect to each other. Once one grasps the micro-story, one can just see the modality involved. But, clearly, this is not so with respect to mental properties. It seems pretty obvious to many people that zombie worlds and various inverted qualia worlds are within the range of minimal physical duplicates of the actual world. No description of the physical particulars, properties, laws or relations entails anything whatsoever about the presence or nature of the mental features of the world in question. The connection between the mental and physical is radically contingent. When physicalists deny this claim, they have to dig their heels in in a question-begging way that is completely unnecessary for the modal claims about Jackson's three paradigm cases.

Third, B* requires a stop clause ('contains nothing else in the sense of nothing more by way of kinds or particulars than it *must* to satisfy (a)') that is not at all necessary for a formulation of B* that is adequate for facts about macro-density, solidity and relational facts about height. Jackson himself states a general principle B that he narrows into B* to focus on the supervenience of psychological facts: Any world which is a *minimal* physical duplicate of our world is a duplicate *simpliciter* of our world. Clearly, B does not require a stop clause to be adequate for the location of density, solidity and relational facts. But the location of mental facts does require the stop clause, hence, B*. But the stop clause is not itself explicit or even implicit in the Grand Story nor is there any strictly scientific argument from the naturalist epistemic attitude for its inclusion in B*. Indeed, it seems that Jackson's employment of it gives perhaps unintended testimony to the fact that the physical world alone is not sufficient to locate mental properties, so something more (no mental substances may be allowed) is required. Thus, the stop clause is ad hoc and question-begging against advocates of AC, but no such charge could be levelled against B and the location of the three paradigm macro-features.

In addition to his failure convincingly to locate mental properties in the Grand Story, Jackson's employment of serious metaphysics is question-begging against advocates of AC. To see this, recall that one epistemic value may be essential to one theory but a different epistemic value may be essential to its rival. When this happens, it is inappropriate to fault a rival theory for not measuring up to an epistemic value that is important if the rival is true. Given the implicit reductionism and micro-to-macro forms of explanation that express the naturalist epistemic attitude and that constitute the core of the Grand Story, it is easy to see why naturalists must prefer serious metaphysics to a shopping list metaphysics. But on a theistic view, for two reasons a shopping list approach is preferable.

First, the freedom and creativity at the core of our notion of a person – especially a Divine Person – provide grounds for preferring a shopping list approach to ontology. There is a positive and negative side to this claim. Positively, if God exists, He may well create a variety of kinds of entities, and it may create various kinds ex nihilo or by actualizing potentialities in precursors that go far beyond what is countenanced in the Grand Story. Given theism, one would expect creative variety in being and there is no bar to holding that various kinds of things are quite discrete. Indeed, early Creationist taxonomists such as Carl Linnaeus exemplified a 'shopping list' to biological taxonomy precisely because, as theists, they employed a top-down typological essentialist perspective that is not at home in a naturalist approach dictated by the Grand Story. Negatively, the theist has no need to begin with a basic account and try to locate other entities in terms of a limited number of basic entities. Such an approach is either eliminativist or reductionist (macro-entities must be located by being entailed by the basic story) as Jackson acknowledges, and this places a premium on explanatory vs. descriptive metaphysics, along with theoretical simplicity and serious metaphysics as a crucial component of a naturalist approach to metaphysics. But the theist is free to describe metaphysical data whether he can locate them or not. Thus, in doing ontology, the theist will prefer the value of descriptive accuracy (it is no accident that Husserl was both a theist and a phenomenologist in ontology) to theoretical simplicity understood in Jackson's characterization of serious metaphysics. So it is question-begging for Jackson to employ serious metaphysics as common ground for the adjudication of naturalism vis-à-vis its rivals, given theism and AC.

John Searle's biological naturalism

John Searle has developed a naturalistic account of consciousness which would, if successful, provide justification for rejecting premise (5) of AC.[15] According to Searle, for fifty years philosophy of mind has been dominated by scientific naturalists who have advanced different versions of strict physicalism because it was seen as a crucial implication of taking the naturalistic turn. For these naturalists, if one abandons strict physicalism, one has rejected a scientific naturalist approach to the mind/body problem and opened oneself up to the intrusion of religious concepts and arguments about the mental.

By contrast, Searle's own solution to the mind/body problem is biological naturalism: While mental states are exactly what dualists describe them to be, nevertheless, they are merely emergent biological states and processes that causally supervene upon a suitably structured, functioning brain. Brain processes cause mental processes, which are not ontologically reducible to the former. Consciousness is just an ordinary (i.e., physical) feature of the brain and, as such, is merely an ordinary feature of the natural world.

Given that he characterizes consciousness as dualists do, why does Searle claim that there are no deep metaphysical implications that follow from biological naturalism? More specifically, why is it that biological naturalism does not represent a rejection of scientific naturalism which, in turn, opens the door for religious concepts about and explanations for the mental? Searle's answer to this question is developed in three steps.

In Step One, he cites several examples of emergence (liquidity, solidity, features of digestion) that he takes to be unproblematic for naturalists and claims that emergent consciousness is analogous to the unproblematic cases.

In Step Two, he formulates two reasons why consciousness is not a problem for naturalists:

1 The emergence of consciousness is not a problem if we stop trying to picture or image consciousness.
2 In standard cases (heat, colour), an ontological reduction (e.g., identifying a specific colour with a wavelength) is based on a causal reduction (e.g., claiming that a specific colour is caused by a wavelength) because our pragmatic interests are in reality, not appearance.

In these cases we can distinguish the *appearance* of heat and colour from the *reality*, place the former in consciousness, leave the latter in the objective world, and go on to define the phenomenon itself in terms of its causes. We can do this because our interests are in the reality and not the appearance. The ontological reduction of heat to its causes leaves the appearance of heat the same. Regarding consciousness, we are interested in the appearances, and thus the irreducibility of consciousness is merely due to pragmatic considerations, not to some deep metaphysical problem.

In Step Three, Searle claims that an adequate scientific explanation of the emergence of consciousness consists in a detailed, law-like set of correlations between mental and physical state tokens. Part of his justification for this is that some explanations in science do not exhibit the type of necessity that explains why certain things must happen (e.g., macro-impenetrability) given that other things have obtained (e.g., micro-structure). Searle cites as an example the inverse square law, which is an explanatory account of gravity that does not show why bodies have to have gravitational attraction.

Several things may be said in response to Searle's position. Regarding Steps One and Two, his cases of emergence (rigidity, fluidity) are not good analogies to consciousness since the former are *easy* to locate in the naturalist epistemology and ontology, but consciousness is *not*. Given a widely accepted physicalist description of atoms, molecules, lattice structure, and the like, the rigidity or fluidity of macro-objects follows necessarily. But there is no clear necessary connection between any physical state and any mental state. For example, given a specific brain state normally 'associated' with the mental state of being appeared to redly, inverted qualia worlds (worlds with that physical state but radically different mental states 'associated' with it), zombie worlds (worlds with that physical state and no mental states at all) and disembodied worlds (worlds with beings possessing mental states with no physical entities at all) are still metaphysically possible. It is easy to locate solidity in a naturalist framework but the same cannot be said for consciousness. This is why there has been turmoil for naturalists in philosophy of mind but not in the philosophy of solidity. Searle's emergent entities follow necessarily given the naturalist Grand Story, but consciousness does not.

Further, the emergence of genuinely new properties in macro-objects that are not part of the micro-world (e.g., heat construed as warmth, colour construed commonsensically as a quality) presents problems for naturalists in the same way consciousness does and, historically, that is why they were placed in consciousness. Contrary to Searle, they were not so placed because of the pragmatics of our interests. For example, historically, the problem was that if so-called secondary qualities were kept in the mind-independent world, there was no naturalistic explanation for why they emerged on the occasion of a mere rearrangement in micro-parts exhaustively characterized in terms of primary qualities. Secondary qualities construed along commonsense lines are not among the primary qualities employed to characterize the micro-world and, indeed, seem contingently linked to the micro-world.

It is this straightforward ontological problem not the pragmatics of reduction or the attempt to image consciousness that presents difficulties for naturalism: How do you get secondary qualities or consciousness to come-to-be by merely rearranging purely physical entities bereft of the emergent features? Given their existence, why are secondary qualities and conscious states regularly correlated with purely physical states similarly bereft?

In fact, the emergence of mental properties is more like the emergence of normative (e.g., moral) properties than the properties of solidity or digestion. Even the atheist J. L. Mackie admitted that the emergence of moral properties provided evidence for a moral argument for God's existence analogous to AC: 'Moral properties constitute so odd a cluster of properties and relations that they are most unlikely to have arisen in the ordinary course of events without an all-powerful god to create them.'[16] Mackie is right on this point. Given theism, if a naturalist were simply to claim that the emergence of moral properties was a basic naturalistic fact, this would be an ad hoc, question-begging ploy of assuming a point not congruent with a naturalistic worldview. Searle's 'explanation' of consciousness is guilty of the same charge.

Regarding Step Three, 'explanations' in science that do not express the sort of necessity we have been discussing are better taken as *descriptions*, not *explanations*. For example, the ideal gas equation is a description of the behaviour of gases. An explanation of that behaviour is provided by the atomic theory of gas. Curiously, Newton himself took the inverse square law to be a mere description of gravity and not an explanation; so Searle's own example counts against him. Further, given theism and AC, along with our earlier discussion of scientific theory acceptance, it is question-begging and ad hoc for Searle to assert that mental entities and mental/physical correlations are basic, since such entities are natural in light of theism but unnatural given philosophical naturalism.

Our current belief that there is no causal necessity to specific mind/brain correlations is not due to our ignorance of how the brain works, but based on an understanding of the radical differences between mental and physical entities. As fellow naturalist Jaegwon Kim notes, the correlations are not explanations. They are the very things that need explaining, and, given a proper understanding of the real questions, no naturalistic explanation seems to be forthcoming:

> How could a series of physical events, little particles jostling against one another, electric current rushing to and fro . . . blossom into a conscious experience? . . . Why shouldn't pain and itch be switched around? . . . Why should *any* experience emerge when these neurons fire?[17]

By misconstruing the problem, Searle fails to address the real issue and, weighed against AC, his position is inadequate.

Colin McGinn's agnostic 'naturalism'

Naturalist Colin McGinn has offered a different solution.[18] Given the radical difference between mind and matter as it is depicted by current or even an ideal future physics, there is no naturalistic solution that stays within the widely accepted naturalist epistemology and ontology. Darwinian explanations fail as well because they cannot account for why consciousness appeared in the first place. What is needed is a radically different kind of solution to the origin of mind, one that must meet two conditions:

1 It must be a naturalistic solution.
2 It must depict the emergence of consciousness and its regular correlation with matter as necessary and not contingent facts.

McGinn claims that there must be two kinds of unknowable natural properties that solve the problem. There must be some general properties of matter that enter into the production of consciousness when assembled into a brain. Thus, all matter has the potentiality to underlie consciousness. Further, there must be some natural property of the brain he calls C* that unleashes these general properties.

The temptation to take the origin of consciousness as a mystery, indeed, a mystery that is best explained theistically, is due to our ignorance of these properties. However, given C* and the general properties of matter, the unknowable link between mind and matter is ordinary, commonplace and necessitates the emergence of consciousness. Unfortunately, evolution did not give humans the faculties needed to know these properties and, thus, they are in principle beyond our grasp. We will forever be agnostic about their nature. However, they must be there since there must be some naturalistic explanation of mind as all other solutions have failed.

McGinn offers two further descriptions of these unknowable yet ordinary properties that link matter and mind:

1 They are not sense perceptible.
2 Since matter is spatial and mind non-spatial, they are either in some sense pre-spatial or are spatial in a way that is itself unknowable to our faculties.

In this way, these unknowable properties contain at least the potentiality for both ordinary spatial features of matter and the non-spatial features of consciousness as judged by our usual concept of space.

In sum, the mind/matter link is an unknowable mystery due to our cognitive limitations resulting from our evolution. And since the link is quite ordinary, we should not be puzzled by the origin of mind, and no theistic explanation is required.

Does McGinn's solution succeed? For at least three reasons, it must be judged a failure. First, given McGinn's agnosticism about the properties that link mind and matter, how can McGinn confidently assert some of their features? How does he know they are non-sensory, pre-spatial or spatial in an unknowable way? How does he know some of these properties underlie all matter? Indeed, what possible justification can he give for their reality? The only one he proffers is that we must provide a naturalistic solution and all ordinary naturalistic ones either deny consciousness or fail to solve the problem. But given the presence of AC, McGinn's claims are simply question-begging. Indeed, his agnosticism seems to be a convenient way of hiding behind naturalism and avoiding a theistic explanation. Given that theism enjoys a positive degree of justification prior to the problem of consciousness (see other chapters in this volume), he should avail himself of the explanatory resources of theism.

Second, it is not clear that his solution is a version of naturalism, except in name only. In contrast to other entities in the naturalist ontology, McGinn's linking properties cannot be known by employment of the naturalist epistemology, nor are they relevantly similar to the rest of the naturalist ontology. Thus, it becomes vacuous to call these properties 'naturalistic'. McGinn's own speculations strike one as ad hoc in light of the inadequacies of naturalistic explanations. In fact, McGinn's solution is actually closer to an agnostic form of panpsychism (see below) than to naturalism. Given AC, McGinn's solution is an ad hoc readjustment of naturalism.

Third, McGinn does not solve the problem of consciousness, he merely relocates it. Rather than having two radically different entities, he offer us unknowable properties with two radically different aspects; for example, his links contain the potentiality for ordinary spatiality and non-spatiality, for ordinary materiality and mentality. Moreover, these radically different aspects of the linking properties are just as contingently related as they seem to be without a linking intermediary. The contingency comes from the nature of mind and matter as naturalists conceive it. It does not remove the contingency to relocate it as two aspects of an unknowable third intermediary with both.

Panpsychism

Currently, there are few serious advocates of panpsychism, though it has been suggested by Thomas Nagel and David Chalmers.[19] Roughly, panpsychism is the view that all matter has consciousness in it. Since each parcel of matter has its own consciousness, the brain is conscious since it is just a collection of those parcels. Consciousness is pervasive in nature so its apparent emergence in particular cases is not something that requires special explanation. One can distinguish two forms of panpsychism. According to the strong version, all matter has conscious states in it in the same sense that organisms such as dogs and humans do. According to the weak form, regular matter has consciousness in a degraded, attenuated way in the form of proto-mental states that, under the right circumstances, yield conscious mental states without themselves being conscious.

The strong form is quite implausible. For one thing, regular matter gives no evidence whatever of possessing consciousness. Further, if all matter has consciousness, why does it emerge in special ways only when certain configurations of matter are present? And if conscious human beings are in some sense merely combinations of little bits of consciousness, how are we to account for the unity of consciousness and why do people have no memory of the conscious careers of the bits of matter prior to their combination to form humans? There is no answer to these questions and few, if any, hold to strong panpsychism.

What about the weak version? Given the current intellectual climate, a personal theistic or a naturalistic explanation would exhaust at least the live – if not the logical – options. It is widely recognized that weak panpsychism has serious problems in its own right; for example, explaining what an incipient or proto-mental entity is; how the type of unity that appears to characterize the self could emerge from a mere system of parts standing together in various causal and spatio-temporal relations; and why certain physical conditions are regularly correlated with the actualization of consciousness when the connection between consciousness and those conditions seems to be utterly contingent.[20]

Moreover, panpsychism is arguably less reasonable than theism on other grounds. I cannot pursue this point here but other chapters in this volume take up other aspects of the case for theism. In light of that case, theism enjoys positive epistemic justification prior to the issue of consciousness, but the same cannot be said for panpsychism.

Also, panpsychism is merely a label for and not an explanation of the phenomena to be explained. As Geoffrey Madell notes,

> the sense that the mental and the physical are just inexplicably and gratuitously slapped together is hardly allayed by adopting . . . a pan-psychist . . . view of the mind, for [it does not] have an

explanation to offer as to why or how mental properties cohere with physical.[21]

Conclusion

Prominent naturalist David Papineau admits that if the naturalist refuses to identity consciousness with strictly physical properties and, instead, admits the reality of consciousness as a range of commonsense mental properties correlated with physical properties, the naturalist is in trouble: 'But then we still seem to face the question: *why* does consciousness emerge in just those cases? And to this question physicalist "theories of consciousness" seem to provide no answer.'[22] Papineau's solution is to deny the reality of consciousness as a genuinely mental phenomenon.[23] Another prominent naturalist – Jaegwon Kim – has observed that 'if a whole system of phenomena that are prima facie not among basic physical phenomena resists physical explanation, and especially if we don't even know where or how to begin, it would be time to reexamine one's physicalist commitments'.[24] For Kim, genuinely non-physical mental entities are the paradigm case of such a system of phenomena. Kim's advice to fellow naturalists is that they must simply admit the irreality of the mental and recognize that naturalism exacts a steep price and cannot be had on the cheap.[25] If feigning anaesthesia – denying that consciousness construed along commonsense lines is real – is the price to be paid to retain naturalism, then the price is too high. Fortunately, the theistic argument from consciousness reminds us that it is a price that does not need to be paid.

3

Naturalism, Free Will and Human Persons

The Ubiquity of Libertarian Intuitions

It is widely acknowledged that worldwide, the commonsense, spontaneously formed understanding of human free will is what philosophers call libertarian freedom: one acts freely only if one's action was not determined – directly or indirectly – by forces outside one's control, and one must be free to act or refrain from acting; one's choice is 'spontaneous', it originates with and only with the actor.

Unless one has an ideological axe to grind, one will be a libertarian. And even if one's ideology requires one to adopt an alternative view of 'free will' compatible with determinism, I believe that one will continue to act on and actually believe the libertarian account in one's daily life, for example while playing backgammon, and in dealings with oneself and others, when one is not, as it were, reminding oneself of one's ideological commitments.

It is not my purpose to argue for libertarianism, and I have already shown why I feel less intellectual pressure to do so than you, the reader, may expect. I simply offer two fairly obvious remarks. For one thing, as John Searle has recently noted, the experience of libertarian free will is compelling, so compelling in fact, that people cannot act as though that experience is an illusion, even if it is one.[1] He reminds us that when we are presented by the waiter with a choice between pork or veal, we cannot bring ourselves to reply, 'Look, I'm a determinist. I'll just have to wait and see what order happens!'

For another thing, a thought experiment will, I believe, make evident the power of libertarian intuitions. Suppose a scientist slips into your room at night while you are asleep, places an electrode in your brain, quietly sets up his computer across the street, and by simply typing a specific word is able to cause any mental state – sensation, belief, thought, desire – to occur in you that he wishes. And suppose, further, that once the mental state happens, it inexorably determines what your body must do. The next day, you arise, take a morning walk, and just as you are about to pass a stranger, the scientist, filled with malicious intent, types in the right word, it causes you to have a desire to hit the stranger in the nose, and this desire deterministically causes your arm to move and your hand to smack the stranger in the face.

Question: Who did this act? Who is responsible for it? Clearly it is not you. The responsible actor is the scientist who hit the stranger through you. You did not have a free choice about the matter. Why? Surely not because the controller (the scientist) is atypical, his desires were contrary to the ones you would have had if left alone, or the causal chain between the scientist's action and yours was deviant. No, it's because the movement of your arm was determined by factors outside your control. Only if your action was not determined and was brought about spontaneously by you such that you could have refrained from bringing it about, only then was it *your* action.

It is, of course, open for a compatibilist to claim that a 'free' act is one that is deterministically caused (or has its probabilistic chances fixed) by one's own prior mental states, for example a belief/desire set, when the chain of events from that mental state to the body movement constituting that act causes the latter in the right way. The weasel word here is 'in the right way', and it rears its ugly head in all sorts of causal-chain analyses in philosophy. In my view, the best compatibilist attempt to develop a causal theory of action is John Bishop's.[2] He begins by claiming that we all operate within a libertarian conception of free will, and his task is to develop a causal theory that approximates the libertarian account as closely as possible while remaining within the compatibilist camp, a requirement Bishop takes to be part of being a naturalist. So he offers an analysis of free action, generates counter-examples, proffers another analysis, generates further counter-examples, until after several epicycles of this, he finally lands on his preferred view. Curiously, it is the concept of agent causation and libertarian freedom that controls this entire dialectic for Bishop, providing the materials for each analysis, as well as for the counter-examples and the sense of adequacy in having solved them with a further analysis. In my view, this employment of the concept of agent causation and libertarian freedom is ubiquitous in compatibilist writings, and, surely, the centrality of the role of the concept of libertarian freedom counts heavily in favour of the view that it is no mere concept; it's the correct view of the matter.

Why are libertarian intuitions so pervasive that they clearly constitute the commonsense default position? I think it is because through first-person introspection, people the world over are simply directly aware of themselves exercising active power in bringing about the effects they endeavour to bring about. When one sees a hammer driving a nail into lumber, they don't just see the hammer moving followed by the nail moving. They also perceive the hammer-moving-the-nail. Similarly, we are directly aware of our own endeavouring-to-raise-our-arm-in-order-to-vote. On the basis of such awarenesses, we form the justified belief that we exercise originative, free, active power for the sake of teleological goals. We are able to distinguish through immediate introspective awareness the difference between an active and a passive thought. The former is a thought we have freely chosen to entertain while a passive thought is one we merely receive, say, while reading a book or listening to a speech. The differences between the two types of thoughts is made evident to direct awareness, and this is one example of our ability to be directly aware of our own exercises of active, free power. On a compatibilist view, the difference between an active and passive thought would lie in their different causal pedigrees, for example the active thought being caused in the right way by the appropriate prior mental state and the passive thought failing to be produced by such a chain. On this view, there simply is no introspective difference between active and passive thoughts. But I believe that awareness of our own mental lives points in the other direction.

Naturalism and Libertarian Free Will

Shortly, I shall unpack the formal elements of a libertarian view of free will that I take to be true and most obvious.[3] Most philosophers are agreed that libertarian freedom and a theory of agency it entails are incompatible with the generally accepted depiction of naturalism presented in Chapter 1. Thus, Roderick Chisholm claimed that 'in one very strict sense of the terms, there can be no science of man'.[4] Along similar lines, John Searle says that 'our conception of physical reality simply does not allow for radical [libertarian] freedom'.[5] And if moral (and intellectual) responsibility has such freedom as a necessary condition, then reconciling the natural and ethical perspectives is impossible. In what may be the best naturalist attempt to accomplish such a reconciliation, John Bishop frankly admits that 'the idea of a responsible agent, with the "originative" ability to initiate events in the natural world, does not sit easily with the idea of [an agent as] a natural organism . . . Our scientific understanding of human behavior seems to be in tension with a presupposition of the ethical stance we adopt toward it.'[6]

Stated formally, a Person P exercises libertarian agency and freely does some intentional act e just in case

(1) P is a substance that has the active power to bring about e;
(2) P exerted his/her active power as a first, unmoved mover (an 'originator') to bring about e;
(3) P had the categorical ability to refrain from exerting his/her power to bring about e;
(4) P acted for the sake of reasons which serve as the final cause or teleological goal for which P acted.

Taken alone, (1)–(3) state necessary and sufficient conditions for a pure voluntary act, for example freely directing my eyes towards a specific desk upon entering a room. Propositions (1)–(4) state necessary and sufficient conditions for an intentional act, that is, a voluntary act done for a reason (e.g., raising my hand to vote).

There are six features of a free act that makes it difficult and, indeed, virtually impossible to reconcile with the naturalist standpoint. First, the free agent is a substance and not an event or bundle of events. But for two reasons, ordinary objects are not substances in a naturalist ontology; rather they are bundles of events or aggregates of parts. For one thing, according to naturalism, all causes and effects are events (or bundles of events). The laws of nature govern causal processes in which a temporal state (an event) of an object (an electron, water molecule, storm cloud) brings about a different temporal state (a subsequent event) according to a natural law. This is called 'event–event causation' and it is the only sort of efficient cause recognized in physics, chemistry, geology, biology, neuroscience or other naturalistically certified hard sciences. Event–event causation governs changes of state in or among objects – nothing more, nothing less. Substances as substances – essentially characterized particulars, substantial things – do not cause things. Strictly speaking, it is not the first billiard ball that moves the second. It is the moving-of-the-first-ball (the causal event) that causes the moving-of-the-second-ball (the effect event). Thus, whatever there is to an 'object' that is more than its event status is otiose as far as causality is concerned, and Ockham's razor and the causal criterion of being (something exists only if it can serve as a cause) have led many naturalists to shave off that excess baggage and reduce macro-objects to bundles of events. For another thing, the Grand Story tells a tale about how macro-objects come-to-be, and that combinatorial tale implies that macro-objects are mere systems, relational collections of parts standing in external relations to each other, and not genuine substances. More on this in Chapter 5.

By contrast, it is the agent as a substantial self or I, not some state in the agent, that brings about a free act. By 'substance' I mean a member of a natural kind, an essentially characterized particular that sustains absolute sameness through (accidental) change and that possesses a primitive unity of inseparable parts (parts that cannot exist and retain their identity when outside the wholes of which they are parts; another term for an inseparable part is 'mode'), properties, and capacities/powers at a time. This strong view of substance is required for libertarian agency for at least three reasons:

1. Libertarian agency is possible only if there is a distinction between the capacity to act or refrain from acting and the agent that possesses those capacities.
2. The type of unity present among the various capacities possessed by an agent is the type of unity (i.e., a diversity of capacities within an ontologically prior whole) that is entailed by the classic Aristotelian notion of substance.

3 Free acts take time and include sub-acts as parts, and an enduring agent is what gives unity to such acts by being the same self who is present at the beginning of the action as intentional agent, during the act as teleological guider of means to ends, and at the end as responsible actor.

But this is not countenanced by naturalism. Thus, naturalist John Bishop frankly admits,

> the problem of natural agency is an ontological problem – a problem about whether the existence of actions can be admitted within a natural scientific perspective . . . [A]gent causal-relations do not belong to the ontology of the natural perspective. Naturalism does not essentially employ the concept of a causal relation whose first member is in the category of person or agent (or even, for that matter, in the broader category of continuant or 'substance'). All natural causal relations have first members in the category of event or state of affairs.[7]

Second, the ontology of naturalism knows nothing of active powers. The particulars that populate that ontology are, one and all, exhaustively characterized by passive liabilities with regard to their causal powers. A passive liability is such that, given the proper efficient cause, it is and, indeed, must be actualized. As such, the actualization of a passive liability is a passive happening, not an *action*. This fact about passive liabilities is what makes them, along with their causes, fitting entities for subsumption under law. And it is precisely as passive and so subsumable that makes their owners bereft of the sort of first-moving, active spontaneity that is a necessary condition for the exercise of free will.

All natural objects with causal powers possess them as passive liabilities. Again, these liabilities are triggered or actualized if something happens to the object and, once triggered, they can produce an effect. For example, dynamite has the power (passive liability) to explode if something is first done to it. And so on for all causes. They are, one and all, passive potentialities. Their actualizations are mere happenings to the relevant object.

But active power is different. In virtue of possessing active power, an agent may *act*, initiate change or motion, perform something, bring about an effect with nothing causing it to do so. Active power is not something admitted in the ontology of the hard sciences, period.

Third, a 'first mover' is a substance that has active power. As such, it is the absolute originator of its actions. It is not just another caused cause, just one more event in a chain of events in which earlier causes bring about later effects that, in turn, bring about later effects to form one big series of passive happenings governed by natural law. No, a first mover is not subject to laws in its initiation of action. Since such an initiation is a first, spontaneous, action not caused by a prior event, it amounts to the absolute origination of initiatory movement. Such an origination comes into being instantaneously and spontaneously, and while the effect it produces (e.g., the earliest stages in the raising of one's arm) may well be subject to natural laws, the initiating event is not since there is nothing prior to its coming-to-be on which a law may operate. Moreover, such a first mover is an unmoved mover, that is, it has the power to bring about an action without having to change first before it can so act.

By contrast, since all events in a naturalist ontology are passive happenings, they all are examples of moved movers: something has to happen to an object first, namely, an event that triggers and actualizes its causal powers, before it can cause something else to happen. In this sense, all naturalistic causation involves changed changers. But a first mover can produce change without having to change first to do so. It should be obvious why such an agent is not an object that can be located in a natural ontology. Unmoved movers with active power are quintessentially unnatural! Indeed, they are exactly like the God of the Bible in this regard!

Fourth, the notion of 'categorical ability' in (3) has two important aspects to it. First, it expresses the type of ability possessed by a first mover that can exercise active power and, as such, it contrasts with the conditional ability employed by compatibilists. Second, categorical ability is a dual ability: if one has the ability to exert one's power to do (or will to do) A, then one also has the ability to refrain from exerting one's power to do (or to will to do) A. This means that the circumstances within (e.g., motives, desires, reasons) and outside (environmental conditions) the agent at the time of action are not sufficient to determine that or fix the chances of the action taking place. Given those circumstances, the agent can either exercise or refrain from exercising his/her active power, and this ability is the essential, causal factor for what follows. Among other things, this implies that libertarian acts cannot be subsumed under natural laws, whether construed as deterministic or probabilistic.

But all the particulars in the naturalist ontology are so subsumable. In fact, all of them are subject to synchronic and diachronic determinism in the following sense:

> Regarding synchronic determinism, at some time t, the physical conditions are sufficient to determine or fix the chances of the next event involving the object and its environment. Regarding diachronic determinism, at any time t, the object's states and movements are determined or have their chances fixed by the micro-physical states of the object and its environment. This latter determination is bottom-up.

Fifth, (4) expresses a view of reasons and irreducible, teleological goals for the sake of which a person acts. In general, we may characterize this by saying that person S F'd (e.g., went to the kitchen) in order to Y (e.g., get coffee or satisfy S's desire for coffee). This characterization of action, according to (4), cannot be reduced to a causal theory of action that utilizes belief/desire event causation such that reasons amount to efficient causes (or causal conditions) for action. To see this, consider these two sentences:

> (1) The water boiled because it was heated.
> (2) Smith went to the kitchen because he wanted to get coffee.

(1) is a straightforwardly (efficient) causal assertion. The event cited after 'because' (the water's being heated) is the efficient cause for the water's boiling. But while grammatically similar, (2) doesn't employ reasons as causes. This can be seen by paraphrasing (2) as follows:

> (2′) Smith went to the kitchen in order to get coffee.

Here, getting coffee is the goal, purpose, end of Smith's free action. Every step he takes (getting out of his chair, walking towards the kitchen, opening the pantry) are means to this end.

If there is anything that naturalists agree upon, it is that there is no such thing as teleology. Matter is mechanistic, not in the sense that it only engages in action by contact and is bereft of forces, but in that it only behaves according to chains of efficient causes. As philosophers Joshua Hoffman and Gary Rosenkrantz note, attempts to slap teleology onto a naturalist framework really amount to abandonment of naturalism:

> Aristotle's account [of natural function and teleology] does *not* provide a naturalistic reduction of natural function in terms of efficient causation. Nor do characterizations of natural function in terms of an irreducibly emergent purposive principle, or an unanalyzable emergent property associated with the biological phenomenon of life, provide such a reduction. Theistic and vitalistic approaches that try to explicate natural function in terms of the intentions of an intelligent purposive agent or principle are also nonnaturalistic. Another form of nonnaturalism attempts to explicate natural function in terms of nonnatural evaluative attributes such as intrinsic goodness . . . We do not accept the anti-reductionist and anti-naturalistic theories about natural function listed above. Without entering into a detailed critique of these ideas, one can see that they either posit immaterial entities whose existence is in doubt, or make it utterly mysterious how it can be true that a part of an organic living thing manifests a natural function . . . [T]he theoretical unity of biology would be better served if the natural functions of the parts of organic life-forms could be given a reductive account completely in terms of nonpurposive or nonfunctional naturalistic processes or conditions.[8]

If there are no purposes, no goals, no ends in the cosmos, then the same must be said for human life and action. The late Harvard evolutionist Stephen Jay Gould understood this. When asked, 'Why are we here?', he changed the subject and told a story of how we got here in solely efficient causal terms:

> We are here *because* one odd group of fishes had a peculiar fin anatomy that could transform into legs for terrestrial creatures; *because* the earth never froze entirely during an ice age; *because*

> a small and tenuous species, arising in Africa a quarter of a million years ago, has managed, so far, to survive by hook and by crook. We may yearn for a 'higher' answer – but none exists [italics mine].[9]

Finally, libertarian acts involve so-called top-down causation in which a macro-object (a particular person) exercises causal influence in the micro-physical world. As John Searle frankly admits,

> [W]e are inclined to say that since nature consists of particles and their relations with each other, and since everything can be accounted for in terms of those particles and their relations, there is simply no room for freedom of the will . . . [Quantum] indeterminism is no evidence that there is or could be some mental energy of human freedom that can move molecules in directions that they were not otherwise going to move. So it really does look as if everything we know about physics forces us to some form of denial of human freedom.[10]

To elaborate, consider the following. If the existence of conscious states such as active power is embraced, as it must be if libertarian agency is in view, then a naturalist will have a difficult time avoiding an epiphenomenal depiction of conscious states according to which they are caused by or emerge from the brain, but they are themselves causally impotent.[11] To see why this is so, consider a person getting a drink of water. Now, according to the causal closure principle (in tracing the causal antecedents of any physical event, one will never have to leave the physical; if one has to do so, this would be tantamount to admitting a miraculous intervention in the flow of events at the micro-physical level), the cause of the person getting the drink is a relevant brain state. If so, what does the mental state of feeling thirst contribute? If it is a real mental state distinct from the brain state, there appears to be no room for it to affect anything, since the relevant brain state is the adequate cause. More generally, consider the following diagram:

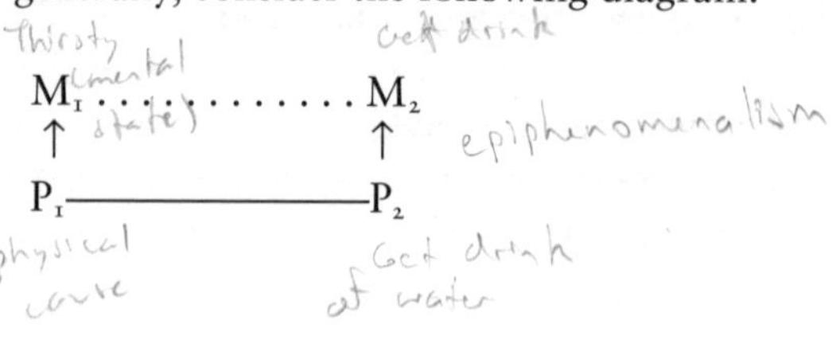

The diagram depicts a sequence of two mental states and two brain states. Let us ask what the cause of M_2 is. If we wish to allow for mental causation, we may say that M_1 is the cause of M_2. However, according to the naturalist principle of supervenience (mental events are determined by and depend upon the relevant physical events upon which they emerge), M_2 supervenes and is dependent upon P_2. Thus, if M_1 is to be the cause of M_2, it will have to cause M_2's subvenient base, P_2. But the naturalist principle of the causal closure of the physical requires that P_1 be the adequate cause of P_2. Moreover, M_1 itself exists in dependence upon its subvenient base, P_1. Thus, assuming the falsity of causal overdetermination (an event has two entirely sufficient causes), we see that there is no room for mental-to-physical causation (M_1 causing P_2) or mental to mental causation (M_1 causing M_2). The sequence of mental events running through a person's consciousness is like a series of causally impotent shadows.

While they may not be familiar with the argument just given, naturalists Cosmides and Tooby seem to grasp that epiphenomenalism follows from evolutionary naturalism:

> The brain is a physical system whose operation is governed solely by the laws of chemistry and physics. What does this mean? It means that all of your thoughts and hopes and dreams and feelings are produced by chemical reactions going on in your head.[12]

The best way for a naturalist to avoid the problem of epiphenomenalism is to identify conscious states with brain states. In this way, conscious states can retain causal power because they just are brain states. Unfortunately, this move amounts to a denial of active power in favour of passive liabilities, and with it, a rejection of libertarian free will.

It should be obvious why free will is a feature of the world that a naturalist must deny. There is not nor will there ever be a plausible explanation as to how one can start with dead, brute, non-teleological, law-governed matter with passive liabilities and generate the sort of ontological agent required for libertarian freedom by simply rearranging parts into new external relations. And as James Rachels reminds us, naturalistic evolutionary theory itself undermines the reality of free will:

> aspects of our behavior which we previously thought were matters of free choice are really the products of deep, genetically controlled forces . . . Humans may fabricate all sorts of other reasons for what they do, but these are mere rationalizations. In reality their conduct is fixed by the territorial imperative built into their genes.[13]

The theist is in no such pickle. He/she takes the fundamental being not to be particles, but a Person who is Himself a libertarian agent. Given that the theist starts with a Being who exhibits the ontological features of a libertarian free agent, it is not difficult to see how such features could be exhibited again at an appropriate time in the development of God's created order. But the naturalist has to pull a rabbit out of a hat with no rabbit in it and without a Magician. That's a pretty tall and dismal order.

Naturalist Responses to the Problem

What is a naturalist to do? Some follow Jaegwon Kim and 'solve' the problem of mental causation by idenfying mental states with brain states and, thus, allow mental states to have causal consequences in the world because, at the end of the day, they are not irreducibly mental but, rather, are physical. So, my desire for a drink of water causes me to get one because that desire-state is identical to a specific brain state.[14] Unfortunately, this is a desperate move. For one thing, the mental qua mental is causally impotent. It is only the mental qua physical that has causal powers, and this is simply to deny the reality of a distinctively mental sort of causation in the universe. Further, at best this merely gives us event–event causation and compatibilism, and this amounts to a denial of libertarian free will.

Timothy O'Connor tries to help himself to emergent properties and claim that when matter reaches a suitable complexity (a notion whose material content is hard to characterize in a non-circular way), active power simply emerges. I have criticized O'Connor elsewhere and, since few have followed him, will not take the time to repeat that criticism here, except to say one thing.[15] For emergentism to work, three things are required. First, it is not enough to embrace emergent active power. One also needs an emergent substantial, unified, enduring subject, and in my view, no one yet has successfully explained how such a subject can emerge from processes that involve the rearrangement of myriads and myriads of tiny particles into constantly changing relational complexes. This will be the subject of Chapter 5. Second, one needs mental potentialities to attribute to matter, and this is to move towards panpsychism and away from naturalism. Such a depiction of matter is at odds with the view that matter is properly and exhaustively characterizable in physical and chemical terms. Third, it is not enough to have mental potentialities in matter. One also needs it to be the case that such potentiality is actualized solely on the basis of a change in the accompanying facts of physics. But the connection between the mental and physical is radically contingent, and this is at odds with the claim that once matter reached the proper structure, that structure all at one go and all by itself necessitated the actualization of a mental potentiality that is itself contingently present.

Realizing these difficulties, Daniel Dennett and John Searle represent more sober attempts to solve the problem of free will in a naturalist framework. Among the reasons for incarcerating people – rehabilitation, deterrence, protection of society, and punishment – only the first three make sense in a naturalist view of things. Genuine retributive justice is a thing of the past. Naturalist philosopher Daniel Dennett tries to preserve a remnant of retributive punishment on a naturalist view, but his solution may fairly be taken as a reductio ad absurdum against naturalism.[16] Dennett acknowledges that both alcoholics and child abusers are equally determined to act as they do by forces outside their control. If we wished, we could continue to peel back the layers of people engaged in each action and find the genetic or other determining factors producing the behaviour. Still, we draw a metaphysically arbitrary line between the two, and we hold child abusers and not alcoholics responsible for their behaviour, preferring to treat the latter as a disease.

What justifies us in drawing the line where we do? Dennett explicitly appeals to a utilitarian justification that he takes to be an aspect of our implicit social contract, claiming that it maximizes the greatest amount of good for the greatest number of people (e.g., it serves to deter other acts of child abuse and retain a stable social order constitutive of the contract) if we act *as if* child abusers are responsible but the same cannot be said for alcoholics. Typical of Dennett, we opt for a voluntaristic stance towards certain acts, such as child abuse – a big *als ob* – even though libertarian freedom is a figment of an outdated worldview.

Dennett's solution is actually a deflation of the problem, a cure that kills the patient. As such, it is merely a denial of free will combined with the dismissive attitude that, at the end of the day, the unreality of free will is no big deal. I leave it to the reader to decide if Dennett is correct about this.

A more promising response has recently been proffered by John Searle.[17] According to Searle, for two reasons, we must posit a substantial ego as a purely formal, transcendental entity, an entity we must take to be real if we are to embrace libertarian action:[18]

1 Reasons-explanations (e.g., I punched a hole in the paper ballot because I wanted to vote for Bush) cite reasons on or for the sake of which we act,[19] but, as such, they are insufficient for explaining why free actions happen. For that we need to postulate a non-Humean (i.e., a non-bundle-of-perceptions), substantial self purely as a formal, transcendental postulate/precondition for the possibility of free action.[20]
2 We experience ourselves acting freely in the space of mental gaps in which an earlier mental state is not sufficient for the occurrence of a subsequent mental state.[21]

But there are serious problems in embracing the reality of free will itself.[22] It is hard to conceive how we can harmonize our conception of ourselves as free with the view that the universe consists entirely of mindless, meaningless, unfree, nonrational, brute physical particles. 'In the end, perhaps we will have to give up on certain features of our self conception, such as free will.'[23] Unfortunately, according to Searle, human rationality presupposes free will because rationality must make a difference in our behaviour; there must be a difference between rational and irrational behaviour and this can be so only if not all of our actions have antecedent causes that are sufficient to determine our actions. Only then can rationality operate, only then is there a certain room for manoeuvre.[24]

Yet it is hard to see how free will can exist in a world where all events, at least at the macro-level, seem to have causally sufficient antecedent conditions. And indeterminacy at the quantum level doesn't seem to help the problem since it is pure chance and randomness which by itself is not sufficient to give us responsible freedom.[25] Moreover, we are strongly inclined to think that determinism governs the occurrence of natural phenomena, given the right causal antecedents, the effect *had* to occur, and this is incompatible with free will.[26] The simple fact is that while we cannot get along without assuming we have free will, it doesn't seem to fit with what we know about the rest of the universe.

At the very least, then, we do not yet know if we have free will and, in fact, it is quite likely that there is no such thing. If, as seems quite likely, the total state of one's brain at t_1 is causally sufficient to determine the brain's total state at t_2, then there is no such thing as free will. So we are faced with this question: Are the causal antecedents of our actions in every case sufficient to determine our actions, or are there some cases where they are not sufficient, and if so, how do we account for those cases?[27] This appears to be a distinctively philosophical question, but as we shall see below, Searle's solution is to dissolve the philosophical problem of free will and replace it with a neurobiological problem.

Given his scepticism, Searle turns to the task of laying out a solution to the naturalist problem of free will. Searle is clear that mere indeterminacy is not sufficient for genuine free will.[28] Still, if free will is to be real, there must be gaps between antecedent causal conditions and resultant effects in three areas:[29] between the reasons for making a decision and the making of it, between the decision itself and the onset of action, and between the onset of the action and the carrying out of the action to its completion. Phenomenologically speaking, says Searle, we do not experience gaps between conscious states and bodily movements or between physical stimuli and bodily movements. But we do not experience the antecedent conditions as sufficient for the effects in these three areas. Instead we seem to be aware of gaps in these areas that can be depicted in Figure 1.[30] We actually experience ourselves – whether veridically or not – as acting in these gaps.[31]

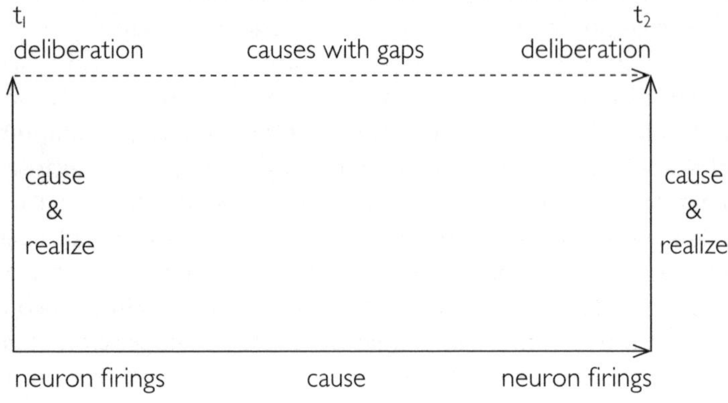

Figure 1

After laying out this background, Searle proffers a solution to the problem of free will in a naturalist world. He begins by trying to deflate the severity of the problem with two moves. First, he asserts that we must abandon the old dualist/physicalist dichotomistic language and replace it with a new vocabulary that describes ordinary matter, including the brain's lower-level structure, in the standard ways, and describes consciousness as a typical higher-level, biological, systems property of the brain. By using this new language, we set aside the idea that consciousness cannot naturally emerge when a suitably structured brain obtains, and we treat consciousness as an ordinary case of emergence, for example just like the emergence of the properties of digestion.

Second, he deflates the distinctive philosophical problem (e.g., given the nature of brute, mindless, deterministic, mechanistic matter, how is it possible for intrinsically characterized, irreducible consciousness to appear by simply rearranging brute matter into different spatial configurations?) and replaces it with a neurobiological problem: What exactly are the neuronal processes that cause our conscious experiences, and how exactly are these conscious experiences realized in the brain?[32] Note carefully, that this question will be answered when detailed correlations are provided between specific brain and mental states, combined with a depiction of indeterminacy necessary for a gap into which free action can be inserted. With this background, Searle tackles the question of how consciousness could move the body,[33] and his answer can be broken down into six steps:

Step one. Given that we have abandoned the old dualist, dichotomistic categories, we can compare consciousness with other higher-level systems properties and find an analogy for how consciousness can move the body. Borrowing an analogy from Roger Sperry, Searle invites us to consider a wheel made entirely of molecules rolling down a hill.[34] The solidity of the wheel affects the behaviour of each molecule in that its trajectory is affected by the entire solid wheel. Given that the wheel is nothing but molecules, when we say that solidity functions causally in the behaviour of the wheel and individual molecules, we are not saying that the solidity is something in addition to the molecules; rather, it is just the condition the molecules are in.

Step two. Searle unpacks the analogy between the wheel and its solidity with the brain and its consciousness. The consciousness of the brain can have effects at the neuronal level even though there is nothing in the brain except neurons (along with other structured entities such as neurotransmitters). And just as the behaviour of the molecules is causally constitutive of solidity, so the behaviour of neurons is causally constitutive of consciousness. Thus, when we say that consciousness moves the body, we are claiming that neuronal structures move the body due to the conscious states they are in. Consciousness is a feature of the brain like solidity is of the wheel. To be sure, consciousness, unlike solidity, is not ontologically reducible to physical microstructures, but this is not because consciousness is some extra thing; it is because consciousness has a subjective, first-person ontology and is not reducible to anything with a third-person, objective ontology. But consciousness is causally reducible to neuronal structures in that the former has no causal powers beyond those of the latter. By way of application, one's conscious intention-in-action causes one's arm to rise, but the intention is a feature of the brain system, and at the level of neurons, it is entirely constituted by neuronal activities.

Step three. Searle reminds the reader that reasons explanations (e.g., I raised my hand because I wanted to vote) do not provide sufficient conditions for explaining action, and thus, one must also postulate a self with free will who acts in the gaps listed above.[35] This self is a purely transcendental postulate in Kant's sense, that is, we must act *as if* such a self exists to make sense of free will, but such a formal postulate is not as such a real entity.[36]

Step four. Searle reminds the reader that our problem is a neurobiological one. If free will is real, it must have a neurobiological reality, and there must be some feature of the brain that realizes free will. Consciousness is a systems feature of the brain caused by lower-level entities (neurons, and so forth) and, in turn, realized in the system composed by these lower-level entities.[37] Given that free will requires higher-level gaps, how might they be realized at the neurobiological level? Unfortunately, says Searle, there do not appear to be gaps in the brain. Now, the problem is this: If the total state of the brain at t_1 is causally sufficient to determine the total state of the brain at t_2, then one has no free will. However, if the earlier state is not causally sufficient for the latter, then given certain assumptions about consciousness, one does have free will. How would we build a conscious robot, where at any instant, every facet of its consciousness is entirely determined by states at the micro-level, yet at the same time, the consciousness of the system functions causally in determining diachronically the next state of the system by processes that are not deterministic but, rather, are a matter of free, rational choice?[38]

Step five. Searle considers two hypotheses as answers to these questions.[39] According to Hypothesis 1, the state of the brain at any time is, in fact, causally sufficient for the next state. At the level of conscious deliberation where there are allegedly gaps such that certain antecedent psychological states are insufficient for bringing about the next state (e.g., between deliberating and deciding, between deciding and initiating action, and between initiating and carrying out an action), each such state is matched at the lower level by a sequence of neurobiological events each of which is causally sufficient for the next. Here we have a neurobiological determinism that 'matches' a psychological libertarianism. But the psychological level is illusory. There is an experience of free will, but no genuine free will obtains. The experience of such gaps is causally impotent and, in fact, there are no such gaps. Each lower-level state is sufficient for the next lower-level state and for the upper-level conscious state that synchronically supervenes on it. Free will is an illusory epiphenomenon on Hypothesis 1.

On Hypothesis 2, the absence of causally sufficient conditions at the psychological level is matched by the same absence at the neurological level. The problem, says Searle, is that we seem to have no idea what this could mean. There just are no gaps in the brain. But maybe we need to revise our description of consciousness as a higher-level phenomenon. We must hold on to the idea that consciousness is a feature of the whole system, it is literally present throughout those regions of the brain where it is created by and realized in neuronal activity, and it is located in certain portions of the brain and functions causally relative to those locations. As with the wheel and solidity example, perhaps conscious volitional features of consciousness have effects on the micro-elements of the brain, even though the system is composed entirely of those elements.

So, on Hypothesis 2,

1 The state of the brain at one time is not causally sufficient for its next state.
2 The movement of a state of the brain to the next state can only be explained by consciousness construed as a higher-level systems feature causally but not ontologically reducible to the lower level.
3 All the features of the conscious 'self' are entirely determined at each instant by the lower level.

The state of the neurons determines the state of consciousness (bottom-up), but any given neuronal state is insufficient for the next such state (lower-level diachronic indeterminism), and the passage of the brain from one state to the next is explained by rational thought processes and volitional choices.

Step six. Currently, says Searle, we have no idea how Hypothesis 2 could be true, but we can set down certain necessary conditions for its being true:

1 Consciousness, as caused by neuronal activity, can cause the body to move.

2 The brain causes and sustains the existence of consciousness and the 'self' (the possession of a unified field of consciousness, the possession of capacities for deliberative rationality, the possession of capacities to initiate and carry out actions) that can make free decisions and carry them out.
3 The brain is diachronically indeterminate such that the conscious self can make/carry out decisions in psychological gaps with respect to which explanations are provided for the sequence of the brain's states. The indeterminacy at the micro-level is necessary but not sufficient for genuine rationality/choice since the former but not the latter is purely random.

How Hypothesis 2 could be true is a mystery, and according to Searle, Hypothesis 1 is more likely to be true.[40]

Because the metaphysics of libertarian freedom (a first-moving substantial, immaterial self, active power, teleological action, top-down causation that violates the causal closure of the physical and seems to run contrary to bottom-up dependency and determination, a non-empirical faculty of awareness in virtue of which one is able to be aware of one's own self and its invisible exercise of active mental power), almost all naturalists reject libertarian free will. However, a small minority has sought to harmonize such freedom with naturalism, with Searle's account being among the most sophisticated and recent of such attempts. Unfortunately, for several reasons, his attempt must be judged a total failure.

For one thing, Searle's rejection of the dualist dichotomistic vocabulary of mental vs. physical amounts to nothing more than an unwarranted question-begging assertion or, worse, an unmotivated recommendation. Everyone who reads Searle calls him a property dualist. And while he claims to be puzzled by this, he shouldn't be. Searle's descriptions of ordinary matter and the lower-level constitution of the brain are just the ones dualists and physicalists accept. And his description of consciousness is just the one dualists and physicalists accept if it is taken to be a set of *sui generis*, irreducible, intrinsically characterized mental properties. Searle's new vocabulary of ordinary matter and higher-level biologically natural properties is just a verbal shift that expresses in different terms what dualists and physicalists have all along expressed in the 'old' vocabulary.

There's nothing new here. There's only one difference in Searle's vocabulary. Most dualists and physicalists use a dichotomistic vocabulary not only to describe two very different sorts of entities, but also to imply that they are so different, that the mental could not emerge from the physical by natural processes. And it is here that Searle's lexicon amounts to nothing more than an assertion: 'Consciousness can emerge from matter.' But this begs the question against the majority who eschew such emergence; Searle's depiction of consciousness and ordinary matter is precisely that of the majority, and he provides no argumentation for his assertion besides offering a few bad analogies for consciousness (see below), such as solidity, or digestion. Alternatively, he may be making a recommendation: 'Let's pretend that mind and matter are close enough in their nature that the former can emerge from the latter under suitable conditions.' But, again, he does not offer adequate reasons for accepting this dictum, so it is inadequately motivated.

Second, Searle's replacement of the philosophical problem with the neurobiological one is faulty for two reasons. For one thing, the philosophical problem has been around a long time, it is a unique difficulty (How can consciousness come from brute matter? What are we to make of the interaction between two such different orders of being?) in no way identical to the neurobiological one, and it is actually conceptually prior to and presuppositional for the neurobiological issue. After all, if one has good reasons for rejecting either emergence or causal interaction, then the scientific question becomes otiose. Additionally, Searle's neurobiological question can be answered by listing a set of precise correlations between mental and physical states of the brain. But the explanatory gap is lurking in the neighbourhood of such efforts, and far from being a solution to anything, such correlations are precisely what need to be explained. Further, the correlations seem to be radically contingent (for example, it seems quite possible that zombie worlds and disembodied existence could obtain, and itches as opposed to pains could be correlated with C-fibre firing). Thus, such contingent correlations cry out for explanation, and none will ever be forthcoming within a naturalist perspective. Moreover, such correlations fall far short of being causal laws which require showing that the effect *had* to occur given the cause. Searle accepts this causal necessitation requirement (given the cause, the effect had to occur[41]), so he cannot avoid the problem by opting for a weaker analysis of causation.

Third, Searle's employment (Steps one and two) of Sperry's wheel as an analogy for top-down causation is deeply flawed. For one thing, the wheel is a whole that is broader than its individual constituent molecules/atoms, but it is not a higher whole whose causal activity on its parts would be a case of top-down causation. Rather, it exhibits outside-in causation at the same level. But consciousness is emergent and *sui generis*. As such, it does ride on top of its subvenient base, so if it exerts causal power, that would, indeed, be a case of top-down causation. For another thing, solidity (and digestion) is a structural property ontologically constituted by subvenient particulars, properties and relations, so it is easy to see why it is causally constituted by these latter entities – solidity just is the subvenient structure into which it is entirely decomposable. But this is not so for consciousness. Given its emergent nature and the transitivity of efficient causality, so-called examples of top-down causation of mental events are both equivocal to the case of solidity and really cases of bottom-bottom causation through mental events. Regarding the former, the causal powers of solidity are literally 'causally constituted' (Searle's notion) by the behavior of its atomic/molecular parts, but consciousness is not so causally constituted because it is not analogously ontologically constituted.

Regarding the latter, Jaegwon Kim has argued, persuasively in my view, that there is no room for top-down causation if consciousness is construed emergently. More than any other naturalist, Kim has pressed the problem of top-down mental causation for naturalism.[42] Earlier I made reference to this issue, but by following Kim's treatment, we can develop this theme in a bit more detail. He correctly notes that the problem of mental causation arises from the very nature of physicalism itself, along with ontologically irreducible consciousness, and not from a Cartesian view of mental substance. Indeed, mental causation is a difficulty in the category of property every bit as much as in the category of substance.

Kim's supervenience argument (aka the exclusion argument) purportedly shows that, given the irreducibility of the mental, there can be no mental causation in a world that is fundamentally physical, and according to Kim, this raises serious problems regarding cognition and agency, two features of our lives that are hard to give up. The supervenience argument, says Kim, may be construed to show that mental causation is inconsistent with the conjunction of four theses:

1 closure;
2 exclusion (no overdetermination);
3 supervenience (not construed simply as property co-variance, but taken to entail dependence and synchronic determination);
4 mental irreducibility.

The fundamental idea of the supervenience argument is that 'vertical determination excludes horizontal causation'. To see this, Kim invites us to consider two physical events, p and p*, along with two mental events, m and m* such that:

1 m and m* supervene on p and p* respectively (where supervenience includes the notion of dependence and determination, even if this is not taken to be efficient causality); and
2 p causes p*.

The argument proceeds in two stages. Stage 1: Focus on m to m* causation. Since m* obtains in virtue of p*, if m is going to cause m* it must do so by causing p*. Stage 2: Kim offers two different ways to complete the argument. Completion 1: Assuming causal closure and exclusion (no causal overdetermination), p will be the cause of p* and there is no room for m to be involved in bringing about p*. We have m and m* supervening on p and p*, respectively, and p causing p*, nothing more and nothing less. Completion 2: Granting that m causes m* by causing p*, it follows that m causes p*. By irreducibility, we have $m \neq p$. So m and p cause m*. By exclusion and closure, m is ruled out and p is selected as the only cause for p*. Completion 2 avoids reference to supervenience. On either way of completing Stage 2, we have $m \rightarrow m^*$ and $m \rightarrow p^*$ giving way to $p \rightarrow p^*$.

So there are strong reasons to hold that top-down causation is disallowed by a naturalist view that entails the standard mereological model. If this is so, then mental causation can obtain only if the mental is not emergent but, rather, in some way or another identified with the physical. But this is not Searle's view and he correctly grasps that free will requires at least active power as an emergent property.

Finally, Searle's position is epiphenomenalist for at least three reasons. First, Searle's commitment to naturalism, especially the atomic theory of matter and evolutionary biology, is one that he himself takes to imply that there is no macro to micro causation and, on this point, most naturalists would agree. Jaegwon Kim says 'a physicalist must, it seems, accept some form of the principle that the physical domain is causally closed – that if a physical phenomenon is causally explainable, it must have an explanation within the physical domain'.[43] He goes on to say that 'Causal powers and reality go hand in hand. To render mental events causally impotent is as good as banishing them from our ontology.'[44] For these reasons, Kim claims that a naturalist should be a strict and not a supervenient physicalist because the latter implies a problematic epiphenomenal view of the mental. Along similar lines, David Papineau has argued that a naturalist should accept the completeness of physics, which amounts to the claim that the physical is basic and causally closed, and, therefore, supervenient physicalism is to be rejected because it implies epiphenomenalism.[45]

Second, Searle makes a distinction between two types of system features that are emergent. Emergent$_1$ features are caused by micro-level entities and do not exercise independent causality. Emergent$_2$ features are emergent$_1$ and are capable of exercising independent causality once they exist. Searle rejects the existence of emergent$_2$ features because, among other things, they would violate the transitivity of causality. Since he holds that conscious states are emergent$_1$, it is hard to see how those states could have causal efficacy.

Third, as we have already seen, Searle holds to the causal reduction of the mental. In causal reduction, the existence and 'powers' of the emergent but causally reduced entity are explained by the causal powers of the reducing, base entities. It is hard to see how he could hold this and avoid epiphenomenalism.

There are also difficulties for Searle's attempt to harmonize his biological naturalism with his treatment of reasons explanations. By explicitly adopting a commonsense approach to such explanations, Searle opens the door for a problem. Recall that he argues, correctly in my view, that properly understood, reasons explanations (Agent S performed act A because of reason R) do not cite causally sufficient conditions in appealing to R. Thus, such explanations are not ordinary causal explanations, and they leave a causal gap which is to be filled by (a transcendental, formally postulated) ego or self who exercises freedom. But this does not explain the role of R in such sentences, and it is evident to common sense – something Searle himself values – that reasons are irreducibly teleological goals/ends for the sake of which agents act. Given that we actually do satisfy such reasons explanations, we seem committed to irreducible teleology; indeed, to a form of teleology such that the presence or absence of reasons such as R make a difference to the causal history of human persons. It is hard to see how Searle can call his view biological *naturalism* if it countenances irreducible teleology.

Finally, Searle's appeal to gaps at the neurobiological level that reflect gaps at the level of consciousness and which entail that the unfolding states of the brain are not sufficient for the next state does not work. As Kim argued above, without such gaps, top-down causation is pre-empted. This is fundamentally due to the ontological dependency of emergent states/events on subvenient ones. The relation of ontological dependency is a transitive one just as is efficient causality. Now, if we grant the presence of the appropriate gaps at the brain level, this doesn't solve anything for two reasons:

1 Given quantum theory, if we accordingly take causal laws to be probabilistic, each state of the brain still fixes the chances of the next state and this would not be the case if top-down causation occurs (in which case, the bottom effect would be guaranteed by the necessitating exercise of active power at the top). So there is a conflict with top-down causation and quantum gaps due to indeterminacy.
2 A conscious state qua event is (a) not a continuant, but rather, a fleeting event and (b) entirely caused by the subvenient event with the result that at the level of consciousness, we have a series of mere shadows as far as causality is concerned. Only a substantial continuant can solve the problem, but Searle eschews such if it is taken to be real.

Searle's effort at establishing a rapprochement between libertarian freedom and naturalism – biological or otherwise – was both valiant and most likely the best a naturalist can do. Unfortunately, the simple fact is that we do have such freedom, and the ontology it entails provides a serious defeater for naturalism and confirmation of the image of God in all of us.

4

Naturalism, Rationality and Human Persons

In the seismic book recounting the shift to theism by famous atheist Anthony Flew – *There is a God* – Roy Abraham Varghese notes that

> the rationality that we unmistakably experience – ranging from the laws of nature to our capacity for rational thought – cannot be explained if it does not have an ultimate ground, which can be nothing less than an infinite mind.[1]

Christian philosopher Victor Reppert agrees: 'the necessary conditions for rationality cannot exist in a naturalistic universe'.[2] And Reppert goes on to argue that the ontology of human rationality provides evidence for theism as its best explanation. But it is not simply theists who acknowledge that human rationality is a problem for naturalism and can be explained by theism. According to naturalist Thomas Nagel:

> The problem then will be not how, if we engage in it, reason can be valid, but how, if it is universally valid, we can engage in it. There are not many candidates to this question. Probably the most popular nonsubjectivist answer nowadays is an evolutionary naturalism: We can reason in these ways because it is a consequence of a more primitive capacity of belief formation that had survival value during the period when the human brain was evolving. This explanation has always seemed to me to be laughably inadequate . . . The other well-known answer is the religious one. The universe is intelligible to us because it and our minds were made for each other.[3]

Naturalist Daniel Dennett queries:

> How could reason ever find a foothold in a material, mechanical universe? In the beginning, there were no reasons; there were only causes. Nothing had a purpose, nothing had so much as a function; there was no teleology in the world at all.[4]

In this chapter I intend to develop these insights along the lines of the previous two chapters. I hope to show that the ontology of human rationality provides evidence against naturalism and for theism, especially Judaeo-Christian theism. I shall proceed in two steps. First, I will develop the ontology of human rationality and explain why that ontology is a defeater for a naturalist worldview and evidence for God. Second, I will present and briefly interact with Alvin Plantinga's argument about the self-defeating nature of naturalism conjoined to evolutionary theory.

The Ontology of Rational Deliberation

Human persons are capable of acts of rational deliberation in which they reason through a chain of inductive or deductive premises and draw the proper conclusion. Whether it's deliberating about the most reasonable way to invest money, function as a juror, or view the ontological argument for God, we engage in rational processes regularly and successfully. Given the ontology of such acts, it is easy to see how they could obtain in a theistic world because the fundamental level of being – God – exhibits this ontology himself. Since they are fundamental to reality, it is not hard to see how they could obtain at certain points in the creation, especially when those allegedly made in God's image appear. But given that brute, non-rational, non-teleological, physical-causal-law-governed material stuff is bereft of this ontology, it is hard to see how that ontology could obtain, given naturalism. The problem for the naturalist is even more acute when we recall that he/she must employ combinatorial processes constitutive of the Grand Story according to which all change is the rearrangement of separable parts into various external, spatio-temporal, causal relations to form differently structured relational wholes.

In this section I want to examine the ontology of rational deliberation in some detail. That examination, I hope, will show why rationality is best explained by theism relative to atheistic naturalism and, indeed, why rationality is just not at home in the latter. I divide this ontology into factors regarding the nature of the rational agent and those regarding the rational deliberative process itself.

The rational agent

1 ***The unity of the agent.*** Regarding the agent, if we study paradigm cases of rationality, it becomes evident that the human person qua rational agent is a non-aggregated, substantial, enduring self with a fundamental, irreducible unity at and through time. Focusing on unity at a time, it will help us to think about two paradigm cases of reasoning.

Case one comes from an argument that has been offered by William Hasker.[5] The argument is an attempt to show that

1 The unity of consciousness at a time is real and irreducible.
2 It is essential to our experience of the world and to various epistemically justified beliefs grounded in such experience.
3 It cannot be explained if one is a brain because a brain is just an aggregate of different physical (separable) parts standing in various external relations to each other.

It is only if the self is a single, simple (uncomposed of separable parts) subject that the unity of consciousness is adequately accounted for.

To grasp the argument as presented, consider one's awareness of a complex fact, say one's own visual field consisting of awareness of several objects at once, including a number of different surface areas of each object. One's entire visual field is composed of several different experiences, for example, an awareness of a desk towards one's left side and an awareness of a podium in the centre of one's visual experience of an entire classroom. Such a unified visual field is essential to the epistemic justification of various perceptual beliefs. On the basis of my awareness of the entire back wall and its colour, I am justified in my belief that the wall is green. On the basis of my awareness of the desk and podium, I am justified in believing that the desk is to the left of the podium.

Corresponding to such a unified visual field, thousands of different light waves are bouncing off different objects (and off different locations on the surface of the same object, say different areas of the desk's top side), they all interact with the subject's retinas, and they all spark signals that terminate in myriads of different parts of the brain. Accordingly, a physicalist may claim that such a unified awareness of the entire room by means of one's visual field consists in the fact that there are a number of different physical parts of the brain each of which terminates a different wavelength and each of which is 'aware' only of part of and not the whole of the complex fact (the entire room).

However, this will not work, because it cannot account for the fact that there is a single, unitary awareness of the entire visual field. It is the very same self that is aware of the desk to the left, the podium at the centre, and, indeed, each and every distinguishable aspect of the room. But there is no single part of the brain that is correspondingly activated as a terminus for the entire visual field. Only a single, uncomposed mental substance can account for the unity of one's visual field or, indeed, the unity of consciousness in general.

And such a substance must be spatially unextended. Why? If it is spatially extended, then irrespective of whether or not it is composed of separable parts, there will be various non-identical regions within that extension with which different aspects of the visual field overlap. The self will be like a movie screen construed as uncomposed. There is no region of the screen that overlaps with the entire movie at a particular time. One cannot merely say that it is the screen itself that exemplifies the movie, because this is not an unanalysable fact. The screen can be reduced to a sum of the iteration of an arbitrary region (e.g., a foot tall and wide), and the movie picture can be similarly reduced such that each such region of the picture overlaps with one and only one such region of the screen. There is no further, relevant screen 'over and above' this reduced one. Similarly, regarding the self, there will be no single entity that has all the different visual experiences or the entire holistic experience if the self is extended.

Here's a second case. Consider the process of reasoning through an instance of *modus ponens* in which at times t_1–t_5 one attends to the first premise (If P, then Q), the second premise (P), the two premises together ((If P, then Q) and (P)), draws a conclusion (Q) and attends to that conclusion precisely *as* the conclusion. At time t_3, one must attend to the two premises simultaneously, become acquainted via rational intuition (Edmund Husserl called it eidetic intuition) with the logical relation between the two propositions in order to *draw* the conclusion and attend to it precisely as such. At t_3, the self that attends to one premise and the self that attends to the other premise stand in absolute identity to 'each other'. Such a self is an irreducible, unified, substantial I.

Let us now focus on unity or strict sameness through change, including part replacement in the brain. Two parallel paradigm cases suggest themselves. The first focuses on cases in which we go through processes to verify (or disconfirm) thoughts (beliefs, sensations) about things in the world. Right now I am looking at a chair in my kitchen from my desk in my office. Suppose I want to know if that very chair has a scratch on the side away from me that is unavailable to my visual access. As I walk toward the chair, I experience a series of chair representations. That is, I have several different chair experiences that replace one another in rapid succession. As I approach the chair, my chair sensations vary. If I pay attention, I am also aware of two more things. First, I do not simply experience a series of sense images of a chair. Rather, through self-awareness, I also experience the fact that it is I myself who has each chair experience. Each chair sensation produced at each angle of perspective has a perceiver who is I. An 'I' accompanies each sense experience to produce a series of awarenesses – 'I am experiencing a chair sense image now.'

I am also aware of the basic fact that the same self that is currently having a fairly large chair experience (as my eyes come to within 12 inches of the chair) is the very same self as the one who had all of the other chair experiences preceding this current one. Through self-awareness, I am aware of the fact that I am an enduring I who was and am (and will be) present as the owner of all the experiences in the series. Indeed, in the middle of the sequence, I am aware of having had certain representations, of currently having a specific representation, and of being about to have future representations.

These two facts – I am the owner of my experiences, and I am an enduring self – show that I am not identical to my experiences. I am the conscious thing that has them. And arguably, I am also aware of myself as a simple, uncomposed and spatially unextended centre of consciousness.

Now consider my act of discovering that the chair's far side has a scratch on it. Does this verify my initial thought, 'The chair in the kitchen has (or fails to have) a scratch on the far side'? Yes, but only if I am an enduring continuant. To see why, let us distinguish an entity – anything whatsoever that actually exists – from an object – anything towards which an intentional act is directed. If there were no intentional agents, there would be entities but no objects. An object is an entity that is being sensed, thought of, and so forth. Let us also call the sequence of experiences from my initial perception and conception of the kitchen chair from my study to the final experience in which the chair's scratch itself is directly present to me a 'fulfilment structure'.

Fulfilment structures are essential to human rationality and they consist in cases of first-person epistemic success where initial thoughts/concepts are verified or disconfirmed by a sequence of relevant first-person experiences. Fulfilment structures are always experiences *for individual selves who live through them*. To be sure, if asked, I may verify the chair's scratch for you, but this derivative case of epistemic success for you is dependent on my first-person fulfilment structure related to the scratch, and in any case, such first-person cases are essential for human rationality. Now in such cases, the self at the beginning of the structure is identical to the self at the end. Otherwise, the self (or self-stage) at the end of the sequence verifies the scratch for someone else (or a non-identical stage).

The second paradigm case involves thinking through the *modus ponens* syllogism as presented above. Not only must there be a unified self at each time in the sequence, but also an identical self that endures through the rational act. Now consider A. C. Ewing's argument:

> To realize the truth of any proposition or even entertain it as something meaningful the same being must be aware of its different constituents. To be aware of the validity of an argument

> the same being must entertain premises and conclusion; to compare two things the same being must, at least in memory, be aware of them simultaneously; and since all these processes take some time the continuous existence of literally the same entity is required. In these cases an event which consisted in the contemplating of A followed by another event which consisted in the contemplating of B is not sufficient. They must be events of contemplating that occur in the same being. If one being thought of wolves, another of eating, and another of lambs, it certainly would not mean that anybody contemplated the proposition 'wolves eat lambs' . . . There must surely be a single being persisting through the process to grasp a proposition or inference as a whole.[6]

If the conclusion of a syllogism is to be grasped as a conclusion, it must be *drawn* from the experiences of each premise singularly and, then, together. As Ewing notes, a successive series of I-stages cannot engage in such acts; only an enduring I can. Moreover, if the rational agent who embraces the conclusion is to be regarded as intellectually responsible for his reasoning, it must be the same self at the end of the process as the self who lived through the stages of reasoning that led to drawing the conclusion. One is not responsible for the acts of others or of other person-stages. So intellectual responsibility seems to presuppose an enduring I.

In Chapter 5, I will offer additional defences of a substantial, enduring mental self, and I will explain why naturalism cannot countenance such a self. But for now, I simply note the basic reason for this inability: If one starts with separable parts, and simply rearranges them according to natural laws into new relational structures constituted by external relations, then in the category of individual, one's ontology will have atomic simples (sans difficulties with such) and mereological aggregates with insufficient unity to avoid mereological essentialism or to ground absolute unity at and through part replacement and the flux of conscious states.

2 ***Free will.*** I will not repeat our discussion of free will in Chapter 3. I simply note that there are several aspects to human reasoning that require free will. You may recall that for the compatibilist, rationality is more basic than freedom (e.g., free will occurs when

an act is caused in the right way by one's own prior rational states). The converse is true for the libertarian. Acts of deliberation presuppose that the rational process is 'up to me' and is not determined prior to or during the process. The conclusion is drawn freely. My act of deliberation itself contributes by way of exercises of active power to what outcome is reached. Acts of deliberation presuppose that there is more than one possible conclusion one could reach, but if determinism is true, there is only one outcome possible, and it was fixed prior to the act of deliberation by forces outside the agent's control. In deliberation, we not only weigh evidence, we also *weight* evidence – freely assign it certain importance in the rational process. Moreover, we stand at the end of our deliberative processes as intellectually responsible rational agents. Our conclusions are ones we or anyone in relevantly similar circumstances *ought* to draw. On the reasonable assumption that in clear cases, ought implies can, then genuine epistemic responsibility requires free will.

Finally, there is a flexible, non-Sphexishness to rational deliberation. In reasoning, there is a non-Sphexishness, a non-rigidity of performance, a flexibility in which one has the ability to choose freely to adjust one's processes or behaviours by choosing to step back from one's immediate context, by simply seeing certain things to be so, by noting what is and is not significant in one's context, by engaging in *ceteris paribus* bracketing, and by rationally choosing to act accordingly. The term 'Sphexishness' comes from the digger or *Sphex* wasp whose deterministic, 'mechanical' behaviour renders it an automaton with no freedom or rationality. During the egg-laying period, the *Sphex* wasp builds a burrow, drags a paralysed cricket into it, lays eggs alongside it, closes the burrow, and leaves. The eggs hatch and feed off the cricket. The wasp's routine is to bring the paralysed cricket to the burrow, set it on the threshold, go inside to see if all is well, exit and drag the cricket inside. If the cricket is moved a few inches away while the wasp is inside, upon exiting, the wasp will again bring the cricket up to the threshold but not inside, and repeat the preparatory behaviour. The *Sphex* becomes trapped in a rigid loop: if the cricket is moved again the behaviour will re-cycle. One wasp that was studied did the cycle 40 times! The *Sphex* is deterministically at the mercy of its environmental input and internal hardware, both of which are outside its control. Speaking of this Sphexish behaviour, Daniel Dennett says, 'The poor wasp is unmasked; she is not a free agent, but rather at the mercy of brute physical causation, driven inexorably into her states and activities by features of the environment outside her control.'[7] This property of deterministic rigidity is Sphexishness.

Given a naturalistic view of human persons, we are just as Sphexish as the digger wasp. In Chapters 1 and 3, I have presented reasons for why libertarian agency is not an option for robust naturalism. We are Sphexish all the way down. In such a world, there is no such thing as genuine rational deliberation at the basic level of analysis.

Dennett attempts to provide a naturalist rejoinder to the problem of Sphexishness, and thereby to retain room for reason and rational deliberation in a naturalist worldview.[8] He acknowledges that abnormal cases of Sphexishness (e.g., the radically insane, retarded, or brain-damaged) undermine the presence of reason. But according to Dennett, while a naturalist may not be able to avoid Sphexishness at the end of the day, he/she can provide an account in which our Sphexishness is so radically different from that of the digger wasp or abnormal cases, that worries about naturalism and rational deliberation may be set aside. Dennett claims that under the demands of evolutionary survival, creatures like us appeared that have self-interests and, in fact, are aware of those interests and guardians of them. We can fend for ourselves. Reason evolved as the ability to order and evaluate our various interests, and select varying degrees of effectiveness in securing them. Thus, there is a clear evolutionary account for this sort of practical reason.

Dennett notes that some draw a distinction in kind between these two categories:

1 acting on account of reasons precisely because they are good reasons, being a semantic engine, acting freely; vs.
2 acting in accordance with good reasons, being a syntactical engine, being determined.

But he recommends that we view these as differing in degrees such that if the members of the list in 2 are highly complicated, unpredictable, and involve feedback loops that re-cycle through the brain, then a naturalist can give an account such that human beings can approximate the members in list 1 close enough to avoid Sphexish worries. For example, under such conditions of complexity, and so on, a person could recognize he was in a vicious loop and step out of it. Again, a highly complicated syntactical engine approximates a semantic engine. And so on.

Does Dennett's account succeed? For two reasons, I do not think so. First, it seems obvious to me that the two lists do, in fact, differ in kind. Artificial intelligence, no matter how complicated, is not real intelligence. Naturalism cannot sustain the reality of the members of list 1 and, therefore, cannot provide enough room for genuine rational deliberation, but only for organisms that imitate it to one degree or another. Second, unpredictability does not entail non-Sphexishness. From the fact that your brain is so much more complicated than that of the Sphex wasp that your behaviour is unpredictable, it does not follow that it isn't mechanical and determined. To return to Dennett's own example, even if we grant that one's feedback loops are such that one can 'recognize' one is in a loop and jump out of it, one still jumps into a new loop, even if it is so complicated that the precise sequence of behaviours constituting the new loop are unpredictable. After all, being determined by a complicated mechanism is still being determined.

*3 **Epistemic powers.*** Epistemic externalism is the most plausible view of the epistemic subject and his/her epistemic states/processes in light of the commitments of naturalism outlined in Chapter 1. And as John Searle notes, for adherents of robust naturalism,

> Every fact in the universe is in principle knowable and understandable by human investigators. Because reality is physical, and because science concerns the investigation of physical reality, and because there are no limits on what we can know of physical reality, it follows that all facts are knowable and understandable by us.[9]

Thus, Robert Stalnaker observes that 'the philosopher who wants to regard human beings and mental phenomena as part of the natural order [must] explain intentional relations in naturalistic terms'.[10] The naturalist will hold to an externalist theory of knowledge or justification (or warrant). This is true for two main reasons, one positive and one negative. The positive reason is that 'A scientific or naturalistic account of [human beings and their mental states] must be a causal account.'[11] Externalist theories in epistemology either implicitly (e.g. reliabilist theories) or explicitly (e.g. causal accounts) centre on the notion of causality.

The negative reason is this: The central notion of 'internal' for the internalist is an irreducibly mental one that makes reference to such things as being a self-presenting property, being a mode of consciousness, being a second-order state directed at a first-order mental state via introspection, being directly present to the cognizer's awareness, cognitive accessibility, being internal to one's point of view, first-person introspection, and the like. Arguably, all these notions are irreducibly mental. And it is difficult to see to what collection of particles, along with their individual or collective movements or causal relations, these mental properties and their instantiations are identical.

Moreover, they are irreducible and cannot be analysed merely as functional kinds with physical realizers if the perspective is to remain an internalist one because if these are reduced to (or replaced by) physicalist (causal/functional) notions, then what is distinctive to internalism will fall out and the view will collapse into externalism. Neither the properties just mentioned nor the way that they are internal to epistemic subjects (e.g., by being self-presenting, being available to private, first-person access) is easily identifiable with

1 a particular, property, or relation that belongs to the ontology of physics, or
2 a functional state or a physical realizer of a functional state.

The mental properties just listed are intrinsic, simple properties, but functional types and the brain states that realize them are relational structures. And it is precisely as intrinsic properties that the mental states so characterized are capable of being directly present to consciousness via a simple act of awareness.

The desire to preserve naturalism notwithstanding, these and other features of the epistemic subject amount to powers/faculties of such a subject that are not countenanced within the constraints of naturalism. In what follows, I want to discuss two sorts of knowledge that exhibit an immediacy that belies any naturalist attempt to reduce them to some sort of physical causal relation: a priori knowledge and introspective knowledge. In each case, there seems to be an epistemically immediate awareness of a relevant object that is possible only if there is no entity between the subject and the object, including no causal chain. It is plausible to think that in cases of a priori knowledge such as '2 + 2 = 4' or 'Necessarily, redness is (an 'is' of exemplification) colourfulness', the relevant abstract objects are immediately given to the knowing subject and, in some cases, incorrigibly known.

I have defended this notion elsewhere, and cannot elaborate that here.[12] Suffice it to say that a 'perceptual' account of rational intuition has a long and sturdy pedigree in the history of philosophy. Thus, George Bealer says that 'By [rational] intuitions here, we mean *seemings*: for you to have an intuition that A is just for it to *seem* [rationally appear] to you that A.'[13]

Similarly, one's own awareness of one's sensations, occurent thoughts, and so forth are such that the relevant mental states are immediately, and in some simple cases incorrigibly, given to the subject.[14]

In each case – a priori knowledge and introspective knowledge – there are two reasons why there can be no causal relation – certainly, no physical causal relation – constitutive of the relevant cognitive acts. First, the abstract objects of a priori knowledge are causally inert, and even if one tries to specify a causal or quasi-causal relation in which they stand to epistemic subjects, that specification will go far beyond the resources of naturalism. And in cases of introspective knowledge, even if there is a causal relation between the mental state and the introspecting subject, this would amount to a mental–physical (or mental–mental) relation that should make a naturalist uncomfortable. In this case we have Descartes' revenge: The mental–physical interaction problem surfaced in the category of individual/substance now applies to the category of property/event.

Second, the sort of epistemic directness and immediacy involved in each case entails that the relevant object is directly present to the subject. This presents a problem for the naturalist. Why? Because he/she will reduce these sorts of cases to the subject (a specific region of the brain?) standing in a physical causal relation to the object (a surrogate for an abstract object, a different region of the brain?). Unfortunately, for any such chain, there will always be the problem of causal deviancy in which case the object is neither directly present (there being a causal chain between the subject and object) nor known incorrigibly (since any chain is possibly rendered deviant by a counterexample, the subject could always be mistaken). Thus, naturalism fails to account for these sorts of knowledge. I should say that these types of knowledge are crucial for rationality. In the a priori case, logic, mathematics, the nature of explanation, evidence, justification, knowledge, truth and so forth are all examples of such knowledge. Regarding introspective knowledge, reasoning itself requires direct access to one's own thoughts/beliefs/sensations in order to engage in rational treatment of these states.

Though he is a rationalist, Laurence Bonjour has attempted to develop a non-perceptual realist account of a priori knowledge.[15] Bonjour queries, just because there is no efficient causal relation between a subject and an abstract object such as a traditional universal, why think that some relation of influence isn't there? Why think that the only way to enter a relation of influence is like individual physical particulars do? Why think that redness and greenness must be concretely involved in causal chains like physical particulars before one can know what they are and that, necessarily, nothing can be red and green all over at the same time? It would be enough if the causal chain contained objects that instantiated the relevant properties. By analogy, claims Bonjour, abstractive theories of concept formation (e.g., Aristotle's) fit in here. This may not be causal influence but it's influence nonetheless, so it suffices.

However, at this point a possible problem arises. If one construes 'causal influence' as being closely analogous to sense perception (e.g., a direct grasping of properties and relations themselves and on this basis judging the relevant propositions to be true) and, even if one admits that this account is in some sense metaphorical, it does seem to require a quasi-perceptual account of rational insight. The problem is that cases of ordinary sensory perception of physical particulars do have as a necessary condition a causal relation between perceiver and perceived, but no such relation obtains in the case of knowledge of abstract objects. Thus, says Bonjour, the analogy with perception should be broken. But if this move is made, if one wishes to retain a rationalist defence of a priori knowledge of abstract objects, one must offer an account of rational apprehension that avoids the analogy with sense perception.

According to Bonjour, to have a rational apprehension of an object is just to think about or represent that object. The way one grasps/apprehends in rational insight is just to think about/ represent an entity. By way of exposition, Bonjour invites us to consider one type of mental state – contemplating an object, which is to say, having it in the mind. In these cases, a subject is aware of the object of thought, of what it is he/she is thinking about. Now the question arises, How is one able to think about an object? In virtue of what is a mental state about, for example triangularity? What is it to be aware of the content of one' own thought, to grasp what one is thinking about? In essence, Bonjour's answer is that it is to have an intelligible conception of the object of one's thought. For this to be the case, some element of thought must be intrinsically meaningful and this is relevant to the defence of moderate rationalism in several ways, one of which is this: The idea of intrinsic thought content suggests how the abstract object involved in a priori justification can be accessible to the mind without appealing to a perceptual or quasi-perceptual view that raises anew the causal objection.

By way of elaboration, Bonjour starts with three initial aspects of such an account:

1 It will be hardcore metaphysics unpopular to post-positivists. We need an account of properties/relations as traditional universals and as objects of thought and of the intrinsic features of thoughts such that the latter are directly accessible.
2 We should not limit ourselves to materialism/naturalism in our approach and, in fact, the account can be used in a reductio against them.
3 Such an account will need contents that represent properties (and not just particulars).

How does a thought simply by virtue of its intrinsic meaning come to be about or have as an element of its content a specific universal?

According to Bonjour, only one answer seems available: The property itself is somehow metaphysically 'involved' in the intrinsic character of the thought. But we can't just say the thought instantiates the property as Aristotle/Aquinas did. Admittedly, says Bonjour, Aristotle and Aquinas did say that thought and object have the property in two different ways, and that notion is in the right direction. Focusing on Aquinas, there are two different interpretations of his view:

(1) The mind and object exemplify the same property but the exemplification relation is different in each case.

Bonjour rejects this as a plausible position on the grounds that there seems to be only one exemplification relation, not two.

(2) The relevant intentional universal and the universal in the object are different and not identical, even though they are intimately related entities.

Bonjour believes that this second interpretation is on the right track. On Bonjour's account, the realist should make the property of the object a component or ingredient or constituent of the thought without saying it is instantiated in the thought. For example, is it by virtue of a thought instantiating a complex universal that 'involves' the universal, triangularity, in the appropriate way, namely as an 'ingredient' of the thought without being instantiated in the thought, that the thought is about triangular things. In this way, claims Bonjour, we can give an account of knowledge of universals without depicting the apprehension of universals as a perceptual relation analogous to visual perception that somehow reaches out into the Platonic realm.

As Bonjour correctly notes, his account entails a metaphysics not acceptable to a naturalist, so even if one accepts this account, one would have ammunition against naturalism. But I believe the perceptual account of a priori intuition is preferable to Bonjour's, and I find at least four problems with his analysis. First, it is not clear that the essence of the comparison between visual perception and rational intuition involves a causal relation, or even some weaker causal-type influence, between the subject and the object.

As a contingent empirical fact, this may be a physically necessary condition for normal acts of visual perception of embodied persons, but there needs to be some argument that rational intuition requires something of the sort and Bonjour gives none. Later in this chapter, I will argue that a subject's standing in a causal relation with an object is neither necessary nor sufficient for having an intentional state – perceptual or otherwise – of that object.

Second, Bonjour appears to conflate grasping an object and being aware of the content of the thought directed on the object. The various constituents of a mental act, along with the other mental entities that are associated with it and which direct the act towards an object, are not the same thing as the object of the act. Put differently, it is plausible to think that neither objects of mental acts nor the constituents (properties, parts) of those objects are constituents of the acts directed upon those objects. Nor does it seem necessary to make a constituent of the object be a constituent of a mental act to explain how an act can be directed upon an object. Moreover, thinking about *modus ponens* is just not the same as being directly aware of an instantiation of it.

Third, Bonjour never explains how it is that the relevant property of the object gets into the mental act in the first place. Perceptual models of rational intuition do just that by actually dismissing the problem: Object x is 'in' mind S just in case x is an object upon which one of S's intentional states is directed. However, Bonjour's non-perceptual account does not have this option available to it, and his non-perceptual view is the weaker for failing on this score.

Finally, it is entirely unclear how a property can be a constituent of a particular (e.g., a concrete particular, a moment, or an event) without doing so by way of exemplification. Throughout history, the overwhelming majority of realists have agreed that qua universals, properties are the sorts of things that enter other things by way of the nexus of exemplification, even though they have different views about the precise nature of exemplification itself. It would be desirable to find a plausible account of knowledge of universals that avoids the introduction of an entirely new and unclear notion of how universals are in things.

I conclude by saying that rational subjects have various epistemic powers that are quite beyond the explanatory resources, the epistemology, the Grand Story, and the ontology of naturalism. However, these epistemic powers are among the sorts of powers God and his image bearers have, so they provide defeaters for naturalism and evidence for biblical theism.

The process of rational deliberation

In addition to the rational agent, there are features of the process of rational deliberation that provide defeaters for naturalism and evidence for biblical theism. Here is a brief study of five such features.

1 ***Teleology.*** Consider the following argument:

(1a) If naturalism is true, there is no irreducible teleology.
(2a) Rational deliberation exhibits irreducible teleology.
(3a) Therefore, naturalism is false.

In Chapter 3, we saw that reasons explanations are irreducibly teleological, and various inductive or deductive thought processes reason through a series of steps *in order to* or *for the sake of* reaching a sound, true, rational conclusion. Besides the analysis of reasons explanations, when one attends to one's own endeavourings, it becomes introspectively evident that the various steps in such processes are formulated for the sake of drawing a particular conclusion. If one pays attention to fairly simple mental states in second-order awarenesses of first-order states, then it seems reasonable to say that unless there are substantial, non-question-begging, overriding defeaters, then one should believe that things are as they seem. For example, a pain is as it seems to be in such acts. Similarly, one's own teleological endeavourings are as they seem.

Additionally, when one attends to the different states containing propositional contents in rational sequences that constitute the inductive or deductive premises of the sequence, it becomes evident that these states are *means – rational means –* to the end of drawing the conclusion. And when one attends to both the drawing of the conclusion and the conclusion so drawn, it becomes evident that the conclusion is the *end* for the sake of which the process was undergone. In fact, if one is reasoning to a conclusion, and one line of reasoning is seen to be (or not to be!) epistemically useful for drawing a conclusion, we are through introspection able to become aware of this and thereupon adopt it or an alternative line of reasoning as a subsequent means to the conclusive end. In this way, the teleological view of deliberation supports the derivation of compensatory counterfactuals. Consider the following:

(T) S D'd (reasoned through a deliberative series) in order to C (draw a conclusion about what insurance policy to purchase).
(T_C) If D'ing had required G'ing (gathering such and such information), then S would have G'd.

An irreducibly teleological interpretation of T provides a powerful, straightforward way of deriving T_C. Moreover, the teleological end is essential to the sequences in the chain (D'ing) being what they are – precisely ordered means to an end. Had S not been directing his behaviour towards C'ing, S would not have D'd.[16]

Reductive analyses of these teleological facts about deliberation cannot appeal to naturalism or physicalism on pain of begging the question, and I know of no good argument that provides a sufficiently strong overrider for the types of evidence for teleology just cited and of which we are aware daily in our thought processes.

2 ***Normativity.*** Being rational, having justified beliefs, drawing correct conclusions from the evidence and related notions are intrinsically normative. When one thinks of these and related notions, it is natural to think of them as being intellectually or epistemically valuable. In other words, there is a close connection with rationality and epistemic value. For example, to have a justified belief is to have something of intellectual worth. How should one understand this connection between justification and epistemic value?

Philosophers differ over this issue. Some have argued that this normativity should be understood in terms of faithfully fulfilling certain intrinsically correct epistemic duties, that is, cognitive rules that specify duties for obtaining rational, justified beliefs. Some of these rules may be 'obtain true beliefs and avoid false ones', 'obtain rational beliefs and avoid irrational ones', 'if something appears red to you, then believe it is, in fact, red until you have sufficient evidence to the contrary', and so on. Being rational is a matter of doing one's intellectual duty, of trying one's best to follow the correct epistemological rules.

There are other, non-deontological views about rationality and justification. On these views, justification does not amount to following correct epistemic rules, but, rather, it involves exemplifying certain states of affairs that are intrinsically valuable. Here are some examples of such states of affairs: holding more true than false beliefs; forming and maintaining beliefs by means of properly functioning sensory and intellectual faculties in an environment for which they were designed; having coherent beliefs; and so on. Here, justification is conceived of as forming and maintaining (and structuring) beliefs in such a way that people embody one or more of these intrinsically valuable states of affairs. But these states of affairs are not to be thought of as rules specifying duties.

The simple fact is that naturalism cannot explain the existence or exemplification of intrinsic value (see Chapter 6 for more on this). This is why the vast majority of naturalists since the 1930s have opted for some form of non-cognitivism or reductive naturalism in metaethics. Nor will it do simply to assert that intrinsic value, in this case, intrinsic epistemic value, simply supervened on certain physical states because (1) supervenience is just a label for the problem to be solved and not a solution and (2) as employed by naturalists, supervenience begs the question against a theistic explanation for which the basic being exemplifies intrinsic values of different sorts.

So most naturalists adopt some sort of descriptive naturalization of rationality and thereby eliminate real, irreducible, epistemically relevant value. On this view, the knowing subject is a natural organism, and 'epistemic' activity amounts to various 'reliable' belief-forming procedures and causal interactions with the environment, all of which may be studied and described by psychology and neuroscience. In this way, the normative element of classic epistemology drops out and the goal is to offer descriptive, scientific theses as to how knowing subjects typically do, in fact, form their beliefs.

To see how the normative element drops out of consideration, consider the following example that appropriates descriptive rationality in ethical reasoning. In a widely used text in ethics, utilitarian Tom L. Beauchamp considers and rejects a pluralistic theory of value because, among other things, it requires commitment to a plurality of intrinsically valuable things and, in light of naturalism and other considerations, it seems to Beauchamp to be futile and presumptuous to attempt to develop a general theory of value.[17] As a replacement, Beauchamp proffers subjective preference utilitarianism according to which the 'value' of an act lies in its maximization of the satisfaction of desires and wants which express individual preferences.

He recognizes that, so defined, this theory suffers from some fairly obvious counterexamples, for example, in a possible world where most prefer child-molestation, it would justify such an act under certain conditions. So Beauchamp supplements the principle of subject preference such that the justification of an act is spelled out in terms of the maximization of those subjective preferences that it is rational to have.

Now just exactly how is 'rationality' functioning here? To answer this, let us distinguish prescriptive and descriptive rationality. Prescriptive rationality is the ability to have intrinsically correct insights into, or form justified beliefs with respect to, what is intrinsically valuable in an ethical sense. This cannot be what Beachamp means since, if it were, his theory would be circular. Clearly, he means descriptive rationality: the ability to select efficient means to accomplish arbitrarily preferred ends and the formation of only those desires that normal people desire which, in turn, would be cashed out statistically or in terms of evolutionary advantage, or in some similar sort of way.

Of course, it is easy to envision worlds in which what is 'normal' – statistically regular or evolutionarily advantageous – would place moral duties to engage in child-molestation and a host of other hideous practices. Beauchamp's response to this argument is simply to assert that no moral theory is required to respond to universal 'idiocy' and leave it at that. But beside the fact that it is Beauchamp's own theory that generates the problem of universal 'idiocy' in the envisioned worlds, his answer singularly fails to respond to a legitimate counterexample that may appropriately be taken as a reductio against his views. In any case, the difference between descriptive and prescriptive rationality is clear, naturalists really are stuck with the former (unless they beg the question by adopting the vacuous supervenience route), and, as a result, demonstrate the inability to have the worldview resources for objective, intrinsically (epistemically) valuable rationality. It would not be too far afield to suggest that self-refutation is lurking in the neighbourhood.

3 ***Mental contents.*** There are three features of mental contents as they figure into rational deliberation for which naturalism cannot account:

1 The nature of concepts/propositions themselves and the fact that they can be true/false.
2 The internal relations in which mental contents sometimes stand.
3 Intentionality.

Let us take these in order.

1 Propositional contents, such as meanings, are intentional qualities (e.g., concepts; propositions which are wholes with concepts, logical relations, etc. as constituents) instantiated as immanent contents in their associated mental events (e.g., specific thoughts, beliefs). And meanings, logical relations, epistemic relations, and so forth are not physical, causal entities. For example, premises in a syllogism do not cause their conclusion, they entail it. The basing relation (e.g., I believe P on the basis of believing Q) is not charactertizable in physical categories. Deontological epistemic rules (e.g., If x appears F to me, then in the absence of an awareness of defeaters, I *ought* to believe that x is F) or epistemically intrinsically valuable doxastic states (e.g., an internally consistent belief state is more valuable epistemically than a contradictory belief state) are not easily characterizable as physical states. The modality of certain meanings (e.g., propositions) and the relations among them (e.g., *modus ponens*) have a necessity throughout all possible worlds (*modus ponens* is true in all possible worlds whatever) that goes beyond mere physical necessity (e.g., given that the laws of nature are such and such and that a chunk of matter is thus and so, then it is physically necessary that such and such happen). And the type of a priori knowledge we have of this necessity is not reducible to a physical causal process.

Let me elaborate a bit on concepts and propositions.[18] A dog and a thought about the dog are different entities, yet they exhibit a special togetherness such that the latter is essentially about the former. In general, there is something about a conceptual act that makes it necessarily of its object, that grounds their relation of togetherness. Call that something 'a concept'. A concept may be acquired, it applies to and is of something other than itself, namely its cases or extension. The 'meaning' of a concept is the properties and other constituents of the concept that are of a specific non-intentional range of properties and other constituents a thing must have to fall under a concept. For example, the 'meaning' of the concept of a unicorn resides in being a structural property consisting of at least two intentional properties – being a concept of a horse and being a concept of a horn – which is thereby of the property of being a horned horse that is exemplified by all and only the members of the extension of the concept.

Many people can have the very same concept, concepts are necessary constituents of human thought and knowledge, and, arguably, it is the relationship among concepts that grounds logical constraints and logical laws among propositions of which those concepts are constituents. Moreover, a concept is an intentional property that is exemplified in various acts of cognition (thinking, reasoning, daydreaming, etc.). Concepts are identifiable by direct reflective awareness (introspection), and they 'mediate' the mind and world. Their identity is necessarily tied to their referents with which they have a natural affinity and, thus, are natural signs.

Propositions are structural, intentional properties composed of concepts and various other mental entities (e.g., being predicated of, being this). Propositions are

1 not located in space or time,
2 not identical to sentences/statements, but are the meanings of such,
3 underivatively true or false;
4 capable of being in and grasped by many minds at once.

Just as our ability to grasp intuitively the nature of a pain (and other so-called states of phenomenal consciousness) is due to the fact that its nature is an intrinsic, non-relational feature of it, so is our ability to grasp the introspectively available nature of the concepts and propositions that constitute our thoughts, beliefs and so forth. Jaegwon Kim disputes this claim and argues that, in fact, a kind of belief, for example that George Washington was the first president of the United States, does not have a uniform, qualitatively introspectable character present in all instances of that kind.[19] His argument turns on the claim that while having this belief, one person might have a mental image of George Washington on a dollar bill, another may have the words 'George Washington' and so on.

But this argument rests on a mistake. The introspectively available character of a concept or proposition constituitive of a particular belief neither is identical to nor does it derive its intentionality from a sense image. As Edmund Husserl and others have seen, such an image may function to help one sustain his attention on George Washington. In this case, one may think in light of the image, but, typically, one does not think with or about the image, which, in any case, does not need to be present in order to have the belief in question. Thus, the variability of a sense image has nothing to do with whether or not there is an introspectively available constancy that constitutes all cases of the belief about George Washington. Further, Kim seems to be guilty of a Humean vivacity test for a phenomenal quale according to which one has such a quale only if it is a vivid sensation like a pain or an image of George Washington. But I see no reason to accept this claim. In fact, if there is no uniform phenomenal character present in all cases of believing (occurrently) that George Washington was the first president of the United States, then how would one be able through introspection to know what one believed? After all, one does not need to wait to observe the functional outputs of such a belief to know its content in the first-person case.

Paul Churchland recognizes that if semantic contents are construed along the lines of my descriptions of concepts and propositions, then a physicalist construal of the mind is out of the question and naturalism is in trouble. So he offers an eliminativist line on semantic contents – for example, thoughts, beliefs and so forth – according to which just as we have eliminated vital spirits in favour of physically acceptable entities that do the same job, we eliminate dualistically construed semantic contents in favour of physically acceptable entities that play the same role.[20] But for two reasons, this strategy fails. First, anything that satisfies the descriptions and roles of concepts/propositions just mentioned will simply be a concept or proposition by another name, and there will be a mere verbal shift. Second, the very notion of playing a role is a mental one. Joe Montana and a certain piece of paper play the roles of quarterback and dollar bill, respectively, because of various semantic, mental states (beliefs, purposes, values, goals, desires, etc.) that constitute them. I have no idea what a role is if it is not so constituted.[21]

2 *In virtue of the propositional content that constitutes them*, for example meanings whose identity is constituted by relations to other meanings; propositions (All S is P) whose form and content individuate them by way of internal logical relations to other propositions (Some S is P) – mental states sometimes stand in internal relations to each other. But brain states do not stand in such internal relations. Thus,

(3a) Some mental states stand in internal relations to other mental states.
(3b) No brain states stand in internal relations to other brain states.
(3c) Therefore, some mental states are not brain states.

Not only is the irreducibly mental nature of certain mental states outside the explanatory resources of naturalism, internal relations also do not have causal power (or contribute causal power to entities that instantiate them) or spatial location, and many naturalists eschew them for these reasons. For example, D. M. Armstrong explicitly rejects internal relations on the grounds that they cannot be spatio-temporally located and, thus, are disanalogous with other entities in the Grand Story. Their lack of spatial location also means they cannot enter into physical causal relations with the brain, which is a necessary condition to be an object of knowledge or justified belief in an externalist epistemology.[22] Thus, the propositional content that grounds these internal relations and the relations themselves play no causal role in the sequential history of brain states that obtain during processes of rational deliberation.

3 *Intentionality*. Intentionality amounts to the ofness or aboutness of a mental state, the non-dispositional directedness of a mental state towards its object. Victor Reppert has advanced the following argument against naturalism:[23]

(4a) If naturalism is true, then there is no fact of the matter as to what someone's thought or statement is about.
(4b) But there are facts about what someone's thought is about.
(4c) Therefore, naturalism is false.

(4a) amounts to the claim that there is no irreducible intentionality in the world nor any adequate surrogate to which intentionality may be reduced (or in light of which intentionality may be eliminated). In addition to providing a defeater for naturalism, it should be obvious that since the basic entity in theism exemplifies intentionality, its appearance in the cosmos is not a problem for, but rather evidence in support of, theism.

Consider the following points about intentionality:

1 When we represent a mental act to ourselves (e.g., an act of thinking about something), there are no sense data associated with it; this is not so with physical states and their relations.
2 Intentionality is completely unrestricted with regard to the kind of object it can hold as a term – anything whatever can have a mental act directed upon it, but physical relations only obtain for a narrow range of objects (e.g., magnetic fields only attract certain things).
3 To grasp a mental act I must engage in a reflexive act of self-awareness (e.g., to grasp my awareness of a tree, I must be aware of an awareness), but no such reflexivity is required to grasp a physical relation.
4 For ordinary physical relations (e.g., x is to the left of y), x and y are identifiable objects irrespective of whether or not they have entered into that relation (ordinary physical relations are external); this is not so for intentional contents (e.g., one and the same belief cannot be about a frog and later about a house – the belief is what it is, at least partly, in virtue of what the belief is *of*).
5 For ordinary relations, each of the participants must exist before the relation obtains (x and y must exist before one can be on

top of the other); but intentionality can be of nonexistent things (e.g., I can think of Zeus).

6 Intentional states are inten<u>s</u>ional (equals cannot be substituted for equals with the guarantee that the same truth value will be preserved – e.g., if Smith knows that Clinton is president, but doesn't know that Clinton is from Arkansas, he won't know that a man from Arkansas is president even though Clinton is identical to a man from Arkansas), but physical states are extensional (if a billiard ball is on the table and the only round object in the room is identical to the billiard ball, then the only round object in the room is on the table).

Physicalists try to reduce intentionality to physical causal relations of input and output. For example, to have a thought of a dog is to have certain inputs come into you (say, you scan the room and 'see' a dog), these inputs, in turn, produce a disposition to behave in certain ways, and the behaviour is produced (you run in the opposite direction while shouting 'Dog!' in English). Thus, the intentionality of thoughts is reduced to/replaced by artificial intelligence and computational models of inputs, internal states, and outputs all standing in functional, causal relations to each other. To have a brain state about an object is just to have a brain state that realizes the appropriate causal, functional role.

Philosopher John Searle has offered a famous counter-argument to this reduction/elimination of intentionality in favour of causal inputs/outputs. The argument is known as the Chinese Room argument, and it seeks to show that the causal analysans is not sufficient for genuine intentionality. In it, Searle depicts a situation where the artificial inputs/outputs are present, there is no semantic meaning, no thought with intentionality, so intentionality cannot be identical to causal inputs/outputs because you can have the latter without the former. Here is the argument:[24]

> Imagine that you are locked in a room, and in this room are several baskets full of Chinese symbols. Imagine that you (like me) do not understand a word of Chinese, but that you are given a rule book in English for manipulating the Chinese symbols. The rules specify the manipulations of symbols purely formally, in terms of their syntax, not their semantics. So the rule might

> say: 'Take a squiggle-squiggle out of basket number one and put it next to a squoggle-squoggle sign from basket number two.' Now suppose that some other Chinese symbols are passed into the room, and that you are given further rules for passing back Chinese symbols out of the room. Suppose that unknown to you the symbols passed into the room are called 'questions' by the people outside the room, and the symbols you pass back out of the room are called 'answers to the questions'. Suppose, furthermore, that the programmers are so good at designing the programs and that you are so good at manipulating the symbols, that very soon your answers are indistinguishable from those of a native Chinese speaker. There you are locked in your room shuffling your Chinese symbols and passing out Chinese symbols in response to incoming Chinese symbols.
>
> Now the point of the story is simply this: by virtue of implementing a formal computer program from the point of view of an outside observer, you behave exactly as if you understood Chinese, but all the same you don't understand a word of Chinese.

The Chinese room with the person inside would simulate a computer to an outside person. For a person outside, the room receives input and gives output in a way that makes it appear that the room understands Chinese. But of course, all the room does is *imitate* mental understanding, it does not *possess* it. Computers are just like the Chinese room. They imitate mental operations, but they do not really exemplify them. Computers and their programs are not minds, because they fail to have consciousness, intentionality, and understanding of real semantic contents. I believe that Searle's argument and the six points listed above are sufficient to show that intentionality is not a physical property or relation and that those states necessarily characterized by intentionality are not physical states. Indeed, it is not even clear what it would mean to say literally that one system of particles is of or about something. At the very least, these points seem to show that the relevant physical, causal entities are not sufficient for intentionality.

It also seems clear that entering into a physical, causal relation with an object is not a necessary condition for having a mental content that is of that object. In this context, there has been a serious lack of consideration of the plethora of information documenting numerous credible near death experiences (NDEs) in which a subject dies, leaves his/her body, and has sensations, thoughts, and so on about different objects, even though the subject does not stand in an ordinary physical relation with those objects, and may not stand in any such causal relation at all.

Consider the following case selected from many credible NDE accounts.[25] The case involves a woman named Kimberly Clark Sharp who worked at Harborview Hospital in Seattle. While she was attempting to resuscitate a clinically dead young patient – Maria – the patient suddenly became conscious, grabbed Kim's arm, and reported that she had left her body, floated out and above the hospital roof, and had seen a large, old blue shoe with a little toe worn to the threads and with the lace tucked under the heel on an upper ledge of the hospital roof! The ledge was not accessible to anyone but hospital personnel nor visible from buildings nearby and Maria had never been to the hospital before. With curiosity aroused about this bizarre story, Kimberly was shocked to find the shoe just as Maria had described in just the correct location! Maria was interviewed by other witnesses that day who corroborate the incident.

Cases like this provide hard evidence that standing in a typical physical, causal relation to an object is not a necessary condition for having a sensation or thought about that object. Indeed, the directedness of intentionality is a function of the constituents intrinsic to our sensations and thoughts – that's one reason why we can know what our mental states are of by simply attending to them – and not a function of external relations, causal or otherwise, they stand in to other things. It is also why we can have a wide range of cases in which first-person epistemic success occurs. For more on this, see below.

Hilary Putnam has advanced an argument to show that it is not the intrinsic features of a mental state that fix its reference but, rather, an external causal relation of the right kind between the mental state and intentional object.[26] According to Putnam, no mental image (the point would apply to thoughts or beliefs) is intrinsically referential. He invites us to imagine a being on some planet where there are no trees but who suddenly gets a mental image which is what we would describe as an image of a tree.

According to Putnam, the image is not a representation of a tree because there is no causal relation between the subject and actual objects. Geoffrey Madell responds to Putnam's argument by claiming that mental images as such are not about anything, and goes on to claim that no amount of causal connection will turn such an image into a representation of an object.[27] According to Madell, 'The image only represents something when the subject whose image it is stipulates that it represents such-and-such, or thinks of it as a representation.'[28]

Madell is correct about the futility of the causal relation, but offers the wrong reason for his observation. The alien's image is, in fact, of a tree and happens to be a hallucination. Suppose that there were, in fact, such trees on the alien's planet but that he had never seen one or entered into a causal relation with a tree. As he sits in his study, the very same tree image occurs to him. He would now have a sensation of a tree and, in fact, could examine the sensation, grasp its intentional object thereby, and know how to fulfil that representation and when that representation had been fulfilled by an awareness of the thing itself. More on this below. For now, I simply note that Madell seems to be confusing a mental image (thought, belief) which is a natural sign with a word which is an artificial sign. If some scribble had occurred to the alien, e.g., an image of 'TREE', then the image would not, in fact, have intentionality until it was assigned. Such artificial signs are derivatively and not intrinsically intentional. But the image of a tree is a natural sign as evidenced by the fact that simple introspective awareness of it could lead to a recognition of its intentional object if presented, but this would not be so for 'TREE'.

4 ***Belief-formation and the flow of rational sequences.*** If the various physical states of our brains follow one another according to prior causally sufficient brain states and physical laws of nature, then even if there is an irreducibly higher level of mental states (e.g., thoughts), there is no room for the presence of one thought (e.g., if P then Q and P) to be responsible for the occurrence of a later thought (e.g., Q), given the dependence of the mental on the physical and the causal closure of the physical. And mental descriptions, for example functional specifications, do not attribute causal powers to the brain events that realize them. How is it, then,

that the specific semantic properties and logical/epistemic relations along with the awarenesses of such, have any role whatever in the actual sequential train of mental states that constitute a chain of reasoning?

The simple fact is that, constituted as they are by

1 semantic contents that can be true or false;
2 logical or weaker epistemic relations (e.g., the basing relation);
3 second-order, non-sensory awarenesses of those contents and relations; and
4 libertarian acts of initiating and carrying out the process, choosing to attend to various states, and drawing a conclusion,

rational processes have a life of their own that is not caused by, dependent on, or consistently type/type correlated with the different brain states that occur during those processes. After all, logical and epistemic relations are just not causal, nor are they in any sense physical because they obtain in worlds without physical entities of any kind.

Unfortunately, the physical constraints just mentioned, and to which I referred in my discussion of Kim's analysis of the problem of mental-to-mental or mental-to-physical causation in the previous chapter, render irreducibly mental contents epiphenomenal. The four features of rational processes listed in the previous paragraph have no room to contribute to what mental state comes after a 'rational' process of deliberation, and the successive stages of such processes at the mental level are analogous to a series of shadows which simply follow each other in time.

5 ***Fulfilment structures and first-person epistemic success.*** We are capable of engaging in first-person examination of our own mental – for example conceptual and propositional – contents, engaging in a series of mental steps that would be relevant to verifying or falsifying those contents, eventually becoming acquainted with the thing itself (the intentional object of the original mental contents), and comparing our initial mental contents with the thing itself in order to experience the truth (or falsity) of those contents. Such cases of first-person epistemic success entail the following:

1. The essence of our mental contents are in the mind and directly available to introspective awareness.
2. Those contents are intrinsically referential and essentially characterized by their intrinsic features, not by external relations in which they stand to other things.
3. Those mental contents suggest a sequence of experiences the subject can live through to verify/falsify the original contents.
4. The subject is not trapped behind his/her mental contents with no access to the things themselves, but rather is able to compare a direct awareness of the intentional object or, better, the intentional object towards which an act of acquaintance is directed, with the mental contents themselves and intuit a match or its absence.

As an example, consider the case of Joe and Frank. While in his office, Joe receives a call from the university bookstore that a specific book he had ordered – Richard Swinburne's *The Evolution of the Soul* – has arrived and is waiting for him. At this point, a new mental state occurs in Joe's mind – the thought that Swinburne's *The Evolution of the Soul* is in the bookstore. Now Joe, being aware of the content of the thought, becomes aware of two things closely related to it: the nature of the thought's intentional object (Swinburne's book being in the bookstore) and certain verification steps that would help him to determine the truth of the thought. For example, he knows that it would be irrelevant for verifying the thought to go swimming in the Pacific Ocean. Rather, he knows that he must take a series of steps that will bring him to a specific building and look in certain places for Swinburne's book in the university bookstore. So Joe starts out for the bookstore, all the while being guided by the proposition *that Swinburne's* The Evolution of the Soul *is in the bookstore*. Along the way, his friend Frank joins him, though Joe does not tell Frank where he is going or why. They arrive at the store and both see Swinburne's book there. At that moment, Joe and Frank simultaneously have a certain sensory experience of seeing Swinburne's book *The Evolution of the Soul*. But Joe has a second experience not possessed by Frank. Joe experiences that his thought matches, corresponds with, an actual state of affairs. He is able to compare his thought with its intentional object and 'see', be directly aware that the thought is true. In this case, Joe actually experiences the correspondence relation itself and truth itself becomes an object of his awareness.

The example just cited presents a case of experiencing truth in which the relevant intentional object is a sense-perceptible one, a specific book being in the bookstore. But this need not be the case. A student, upon being taught *modus ponens*, can bring this thought to specific cases of logical inferences and 'see' the truth of *modus ponens*. Similarly, a person can form the thought that he is practising denial regarding his anger towards his father, and through introspection, he can discover whether or not this thought corresponds with his own internal mental states.

In first-person fulfilment structures, mental contents are intrinsically referential, and first-person inspection of them allows one to grasp the intentional object and recognize if and when those mental contents are fulfilled. I believe that three main naturalist accounts of propositional contents – functionalization, indicator meaning, and externalism regarding mental content – all fail to pass the first-person test, and render such epistemic success unintelligible – though arguing for this claim must be left for another occasion.

Plantinga and Evolutionary Naturalism

Alvin Plantinga had developed arguments that try to show not that evolutionary naturalism is false, but that, even if it is true, it is still 'irrational' to believe it.[29] Let R be 'human beings have reliable cognitive faculties', N be naturalism and E be evolution. Plantinga argues for three theses:[30]

(P1): *The Inscrutability Thesis:* P(R/N&E) is low or inscrutable.

(P2): *The Reliability Defeater:* If Person S accepts N&E and the Inscrutability Thesis, she has a purely alethic rationality defeater for R.

(P3): Therefore, *the Naturalism Defeater:* If S accepts the Reliability Defeater, she has a purely alethic rationality defeater for all of her beliefs, including N&E.

Regarding (P1), Plantinga begins by pointing out that, according to naturalistic evolutionary theory, human beings, their parts, and cognitive faculties, arose by a blind, mindless, purposeless process such that these things were selected for solely in virtue of survival value and reproductive advantage. If our cognitive faculties arose this way, then their ultimate purpose (assuming they have one) is to guarantee that we *behave* in certain ways, that is, that we *move* appropriately in feeding, fleeing, fighting, and reproducing such that our chances of survival are enhanced. From this perspective, beliefs, and certainly beliefs that are true, take a hindmost role if they play any role at all. Thus, naturalistic evolutionary theory gives us reason to doubt that our cognitive systems have the production of true beliefs as a purpose or that they do, in fact, furnish us with mostly true beliefs.

But could not someone object to this in the following way? 'Surely an organism with trustworthy sensory and cognitive faculties would be more likely to survive than those without those faculties and, thus, the processes of evolution would select for trustworthy faculties and make their existence likely.' According to Plantinga, this is not so. That is, the probability that our faculties would be reliable, given the truth of evolutionary naturalism and the existence of the faculties we possess, is either

1 very low indeed, or
2 something about which we should remain agnostic.

Why does Plantinga think this? Evolution is likely to select for behaviour that is adaptive, but we cannot say the same for faculties that produce true beliefs because, given evolutionary naturalism, at least five different scenarios regarding our beliefs (or those of a hypothetical creature or, say, a monkey) and our noetic faculties are possible and cannot be ruled out.

First, evolutionary processes could produce beliefs that have no causal relationship whatever to behaviour and, thus, no purpose or function. In this case, evolution would select for adaptive behaviour but beliefs would be mere epiphenomena, entities that 'float on top' of physical states in an organism with no purpose or function. Beliefs would not cause or be caused by behaviours and, thus, would be invisible to evolution. We can add a further point to Plantinga's argument here. Given evolutionary naturalism, it is not clear that beliefs or, indeed, any conscious states at all are required for survival. Zombie organisms whose causal inputs went straight from bodily inputs to outputs without running through conscious intermediaries would provide the outputs necessary for adaptive selection. So beliefs themselves seem entirely superfluous to evolution.

Second, evolution could produce beliefs that are effects but not causes of behaviour (in option one, beliefs were neither). In this case, beliefs would be like a decoration and would not be a part of a causal chain leading to action. Waking beliefs would be much like dreams are to us now. As Jaegwon Kim has argued, given the principle of the causal closure of the physical and the supervenience of the mental on the physical, there is no room for mental states such as beliefs to have causal power.[31] Thus, if beliefs exist, they are causally impotent epiphenomena with no relevance to evolutionary struggle.

Third, evolution could produce beliefs that do have causal efficacy (they are caused by and, in turn, cause behaviours), but not in virtue of what they essentially are as beliefs; that is, not in virtue of their semantics or mental contents, but in virtue of the physical characteristics or syntax that are associated with (or part of) them. Plantinga illustrates this with a person who reads a poem so loudly that it breaks a glass, but this causal effect is not produced by the meanings or contents of the poem (they, like beliefs in this third option, are causally irrelevant), but by the sound waves coming from the reader's mouth.

Fourth, evolution could produce beliefs that are, in fact, causally efficacious syntactically and semantically (in virtue of their content), but such beliefs and belief systems could be maladaptive (maladaptive systems such as being an albino can be fixed and survive) in at least two ways. First, beliefs could be energy-expensive distractions causing creatures to engage in survival-enhancing behaviour but in a way less efficient and economical than if the causal connections producing that behaviour bypassed belief altogether.

In support of Plantinga's point, some scientists have argued that the possession of rational abilities (e.g., belief-processing systems) can be a disadvantage because such systems require increased information-processing capacities associated with the nervous system and this is a reproductive liability prenatally (such a system requires a longer and more vulnerable gestation period) and postnatally (it takes longer to raise and teach the young). Second, beliefs could directly produce maladaptive behaviour but the organism could survive anyway, perhaps due to other, overriding factors.

Finally, evolution could produce beliefs that are causally efficacious in virtue of their contents and that are adaptive. However, in this case we can still ask: What would be the likelihood that the noetic faculties producing such beliefs would be reliable guides to having *true* beliefs? Not very high, says Plantinga, and to see why, we need to note that beliefs don't produce behaviours directly; rather, entire sets of beliefs, desires, and other factors (e.g., sensations, acts of will, or persons themselves) are among the things that produce behaviour. Plantinga invites us to consider Paul, a prehistoric hominid whose survival requires that he display various types of tiger-avoidance behaviour (e.g., fleeing, hiding). Call these behaviours B. B could be caused by Paul's desire to avoid being eaten plus the true belief that B will increase his chances of avoiding such a fate.

However, indefinitely many other belief–desire systems could easily produce B as well, even if they contain false beliefs (and wrong desires or inaccurate sensory experiences). For example, perhaps Paul likes the idea of being eaten but always runs away from tigers, looking for a better prospect because he thinks it unlikely that the tiger before him will eat him. Or perhaps he thinks a tiger is a large, friendly pussycat and wants to pet the tiger before him, but also believes the best way to pet it is to run away from it. Or perhaps he confuses running toward it with running away from it. All of these belief–desire sets would get Paul's body in the right place so far as survival is concerned, but most of them will not need to contain true beliefs to do this.

To elaborate on Plantinga's point, from an evolutionary perspective, organisms are black boxes in so far as their beliefs, desires, sensations, and willings are concerned. Organisms that move the right way (for survival purposes) given the right circumstances, need not have true beliefs about or accurate sensations of the world around them. Thus, the possession of trustworthy faculties that regularly produce true beliefs is not required by the demands of survival. This is especially true when it comes to the ability to have true beliefs about abstract issues or to engage in intellectual theorizing, such as philosophical reflection, scientific theorizing, and so forth, including the ability to argue for or against evolutionary theory itself. These abilities go far beyond what would be required within the constraints of reproductive advantage and survival.

Regarding (P2) (*the Reliability Defeater*), Plantinga points out that each of these five scenarios is possible. And given no further evidence either way about the reliability of our cognitive equipment, the likelihood that those faculties would be reliable, given evolutionary naturalism and the faculties that we have, would be either very low or something we would simply have to be agnostic about. Thus, evolutionary naturalism serves as an undercutting defeater that removes our grounds for trusting in the reliability of our noetic equipment. Plantinga likens this to a case where a person enters a factory, sees an assembly line carrying apparently red widgets, and is then told that these widgets are being irradiated by various red lights that make everything look red. A given widget before the person could still be red, but the person would have no grounds for believing this. She has an undercutting defeater for such a belief.

Someone could respond in a manner reminiscient of G. E. Moore that we have such obvious evidence for the reliability of our cognitive faculties that Plantinga's argument must be wrong. However, Plantinga responds by claiming that while it may be prudential to a person's well-being to continue to believe and act as if his/her faculties are reliable, this claim fails to provide the sort of warrant needed for knowledge since the claim itself is subject to (P1) and (P2).

Regarding (P3), Plantinga's argument may be employed as an inference to the best explanation for theism over evolutionary naturalism or as a sceptical threat argument against evolutionary naturalism, the latter being Plantinga's favoured interpretation. Regarding the latter, the naturalistic evolutionist uses reason to argue for this view, but he then comes to have a defeater for the reliability of his rational faculties. This provides him with a defeater of naturalistic evolution. But given that this defeater for naturalistic evolution relies on his reasoning and beliefs, he has a defeater for this defeater of naturalistic evolution. He now has no defeater for believing both that his rational faculties are reliable and that naturalistic evolution is true. But he is now in his original position, namely, that of believing naturalistic evolution which provides a defeater for the reliability of his rational faculties. Plantinga concludes: 'So goes the paralyzing dialectic. After a few trips around this loop, we may be excused for throwing up our hands in despair, or disgust, and joining Hume in a game of backgammon.'[32]

Conclusion

In this chapter I have argued that the ontology of rationality is something God possesses and, thus, it is not surprising that we find that ontology obtaining elsewhere in the cosmos, especially where persons made in his image appear. This ontology is predicted from biblical theism and its reality – given it is not reducible or eliminable – provides confirmation of God's existence and evidence against naturalism. Several features of the rational agent and the process of rational deliberation were presented, and I argued that these features are neither reducible to nor eliminable in favour of a naturalist ontology of human rationality. I then discussed Plantinga's argument against evolutionary naturalism, with some supplementary considerations of my own, and defended it as a persuasive argument.

5

Naturalism, a Substantial Soul and Human Persons

Most philosophers agree that the vast majority of people throughout history have believed in a substantial, immaterial self/soul. Some form of dualism appears to be the natural response to what we seem to know about ourselves through introspection and in other ways. In this regard, Jaegwon Kim's concession may be taken as representative: 'We commonly think that we, as persons, have a mental and bodily dimension . . . Something like this dualism of personhood, I believe, is common lore shared across most cultures and religious traditions . . . .'[1] Along similar lines, Frank Jackson acknowledges: 'I take it that our folk conception of personal identity is Cartesian in character – in particular, we regard the question of whether I will be tortured tomorrow as separable from the question of whether someone with *any* amount of continuity – psychological, bodily, neurophysiological, and so on and so forth – with me today will be tortured.'[2] People don't have to be taught to be dualists like they must if they are to be physicalists.

But it is not only the masses who embrace dualism. A growing number of first-rate intellectuals are dualists as well. Indeed, no less a philosopher than Roderick Chisholm proclaimed:

> I will defend the thesis according to which there is something that is metaphysically unique about persons: we have a nature wholly unlike anything that is known to be true of things that are known to be composed physical objects . . . And I will argue that the doctrine of the simplicity of the soul is, in William James' terms, very much of a live option.[3]

In this chapter I will clarify what it means to say that there is a simple, substantial, immaterial self/soul and explain why such an entity is a defeater for naturalism. Second, I will offer arguments for the reality of such a soul, and, third, examine alternatives to it.

Naturalism and a Simple Soul

Before we can fruitfully discuss the soul in what follows, it will be useful to get before us a relevant lexicon.

Part/whole relations are important for treatments of substances, and there are two kinds of parts relevant to our discussion – separable and inseparable.

> P is a *separable part* of some whole W $=_{def.}$ p is a particular, p is a part of W, and p can exist if it is not a part of W.

> P is an *inseparable part* of some whole W $=_{def.}$ p is a particular, p is a part of W, and p cannot exist if it is not a part of W.

In contemporary philosophy, inseparable parts were most fruitfully analysed in the writings of Brentano, Husserl and their followers.[4] The paradigm case of an inseparable part in this tradition is a (monadic) property-instance or relation-instance. Thus, if substance s has property P, the-having-of-P-by-s is

1 a property-instance of P;
2 an inseparable part of s which we may also call a mode of s.

Assuming for the sake of argument that a lump of clay is a substance (most likely, it is an ordered aggregate, not a substance; see below) and that it has a spherical shape, then the lump is a substance, the property of being spherical is a universal attribute, and the-having-of-sphericity-by-the-clay is a mode (inseparable part) of the clay and a property-instance of sphericity.

Setting aside properties, there are two ways something can be simple in the sense relevant to what follows: by being uncomposed of separable parts or by being metaphysically indivisible. I use 'metaphysically indivisible' to mean what many philosophers say by 'indivisible in thought'. Something could be metaphysically divisible but not physically divisible (if, say, such division annihilated the whole), but not conversely. Moreover, all particulars that are metaphysically indivisible are uncomposed, but not conversely (an extended whole with no separable parts could still be divided). According to our usage, a substance with inseparable parts is simple.

A *substance* is $=_{def.}$ an essentially characterized particular that

1 has (and is the principle of unity for its) properties but is not had by or predicable of something more basic than it;
2 is an enduring continuant;
3 has inseparable parts but is not composed of separable parts;
4 is complete in species.[5]

As I use the term, a bare particular or Lockean substratum does not count as a substance. Regarding condition 4, a thing's species (i.e., essence) answers the most basic question, 'What kind of thing is this?' where by most basic I mean (a) an answer to this question is presupposed by an answer to any less basic question of this form (for Socrates is a human kind of thing more basically than he is a white kind of thing); (b) an answer to this question is true of the object in every possible world in which it exists. A hand is not complete in species because 'being a hand' does not adequately capture the sort of thing it is. Rather, being a human hand or a gorilla's hand is required. But being human is complete in species.

A *material substance* is $=_{def.}$

1 a substance;
2 spatially located, extended, can possibly move, and in its entirety cannot be located in more than one place at once;
3 metaphysically divisible;
4 essentially characterized by the actual and potential properties of an ideal chemistry and physics.

I prefer to analyse substances, including material ones, within a framework of properties, natural-kind essences and individuators (bare particulars or haecceities) and not within an ontology of separable parts or stuff. The difference between a substance and stuff is typically illustrated by two ways of interpreting 'Mary had a little lamb.' If 'lamb' is used as a count noun, it refers to an individual substance – a particular sheep – of which the question 'Where is it?' makes sense. If 'lamb' is used as a mass term, it refers to an amount of stuff – a few ounces, for example – of which the question 'How much did she have?' makes sense. Stuff, in turn, can be construed as atomless gunk or ontological goo. Setting aside issues of temporal parts, atomless gunk is construed in particulate terms as follows: x is composed of atomless gunk $=_{def.}$ x is a particular and all of x's separable parts have proper separable parts. Ontological goo is construed in non-particulate terms as follows: x is composed of ontological goo $=_{def.}$ x is a particular, x is spatially continuous and non-gappy, and x contains an undifferentiated ontological blob. It has been said, not unfairly, that a trope ontology is a goo ontology.

A *mereological aggregate* is $=_{def.}$

1 a particular whole;
2 such that it is constituted by at least substantial separable parts and external relation-instances between and among those substantial separable parts (there are differences as to whether such aggregates have additional constituents, e.g., boundaries).

A *spiritual substance* is $=_{def.}$

1 a substance;
2 metaphysically indivisible in being (though it may be fractured in functioning);
3 not spatially extended (though some characterizations hold that it may be spatially located);
4 essentially characterized by the actual and potential properties of consciousness.

A soul is a spiritual substance. I define a spiritual substance to allow for the possibility – which I take to be actual – of animal souls. And while a small minority thinks that spiritual substances are composed of spiritual stuff, I am not among them, preferring instead to identify such a substance with a natural-kind essence, the nexus of exemplification and an individuator.

A *person* is $=_{def.}$

1 a spiritual substance;
2 essentially characterized by the actual and potential properties of consciousness like that of a paradigm case, namely God or a properly functioning angel or human being.

A *human being* is $=_{def.}$
1 a person;
2 essentially characterized by the actual or potential properties apt for embodiment of a certain characteristic sort.

There is a genus/species or determinable/determinate relationship between personhood and humanness. The former is to the latter as being coloured is to being red or being shaped is to being square. All humans are persons, but not conversely. Being a human is a way of being a person.

There are two reasons why a substantial, simple soul is not an option for a naturalist. First, if by some sort of magic, a simple soul could be an emergent entity, then given the naturalist commitment to the closure of the physical (all physical events that have causes have entirely physical causes; when tracing the causal antecedents of a physical event, one need not – and, indeed, cannot – leave the physical realm), the soul would be an epiphenomenon with no causal powers. Such an entity would be otiose and, in any case, most naturalists banish entities with no causal power from their ontology, so an epiphenomenal soul is tantamount to a nonexistent entity. And the causal closure principle is not arbitrary for a naturalist. It is required because

1 the naturalist epistemology certifies only the hard sciences, and all other causal accounts (e.g., mental-to-physical) are epistemically opaque and methodologically useless;
2 the Grand Story presents a creation myth told in terms of entities and their various combinations at the level of physics and chemistry, and to require a neuroscientist to have to go to the psychology department before she can provide causal laws relating to changes in the brain would be to deny the creation myth;
3 the determinism of higher levels and their dependence upon

the basic level of micro-physics leaves no room for top-down causation.

Thus, Jaegwon Kim speaks for most naturalists when he says:

> If the immaterial mind is going to cause a neuron to emit a signal . . . then it must somehow intervene in these electrochemical processes. But how could this happen? At the very interface between the mental and the physical where direct and unmediated mind–body interaction takes place, the nonphysical mind must somehow influence the state of some molecules, perhaps by electrically charging them or nudging them this way or that way. Is this really conceivable? . . . Even if the idea of a soul's influencing the motion of a molecule . . . were coherent, the postulation of such a causal agent would seem neither necessary nor helpful in understanding why and how our limbs move . . . Most physicalists . . . accept the causal closure of the physical not only as a fundamental metaphysical doctrine but as an indispensable methodological presupposition of the physical sciences.[6]

Here's the second reason. Given the combinatorial processes constitutive of the Grand Story, apart from atomic simples (if such there be), all larger wholes are mereological aggregates composed of separable, substantial parts that stand in various external (e.g., spatio-temporal, causal) relations to each other. And as we saw above, mereological aggregates are not simple substances, and certainly not simple souls or egos. In such an ontology, macro-substances are replaced with structures constituted by myriads of relation-instances and separable parts. Thus, Stewart Goetz and Charles Taliaferro were right on target when they noted that

> The unified incorporation of all phenomena in a natural scientific philosophy means that the difference between being a fully conscious human being . . . and any inanimate matter and energy is chiefly a matter of complexity, configuration, and function rather than of nature or substance.[7]

Daniel Dennett says that 'We now understand that the mind is not . . . in *communication with* the brain in some miraculous way;

it *is* the brain, or, more specifically, a system or organization within the brain . . . .'[8] And Carl Sagan flatly asserts: 'I am a collection of water, calcium and organic molecules called Carl Sagan. You are a collection of almost identical molecules with a different collective label.'[9] The terms 'configuration', 'system', 'organization', 'collection' capture nicely the non-substantial, relational nature of such aggregates.

A Case for a Substantial, Simple Soul

In this section I want to present four arguments for a substantial, simple soul.

Our basic awareness of ourselves

There are certain things about ourselves that we know and about which we have a right to be sure. When I say we have a right to be sure of them, I do not mean that they are indefeasible or that we should terminate enquiry about them. Rather I mean that our knowledge of these things confers this right and also the knowledge that we do, in fact, know these things. We, thus, have the intellectual right to rely on this knowledge in assessing other issues, to employ things entailed by this knowledge in developing our views of the world and so forth.[10] Before I lay out some of these items, there is something we should consider as a preliminary for understanding how they figure into the case for the simplicity of the soul.

It often happens in science that a range of apparently unrelated data can be unified if a theoretical entity is postulated as that which is causally responsible for that range. The postulation of electrons unified a wide range of phenomena by depicting them as effects of the electron's causal powers.

Sometimes a range of apparently unrelated items of knowledge can be unified if one has knowledge by acquaintance with some relevant object. For example, there are many things I know about a certain spatial region R in the philosophy classroom in which I usually lecture. For example, I know that everyone walks around R and not through it. R is rectangular in shape, about four feet tall and two feet in width and breadth. R does not contain metal in it, R contains something that is darker than yellow, if a book is placed near the top of R it will hover in stable suspension off the floor. I know all these things. But rather than being a set of isolated pieces of knowledge, there is a unifying pattern to them. Indeed, I know each of them in virtue of knowledge by acquaintance of the podium that overlaps R. It is on the basis of that acquaintance that I know the items in question.

There are many apparently unrelated items of knowledge I have of myself. I know my foot itches and at the same time I am thinking about self-knowledge. As I walk towards my kitchen, I am aware of being the same self that lives through and owns each successive sense experience of the kitchen. In the middle of the sequence, I am aware of having had earlier experiences, of currently having a particular experience, and of being about to have an anticipated experience. I am aware of my unified visual field as I look at the room from my desk, and I am aware that the field belongs to me.

I am aware of the difference between a passive thought and an active one I choose to entertain and, in general, I am aware of being a passive causal patient to which something is done, and an active agent where I exercise my active power and cause things to happen. In general, if person s is aware of x's causing y, then s is aware of x. For example, if I am aware of a hammer's causing a nail to move, I am aware of the hammer. Similarly, if I am aware of my causing my arm to move, I am aware of me.

I know that satisfaction of various psychological criteria – for example, sameness of memory, personality, character; living through a fairly continuous change of such – is neither necessary (e.g., I could survive amnesia) nor sufficient (e.g., someone else could come to have my psychological traits) for being me. I also know the same thing regarding satisfaction of whole or partial bodily (e.g., brain) criteria. Body switch cases are perfectly possible, and I have no difficulty at all acknowledging that if He wished, God could put me in your body and conversely. Indeed, I know that my persistence conditions are not the same as those for my psychological traits, my body, or a proper part of my body such as my brain. Recently on the news, an operation was reported in which a little girl survived a procedure in which 52 per cent of her brain was removed. I know this could – and did – happen. I also know that all the proper parts of my body could be continuously replaced with, say, synthesized materials that could function like their organic counterparts, so while my body would not survive, I would, say, by being directly sustained in existence by God. I know that no amount of bodily/brain or psychological information entails which individual is present.

I also know that disembodied survival is possible. Consider the well-known account of a woman named Viola who was checked into a hospital in Augusta, Georgia, in 1971 for routine gall bladder surgery. Six days after the surgery on 5 May, her condition had worsened to the point that she was operated on again and died at 12.15 pm on the operating table. When the doctor said she was dead, Viola was confused. She had been in excruciating pain, when she suddenly felt a ring in her ear and, then, she popped out of her body! She found herself floating near the ceiling and gazed around the operating room, noting a number of things, including her own lifeless body! Though the room had been sealed off for surgery, she could hear voices in the outside hallway and passed through the wall where she saw her anxious family. Immediately, she noticed her daughter, Kathy, who was wearing an outfit Viola did not like (Kathy had rushed to the hospital and put on the mismatched outfit hurriedly and without thinking.) She then noticed her brother-in-law talking to a family neighbour, 'Well, it looks like my sister-in-law is going to kick the bucket. I was planning on going to Athens, but I'll stick around now to be a pallbearer.' Viola was infuriated by the insensitive comment.

She also sensed *presences* around her that she took to be angels. And get this: she could travel anywhere her thoughts directed her, so she found herself instantaneously in Rockville, Maryland, where she saw her sister getting ready to go to the grocery store. Viola noted carefully the clothes her sister was wearing, the search for misplaced keys, a lost grocery list and, finally, the car she drove. Moments later, she was whisked through a tunnel. Space forbids me to describe all she saw, but I must mention one thing. She met a baby who told Viola he was her brother. Viola was confused because she did not have a brother. The baby then showed himself to her dressed in quite specific clothing and told her that when she went back to tell her father about all this, she describe the clothing.

When Viola came back into her body, each and every detail I have shared was verified by the people involved, often with additional eyewitnesses. Viola's dad confirmed that only he, Viola's mother, and the doctor knew about the brother who had died as an infant but about whom the father and mother had decided to remain silent (which they had done). I believe the evidence is sufficient to justify the claim that this story is true. But one thing seems certain. It is perfectly coherent to me and I know it is at least metaphysically possible and cannot be ruled out prior to investigation of the eyewitnesses and so forth.

While my functioning may come, go, or wax and wane in degrees, I am such that I cannot be present as a percentage of a person; for example, I cannot be 75 per cent present in, say, a room. I am an all or nothing sort of thing. Moreover, my identity to myself, in contrast to the degree of similarity between two different objects, does not come in degrees but is, rather, an absolute fact. My body can gain and lose parts while I retain absolute sameness through such a change. In these ways, I am not like a material object, especially a composed one.

In introspection, I am aware of being fully present at each part of my body and, thus, I am still entirely there even if I lose a limb. And I am unextended such that my visual field does not overlap with me as a motion picture does with a screen; that is, different regions of my field do not overlap with different regions of my self. I in my entirety am the possessor of my entire visual field or, indeed, my entire conscious life at a given moment (or through time for that matter). I am aware that my various mental states – sensations, thoughts, beliefs, desires, volitions – are states within me, that when they obtain, they are the actualization of capacities for them within me, and that I could not be identical to myself if I did not have the ultimate capacities for these sorts of conscious states.

I am aware of being uncomposed of separable parts. To see this, consider the following. The union of two or more thinkers (conscious beings) does not itself think (is not itself conscious). Thus, if I shake hands with you or if I am part of a large group, then there is no thinker over and above the individual persons in the two cases. My knowledge of this fact (that the union of two or more thinkers does not itself think) does not depend on the composing items, in this case, persons, being thinkers themselves. No, my knowledge of this fact is a species of the following genus: For any x and y, the union of x and y is not itself a thinker. I know this because it is directly evident to me that an object composed of separable parts lacks the sort of simple unity necessary for a conscious, thinking being.

If you think about it, these all seem to be things about which we have a right to be sure and, in fact, these intuitions are almost impossible to set aside. They are so deeply ingrained in all of us that they form the core of what is sometimes called Folk Ontology – the spontaneous, natural ontology of ordinary people. Can we unify these apparently diverse items of knowledge? Is there a depiction of the self that underwrites and makes sense of them? I believe there is an affirmative answer to both questions: We are simply directly aware of ourselves through various acts of introspection, and in such awarenesses, we are directly aware of ourselves as simple spiritual substances of such a nature as to be called persons. In the fundamental sense, all these items of knowledge are mine in virtue of, on the basis of, my direct acquaintance with myself. Such an acquaintance does not present me with a material object or aggregate of such objects, a sense datum, a bundle of sense data or a stream of successive sense data. Rather, it presents a simple spiritual substance to me and, on this basis, I have the other items of knowledge listed.

Before we move to the second argument, it is important to reflect upon the dialectical situation we have reached. According to the first argument, the dualist view of the soul is grounded in direct awareness of one's self and in the fact that such an awareness provides a unifying basis for the other items we seem to know. And it is admitted by almost all parties to the dispute that these items of Folk Ontology just cited are, indeed, at the core of the commonsense view. However, so far as I can tell, the physicalist who denies such an awareness or the purported items of knowledge associated with it, does so on the basis of the fact that they cannot be true, given the fact that naturalism must be the case. It should be clear that the naturalist does, but the dualist does not, beg the question.

Lest you think I am misrepresenting the dialectical situation, no less a thinker than Jaegwon Kim has noticed the same dialectic in a closely related area of reflection: the nature of phenomenal consciousness and its contingent relationship to the physical. Among other things, says Kim, the dualist will present inverted qualia and zombie worlds as thought experiments for dualism. For what it's worth, I believe there is a unifying sort of knowledge for these and related dualist thought experiments: direct acquaintance with phenomenal conscious properties, knowledge of physical properties, and the awareness of the contingency of their relationship to each other. But be that as it may, Kim says the following:

> The case against qualia supervenience therefore is not conclusive, though it is quite substantial. Are there, then, considerations in favor of qualia supervenience? It would seem that the only positive considerations are broad metaphysical ones that might very well be accused of begging the question.[11]

Kim goes on to say that these broad metaphysical considerations amount to the assumption that physicalism must be true.

Sameness through mereological replacement

We have very strong, deep intuitions that we are enduring continuants even though we undergo various changes and our bodies experience part replacement. Indeed, we seem to be directly aware of our continuity, and our practice of fearing the future and being responsible for the past seems to presuppose that it will be and was we ourselves who face that future and acted in that past.

Similarly, we have strong, deep intuitions that various kinds of wholes have an insufficient sort of unity to prevent their identities from evaporating on the occasion of part replacement. At one end of the spectrum lie sets and mere heaps (e.g., a mound of sand) that cannot sustain absolute identity through membership change or part replacement, respectively. At the other lie conscious, living organisms of which we are strongly inclined to think that they can survive at least certain sorts of such changes. Recently, Alvin Plantinga has presented an argument lurking in this neighbourhood that I find to be quite persuasive.[12]

Plantinga employs a replacement argument to demonstrate that it is broadly logically possible for one to exist when one's body does not, though he does not explicitly argue that one could exist disembodied with no body at all (though he believes that to be the case). Putting his argument in the first person as he does, according to Plantinga, I am a substance; if I am a physical substance, I would be my body, or a proper part of it or an object distinct from my body but composed of the same matter and collocated with it. But I am none of these things. Call any of these relevant objects 'B'. It is possible that I continue to exist when B doesn't, so I am not identical to B. At the macro-level, science could advance such that I continue to read the paper throughout a process during which each macropart of my body is replaced by others in a microsecond and the original parts are annihilated. If the process occurs rapidly, my body will not continue to exist but I do since I continue to read the paper. Plantinga advances the same argument for the brain. And the same goes for a material object constituted by the same matter as and collocated with my body. It, too, would be annihilated if God destroyed all of its parts, whether micro- (e.g., cells) or macro-level parts.

But, asks Plantinga, would the replacement really kill B? After all, all the matter of the body is replaced regularly and the body seems to survive. Why should merely shortening the time interval make a difference? Plantinga's answer is that speed kills. It takes time for new parts to be assimilated into the bodily whole, so he makes the replacement time quicker than the assimilation time.

Peter van Inwagen has responded to Plantinga's replacement argument.[13] According to van Inwagen, the replacement scenario isn't possible because I am identical to my body. To keep this from being a question-begging assertion, van Inwagen invites reflection on this question: Is it more plausible to suppose that it [Plantinga's scenario] is possible than it is to suppose that I am identical with my body? I believe the answer to this is not only 'yes,' but clearly so. The intuitions shared worldwide by most people that I list above, including the NDE I described, seem to be quite reasonable to most folks. Moreover, when most people introspect, they do not confront their 'composed animality', as van Inwagen has suggested, but their own unified, simple conscious self.

Van Inwagen agrees that if the replacement of parts in Plantinga's envisioned thought experiment is more rapid than the assimilation time, then B is destroyed. But why think, he queries, that I continue to exist throughout the process? For van Inwagen, Plantinga seems to argue for this on the basis of continuous consciousness, i.e., that a single episode of consciousness exists throughout the entire replacement process and a necessary condition for this is that a single person must be the subject of that episode. But, perhaps, there just is no single person who endures this process, or maybe there is not a single conscious episode, but a series of discrete conscious states. I have already dealt with the continuity of consciousness and the self that underwrites that continuity in Chapter 4, so I refer the reader to that discussion. And it seems to be a fundamental datum of self-awareness that I am an enduring continuant throughout processes like reading the paper. Nothing, it seems, is more evident than the fact that as I experience a series of notes in a tune, I am the unifying I for the extended experience.

Plantinga has responded to van Inwagen's argument in the following way:[14] Let t and t* be the beginning and end of the replacement scenario, respectively. According to Plantinga, van Inwagen thinks his argument is this one:

(1) The Replacement Scenario is possible.
(2) If the Replacement Scenario were actual, I would exist at t, during all of t to t*, and at t*.
(3) If the Replacement Scenario were actual, B, my body, would not exist at t*.
(4) Therefore, possibly, I exist when B does not and I am not identical to B.

Van Inwagen attacks (2), but Plantinga claims that (2) isn't part of his argument and van Inwagen has misunderstood his case. Rather, the case goes like this:

(1*) Possibly, the Replacement Scenario is actual and I exist and am conscious at t, from t to t*, and at t*.
(3) If the Replacement Scenario were actual, B, my body, would not exist at t*.
(4) Therefore, possibly, I exist when B does not and I am not identical to B.

Here, (2) is not asserted or presupposed. Accordingly, Plantinga sees no reason to reject the modal intuition that lies under the

Replacement Argument. I leave the reader to evaluate this dialectic, though my sympathies clearly lie with Plantinga. I want to close this discussion with two final reflections. First, it would be open to a Plantingan critic to argue that we are atomic simples or composed material objects that in some way or other can endure the sort of part replacement in the thought experiment. In the next section I will consider these alternatives to dualism.

Second, Stewart Goetz has argued, correctly in my view, that intuitions about what is possible are grounded in awareness of what is actual. Thus, Plantinga's argument is actually grounded in a direct awareness of one's substantial simple self, and on the basis of acquaintance with the self's properties, for example being simple rather than being complex or composed, Plantinga's modal intuition of possibility is justified.[15] Still, for the purposes of argument, one could set aside claims about direct awareness of one's self and use Plantinga's argument as an independent one for those who find his modal intuition to be a more plausible starting point than direct awareness of one's self.

An argument from the concept of a spiritual substance

Stewart Goetz has advanced the following argument for the non-physical nature of the self:[16]

(1) I am essentially a simple entity (I have no separable parts).
(2) Any physical body is essentially a complex entity (any physical body has separable parts).
(3) Principle of Indiscernibility of Identicals.
(4) Therefore, I am not identical with my (or any) physical body.

Goetz's primary justification for (1) is that through direct awareness, I am aware of myself as having the property of being simple. I would rather put the point by saying that through direct awareness, I am aware of myself as a simple substance, but I agree with the thrust of Goetz's argument. Point (2) is the main weakness in the argument, which Goetz acknowledges. Thus, he cannot rule out the possibility that he is identical to a proper part of his body that is an atomic simple such that it has an objective nature that can be described from a third-person perspective, a subjective, non-physical nature that is knowable without sensory observation.

E. J. Lowe has advanced a different argument for a similar conclusion. Let us assume that within a composed object, the mereological sum of two proper parts is also a part (proper or improper), that something cannot have just one proper part, that two objects with the same proper parts are identical, and that parthood is transitive. Then,

(1) I exist, as does my body.
(2) I am not identical with my body.
(3) I am not identical with any proper part of my body (e.g., my brain).
(4) I do not have any proper part which is not a proper part of my body.

Given our assumptions and (1)–(4), Lowe concludes:

(5) I have no proper parts: I am an altogether simple entity.

Point (1) is pretty self-evident. Lowe's argument for (2) is that I and my body have different persistence conditions. Regarding (3), he claims that the best candidate for the proper part to which I am identical is my brain, but again, I and my brain have different persistence conditions. One could reject (3) on the grounds that the best candidate for the associated proper part would be one of the body's atomic simples and my persistence conditions are the same as the atomic simple to which I am identical. More on this below. A naturalist would surely accept (4) so let us grant it.

Where does all this leave us? Lowe agrees that the argument is consistent with the self being an immaterial, non-extended substance, but the former does not entail the latter. For his own part, Lowe believes the self is a subject of experience such that it has, among other things, numerically the same weight as its body and occupies the same space as its body without being identical to or composed of that body. The self inherits its weight and location from the body, but not its thoughts and conscious life. Even though an embodied person is a physical, spatially extended object, Lowe does not have a view about the possibility of disembodied existence.

According to him, the only properties that can confidently be said to be essential for persons are mental properties.

I believe that the arguments by Goetz and Lowe are good ones, but I leave to the reader the task of deciding for himself or herself just what the force of these arguments is. However, for my purposes, both arguments fall short of being entirely satisfactory since they leave open the possibility that the self is either a spiritual substance or a physical simple of some kind. Is there anything that can be said to tip the scales in favour of the spiritual substance view? I believe there is, and to get at the issues, I want to digress a bit and look at a similar dialectic held in the late 1800s between Mormon materialist Orson Pratt and substance dualist T. W. P. Taylder. I believe that those who think that thinking matter is possible, such as advocates of minded atomic simples or Lowe's conscious simples, make two mistakes exemplified by Pratt: they use 'immaterial' as an infima species and not as a genus and they render materially vacuous the very notion of an immaterial substance (aka a spirit).

In addressing Pratt's materialism, I shall concentrate my efforts on his 1849 publication *The Absurdities of Immaterialism*. Written in part as a response to a critique of Mormon physicalism by British minister and substance dualist T. W. P. Taylder, *The Absurdities of Immaterialism* is, in the words of contemporary Mormon scholar David J. Whittaker, 'considered his [Pratt's] most important philosophical treatise'.[17]

In his approach to characterizing matter and spirit, Pratt adopts a methodology according to which one starts with a definition of matter and spirit. On this point, Pratt was in agreement with his antagonist, the Reverend Taylder. According to Taylder, an immaterial substance/spirit is to be defined as something that exists that 'is *not matter* and is evidently *distinct* from matter, which is *not dependent* on matter for its existence, and which possesses properties and qualities *entirely different* from those possessed by matter'.[18] Pratt thinks that something like this is what the immaterialist needs to defend the reality of an immaterial spirit. But Pratt thinks that nothing could possibly exist that was *entirely different* from matter.

Rejecting Taylder's claim that material and immaterial substances must have no properties in common, Pratt adopts a different approach to defining these terms. He claims that all one needs to do to distinguish matter from spirit is to show that they have some differences, not that they need to be entirely different. But, Pratt argues, given that two substances have some different properties, it does not follow that one is material and the other is not. For example, iron, gold and a host of other substances have some properties that differ from the others, but all this shows is that they are all different kinds of matter.[19] Similarly, from the fact that spirit has some properties that differ from other material substances, it only follows that spirit is a certain type of matter.

Perhaps following John Locke, Pratt thought that the notion of thinking matter is clearly coherent, possible and, in fact, actual.[20] Just as the properties of stone and wood are different yet each is still a material substance, so it is with gross and spirit matter. From the fact that mental properties, for example the powers of thought, feeling and free choice, characterize spirit and not unintelligent matter, it only follows that spirits are certain kinds of material substances, not that they are immaterial ones.

What is the difference between gross and spirit matter? Minimally, spirit matter is more refined and purer than gross matter. As *Doctrine and Covenants* 131:7 says, 'There is no such thing as immaterial matter. All spirit is matter, but it is more fine or pure, and can only be discerned by purer eyes.' In addition to this, Pratt claims that spirit matter is free, intelligent and teleological, while gross matter is determined, unintelligent, and mechanistic, and that spirit matter has other properties of consciousness, for example, powers of perception.[21]

As will be clarified in more detail later, whenever a thinker allows for the possibility that there is such a thing as thinking matter and uses mental properties to characterize matter, if that thinker is not careful, he or she will have no way to give content to the notion of immaterial spirit and will come perilously close to using 'spirit matter' or 'thinking matter' as just another word for what dualists mean by 'immaterial spirit'. Indeed, in one place Pratt says that the only difference between Taylder's notion of an immaterial self or soul and his own conception of an atom of spirit matter is the name each uses.[22] However, Pratt does not leave the issue there. He offers a further characterization of spirit matter that clearly distinguishes it from what dualists have traditionally meant by soul or spirit. According to Pratt, spirit matter qua matter has the essential features of matter, namely, extension and location, solidity, and so forth. For Pratt, 'mind is an extended material substance'.[23] Finally, no two particles of spirit or gross matter may occupy the same place at the same time.[24]

Given all that has been presented, a certain picture of human persons emerges. Put briefly, a human person is a combination of a fleshly body composed of corpuscles of gross matter, and a spirit body composed of corpuscles of spirit matter. Personal identity is the result, not of sameness of changeable fleshly body, but of the unchangeable substance called 'spirit' (i.e., spirit body) which thinks, feels, reasons and so forth.[25] The spirit or spirit body pre-exists its entrance in the fleshly body and departs that body at death, it can condense and has elastic properties, and very much like particulate notions of the ether, it is in the body in a straightforwardly spatial sense: the various particles of spirit matter occupy the porous places between the various particles of a person's fleshly body.[26]

Among other things, Pratt's approach to immaterial substances exhibits two serious flaws: Pratt employs 'immaterial' as an infima species and not as a genus and he gives an inadequate treatment of the notion of an immaterial spirit, along with a failure adequately to distinguish it from spirit matter.

To understand the first charge, we need to get clear on the notion of a genus (plural: genera) and an infima species. Things can be classified in increasingly lower or higher categories. For example, we may classify the colour of a fire engine in this way: a sense-perceptible property, a colour property, redness, a very specific shade of redness. Similarly, we may classify a dog as an animal, a mammal, a canine, a dog. An infima species is a terminus point in a hierarchy of classification, a lowest-level classification beyond which there is no other. In our examples, being a specific shade of red and being a dog are infimae species. For our purposes, all the higher levels may be called *genera*. Thus, being a mammal or being a colour property are genera.

In his debate with Taylder, Pratt was correct in his claim that immaterial substances, if such there be, could not be entirely different from matter. Assuming immaterial and material substances exist for the sake of argument, both would be self-identical, both would have the property of being dependent on God, both would be substances, both would have existence, and so forth. So there would be at least some things they would hold in common. But Pratt seems to misunderstand Taylder's point and, in any case, he errs in applying this insight. When Taylder says that spirit 'possesses properties entirely different from matter', I do not think he means that spiritual and material substances have no properties whatever in common. Rather, I think he means, or at least he should have meant, that 'material' and 'immaterial' characterize different genera for classifying substances and, thus, they must have no properties in common relevant to the distinction in genera. This is not as difficult to understand as it sounds. A lizard and a dog may have some things in common, for example each is a living thing, but the genera 'being a reptile' and 'being a mammal' are different and, as such, the properties that constitute each must be entirely different. The features of being a reptile and being a mammal must be different or else they would not amount to distinct, contrasting genera. From this, it does not follow that individual reptiles and mammals have nothing in common (lizards and dogs are alive, gold is not). It is important to observe the following: In so far as they are genera, just as being a reptile and a mammal can be given material content by specifying the properties that constitute each, the same could be proffered for being a spirit (an immaterial substance) and being a material substance, such as an atomic simple.

Furthermore, given that being a reptile and being a mammal are genera, it follows that there are various kinds of reptiles and mammals, that is, various infimae species that fall under each. Similarly, if being immaterial and being material are genera, there would be various kinds of immaterial substances and material substances. Examples of the former may be being a number, a mathematical point, an angel, God, a human spirit, and various kinds of animal souls. Examples of the latter are being gold, being sodium, being iron.

Unfortunately, whereas Taylder correctly uses 'immaterial' as a genus, Pratt seems to attack a straw man by taking it to be an infima species. Pratt claims that just because two substances have different properties, it does not follow that one is material and one is not. So far so good. From the fact that one animal has different properties from another, it does not follow that one is a mammal and the other is not. One could be a dog and the other a cat, though it still might be the case that one is a dog and the other is a lizard.

But when Pratt gives illustrations of his claim, he selects different infimae species under the genus 'material substance'. For example, he claims that just because the properties of stone and wood or iron and gold are different, it does not follow that they are not all material. From this, it would seem that he likens 'being immaterial' to 'being gold' or 'being iron' and the latter are infimae species. For Pratt, being material is the genus and being spirit, being gold, being iron are all different kinds of material substances. In my view, Pratt fails to give adequate arguments for this move and largely rests his case on the analogies just mentioned. But it seems to me that they fail to address Taylder's point because his arguments employ 'immaterial' as a genus, and Pratt simply assumes that it is an infimae species to rebut Taylder. It would seem that those who believe that thinking matter is possible would have to follow Pratt here. For on this view, there are two kinds of conscious substances: conscious material substances (e.g., conscious atomic simples) and conscious spirits/immaterial substances.

Who is correct here? Is 'immaterial' a genus or an infima species under the genus 'material substance'? I shall address this question after I focus on Pratt's inadequate treatment of spirit, especially his failure to distinguish it from spirit matter.

Note, again, that Pratt thinks that thinking matter is possible. By this he means that the various mental properties of consciousness – sensation, other forms of awareness, thought, belief, desire, volitional choices done for the sake of ends – could characterize material substances. If this is so, then granting the reality of immaterial spirits for the sake of argument, one cannot use mental properties to characterize the nature of a spirit, since those properties are consistent with both a spirit and a material substance. To get at the nature of spirit, one must look elsewhere, but here is where the difficulty lies.

To see the problem, let us begin with an analysis of the notion of a substance.[27] In general, a substance is a primitive, underived unity of actual and potential properties or parts at a time, it sustains absolute sameness through accidental change, and it has an essence that answers the most fundamental question, 'What kind of thing is this?' and that grounds its membership in its infima species. For purposes of illustration, God, an angel, a human spirit, a dog, an atom of gold are all substances. Being red is a property and not a substance, being larger than is a relation and not a substance, being a flash of lightning is an event and not a substance.

Note that the characterization just given is a formal one, that is, it merely states necessary conditions for any thing to count as a substance without giving material content necessary to distinguish one kind of substance from another. When it comes to characterizing specific kinds of substances, it seems that there are only two things one can do: state the formal criteria and list a set of dispositions or potentialities as the material content for a specific kind of substance. For example, a characterization of an atom of gold as a substance might go something like this: It is a primitive, underived unity of actual and potential properties or parts at a time (having the power to melt at such and such degrees, dissolving in aqua regia, having atomic number 79, which, in turn, is the potential to attract a certain number of electrons, to resist inertial changes to degree thus and so), it sustains absolute sameness through accidental change, and it has an essence (being gold) that answers the most fundamental question 'What kind of thing is this?' and that grounds its membership in its infima species (the natural kind *gold*).

Note that the formal aspects of the definition of gold are the same as those for a substance in general and the material content is listed in parentheses. Note also that the various properties listed in parentheses that give material content to 'being gold' so as to distinguish it from 'being iron' are dispositions or potentialities, properties that are actualized by a gold atom if certain conditions obtain (e.g., gold will dissolve in aqua regia if placed in it). Substances are more than their potentialities; indeed, it seems reasonable to say that something can have potential properties only if it has actual properties: No potentiality without actuality! Unfortunately, it is very difficult to say what the essence of a substance is without making reference to its potentialities. Thus, we say that gold is *that which* has the potential to do x, y and z; iron is *that which* has the potential to do f, g and h; and so on.

By way of application, it is hard if not impossible to characterize adequately a specific kind of substance without reference to the various potentialities it has by its very nature and which distinguish its essence from the essence of other kinds of substances. But now a difficulty arises for Pratt and, indeed, for all those who think that thinking matter is possible. By taking the various potentialities for thought, feeling, sensation and so forth to be consistent with being a material and an immaterial substance, the very notion of being a spirit is rendered vacuous and surely this is too strong. Even if there are no spiritual substances, surely the claim that there are is intelligible and filled with content, yet the thinking matter thesis renders empty any attempt to give content to the notion of a spirit. During the days of John Locke (who first introduced the thesis that thinking matter is possible), those who accepted the possibility of thinking matter had a terrible time giving any content to the notion of a spirit. About all they could say was that it has bare being. But this is hardly informative and, in any case, it could be used to characterize the number two or any other 'immaterial' entity. Even if there happen to be no spirits, it is surely wrong to say the very notion of a human spirit or of God as a spirit is vacuous and only capable of formal characterization.

Most dualists would characterize a spirit as an immaterial (i.e., at least unextended, without solidity, and not composed of separable parts) substance with the formal characteristics of a substance in general and with the ultimate potentialities of sensation, emotion, thought, free action for a purpose, belief, moral awareness, and so forth. Notice that the material content to being a spirit has a negative component (being without solidity, unextended). But that is not a sufficient condition to have an intelligible concept of spirit, especially one adequate to distinguish it from other entities that satisfy the negative component. And it is precisely the capacities for consciousness that provides that material content. But if those capacities are consistent with a material substance, then one cannot appeal to them to characterize a spirit.

Suppose one were to say that a mind is anything with the powers of consciousness and a spirit was an unextended mind. We are now in a position to see that such a notion of spirit is vacuous. Why? Because the component of the definition that carries weight is 'being unextended'. This is because the powers of consciousness are consistent with not being a spirit – for example being a conscious atomic simple – and, thus, they cannot be what constitutes a spirit and makes it unique. But when one says that God is a spirit, one does not mean merely that God is unextended. The content of 'spirit' in such a case is precisely the fact that God possesses and is essentially characterized qua spirit by the powers of conscious life.

Not only does Pratt's thesis of thinking matter render the notion of an immaterial spirit vacuous, it also seems to imply that his notion of spiritual matter is just an immaterial substance by another name. Note that Pratt clearly has a dualism of spirit and gross matter. His characterization of the difference comes perilously close to the dualist distinction between material and immaterial substances. Indeed, in one place Pratt admits that his notion of an atom of spirit matter is merely a verbal difference in the name he uses in comparison with the traditional notion of an immaterial spirit.[28] Such is the dilemma facing all those who think that thinking matter is possible. They, including Pratt, must find some way to distinguish thinking matter from immaterial spirit or else they offer a distinction without a difference.

By way of application, it is false to employ 'immaterial' as an infima species to claim that a spirit is a *kind* of material substance. Rather, 'immaterial' is a genus, and there are various kinds of spirits – human, angelic, divine. And the admission of thinking matter renders the notion of a spirit materially vacuous. And while there are differences between Pratt and contemporary advocates of conscious atomic simples, I believe that our discussion of the dialectic between Pratt and Taylder applies to these contemporary advocates. It is for these reasons that I believe the arguments by Goetz and Lowe support the self as a spirit and not an atomic simple or some such thing.

An argument from paradigm cases

John Calvin once remarked that 'No man can survey himself without forthwith turning his thoughts towards the God in whom he lives and moves.'[29] Along similar lines, the great Old Testament scholar Franz Delitzsch claimed, 'In order to apprehend the nature of the . . . human soul, it is first of all essential to apprehend the nature of God.'[30] More recently, Alvin Plantinga has argued that Christians ought to take the commitments that constitute Christian theology as items of knowledge to be employed in forming an integrated worldview, doing research, and so forth. Among the things that Plantinga takes to be central to theological knowledge is the proposition that God is a person. Says Plantinga,

> How should we think about human persons? What sorts of things, fundamentally, *are* they? What is it to be a human, what is it to be a *human* person, and how should we think about personhood? . . . The first point to note is that on the Christian scheme of things, *God* is the premier person, the first and chief exemplar of personhood . . . and the properties most important for an understanding of our personhood are properties we share with him.[31]

In the spirit of Calvin, Delitzsch and Plantinga, we offer the following argument for dualism.

(PC1) God and angels are paradigm case persons.
(PC2) If something is a person then it resembles the paradigm cases in a relevantly similar way.
(PC3) The relevantly similar way of resemblance is (1) being a spiritual substance; (2) essentially characterized by a certain range of actual and potential properties of consciousness.
(PC4) A human person is a person.
(PC5) Therefore, a human person is (1) a spiritual substance; (2) essentially characterized by the actual and potential properties of consciousness.

In different ways, the premises most likely to come under attack are (PC1) and (PC3), so let us take them in order. Given Christian theism, it seems clear that God is the paradigm case of a person, and even on an atheistic view, if the concept of God is coherent, the claim may still be granted. But what about angels (or at least the concept of an angel)? I believe they should be included as paradigm cases of persons for two reasons. First, since the nature of human persons is at issue, it is problematic, maybe even question-begging, to list them as paradigm cases. So it's best to employ examples of persons outside the human family, and angels fit the bill. Second, angels do not face two problems present for human persons. For one thing, they do not develop as humans do so there is no issue regarding an angel being a potential person. For another, their identity conditions clearly involve sameness of spirit/soul. Bodily criteria are out of the question and psychological criteria are otiose. So angels are relatively free of personhood problems that apply to discussions of human persons.

The real problem is likely to be (PC3), particularly the idea that the relevant sense of resemblance includes being a spiritual substance. One way to attack this claim is to try to break the analogy between humans and God, and that is just what Kevin Corcoran does in his response to a similar paradigm case argument.[32] According to Corcoran, while we are persons, we are *embodied* persons unlike God the Father. And God's experience of the natural world, being unmediated by a body, must be quite different from human consciousness or awareness, which is mediated by a body.

I believe there are adequate rejoinders to each objection. We can explain our differences with God and angels due to embodiment by pointing out that there are no such things as persons simpliciter, but only kinds of persons, and that if we take being a person and being a human as a determinable/determinate relation, then (1) we do not need to adjust our ontology in this specific case but, rather, we employ a pattern of property relations that runs throughout reality to understand humanness and personhood; and (2) we can make sense of how there could be various kinds of persons (divine, angelic, Martian, human) in virtue of sharing the same genus with different species. We can then treat a human person as a person (a kind of spiritual substance) with at least the potentialities for animating and forming a human body. In this way, we retain human personhood in the Intermediate state and we have a clear way to distinguish human from angelic persons or God.

Moreover, the nature of a conscious state is a function of the state's intrinsic constituents, not a function of the fact that it is mediated bodily or the specific nature of that mediation. Based on strong conceivability, there are possible worlds where visual sensations are mediated by the ears and sounds are mediated by the eyeballs. And the vast literature supporting Near Death Experiences clearly indicates that there are actual cases in which disembodied human persons continue to have the same sorts of conscious states, including sensations, with no bodies at all.

Finally, there are two features of the sorts of mental properties human persons exemplify that seem to indicate that human persons are simple, unextended substances constituted by the capacities for those mental properties. First, they are intrinsic properties. When a mental property is exemplified, the property is an immanent constituent that constitutes the nature of its property-instance. And the substance that has that property-instance is intrinsically characterized by the property. Further, the substance is necessarily the kind of thing that can have the property-instance in question. Indeed, as I have argued elsewhere, such property-instances are characterizing modes of the substances having them.[33] The substance is the kind of thing it is in virtue of the sorts of modes it can have.

Second, these mental properties are possibly exemplified by pure, unextended spirits and, in fact, actually are so exemplified in angels and God. And given the possibility of God and angels having such properties, it is accidental to them that they have an extended object that exemplifies them. Further, in my view, just as it is necessarily the case that a colour cannot be exemplified by an unextended object, so it is necessarily the case that mental properties cannot be exemplified by extended objects. At least the properties involved in volitional acts, propositional attitudes, and various sensations such as being an appearing of red are not such that they have property-instances that are extended. Thus, the particular that instantiates those properties is not extended to the extent that the property-instances characterize them. As Roderick Chisholm has pointed out, some of our mental properties are known to be such that simple substances can have them and are not known to be such that compound substances (and for Chisholm, a compound object is extended) can have them.[34] When combined with justified beliefs of a dualist nature in the history of the Church, there is a considerable burden of proof on the Christian materialist who believes we are constituted by an aggregate, and that burden has not been met.

Alternatives to a Substantial, Simple Soul

In this chapter's final section, I want to examine two major alternatives that serve as rivals to a substance dualist depiction of the self. Each view claims to have the ontological resources to analyse the self as a conscious, enduring continuant without employing substance dualism.

Mereological aggregates and material composition

In the last 15 to 20 years, reflections on material composition have become all the rage and, accordingly, a growing number of thinkers have attempted to use material composition as a way of fleshing out a Christian view of the human person. In this section, I want to interact briefly with a prominent advocate of a constitution view of human persons, namely the views of Lynne Rudder Baker.

Baker claims that I am most fundamentally a person, and a person (human or non-human) is an entity with the potentiality for a first-person perspective.[35] The first-person perspective is a property persons have which is grounded in the causal powers of the brain and constitutive of persons. The capacity to conceive of oneself as oneself is necessary and sufficient for having a strong, robust first-person perspective. A human person is a person wholly constituted by a body that is a human organism, an animal of the species *Homo sapiens*. So the person's relationship to his/her body is that the latter constitutes the former.

According to Baker, constitution is not identity. Why? Consider David the statue and 'Piece' the lump of marble that constitutes David. These cannot be identical because they have different modal properties (e.g., if the lump changes shape, Piece could survive but David would not). Constitution is a type of unity relation whose relata are not identical or two independent (separable) particulars. David and Piece spatially coincide, have many properties in common (size, mass, colour), are such that David's aesthetic properties depend on the properties of Piece, and David does not have Piece as a proper part. Constitution is a relation between identity and separable existence. If x constitutes y, then there is a unified individual whose identity is determined by y. The identity of the constituting thing (x) is submerged or encompassed by the identity of what it constitutes (y). Baker lists the following examples to illustrate the ubiquity of the constitution relation: pieces of paper constitute dollar bills and DNA constitutes genes.

According to Baker, things can have properties in different ways:

derivatively and non-derivatively. For example, Piece has many properties (e.g., being a statue) derivatively (i.e., in virtue of constituting David) and some non-derivatively (mass). David has properties derivatively, that is in virtue of being constituted by Piece (e.g., being made of marble) and some non-derivatively (being a statue). Yet derivative properties are not additive (e.g., there is not twice Piece's mass present). X's having P derivatively just is x constituting some y that has P non-derivatively.

Since the relata of the constitution relation can belong to many kinds, it is the primary kind that determines an object's persistence conditions. Certain circumstances are sufficient conditions for an object x constituting an object y, where x and y are non-identical and belong to different kinds, namely, a whole class of new kinds of causal powers are present.

Regarding human persons, the mereological sum of atoms/molecules constitutes the body at a given time but is not identical to that body. And the human body (the human organism) constitutes the human person. A human person is a particular that is wholly constituted by a human organism/body and that has a capacity for a first-person perspective. Baker also rejects mereological essentialism and claims that material objects are enduring continuants and not sums of temporal parts; thus, human persons are such continuants.

And while a person is essentially a person, a human person is not essentially a human. What makes human persons human is that they are constituted by biologically human bodies, that is, an animal or organism. Still, it may be possible for a human person to come to be constituted by a non-biological body and still exist if, for example, one's body were gradually replaced entirely by bionic parts without loss of one's first-person perspective. In fact, because constitution is not identity, one could survive the death of one's body in an intermediate state by being constituted by a new kind of body.

While there is much to admire in Baker's account, at the end of the day I believe it fails to deliver a coherent account of human persons as conscious, unified enduring continuants. I want to raise three objections with her account.

First, there are two problems with Baker's use of 'a first-person perspective.' For one thing, if there is such a property, it is an impure one. An impure property, such as being identical to Socrates or to the left of a desk, requires reference to a particular to be described. Such a property cannot constitute such a referent without being circular: the property presupposes and, therefore, cannot constitute the particular – Socrates, the desk, or an individual person – to which reference is made.

For another thing, there most likely is no such property. In general, one may give a reductive analysis of the first-person perspective as follows: S has the property of being a first-person perspective if S is a personal, viewing kind of point, that is, S is a kind of substance (point), a sentient (viewing) substance, with the properties (including ultimate potentialities) characteristic of persons (e.g., self-awareness and so on). The first-person perspective is not a property persons have, it is the thing persons are – centres of a personal kind of consciousness. Persons qua substantial, unified centres, exemplify ordinary mental properties – being-a-thought-that-P, being-a-sensation-of-red, being painful. But they do not have in addition to these the property of being a first-person perspective. When a substantial personal ego exemplifies an ordinary mental property, that is ipso facto a first-person perspective. There is no additional fact that needs grounding in a superfluous property – being a first-person perspective. The 'first-person perspective' is just a way of describing/referring to an ontologically prior substantial, sentient person with ordinary mental properties to which that perspective can be reduced.

Second, it is unclear to me that Baker has made it intelligible that a human person could be a continuant even though his original body ceases to exist (through significant part replacement or through death) and another body comes to constitute that person. Following Dean Zimmerman, as Stewart Goetz and Charles Taliaferro point out, organisms and aggregates of matter cannot lose all their parts at once, and there are limits on how latter stages can evolve out of earlier ones.[36] But Baker's persons seem free of such limitations. They can miraculously jump from one body to another with radically different traits. But mere hunks of matter or organisms cannot do this. Such 'bodies' that can pass from organic matter to bionic parts are really souls by another name, and, indeed, one suspects that Baker's account of persons is really a substance dualist one with an unclear account of personal identity in these cases.

Baker does offer a criterion for personal identity over time:[37] 'person P_1 at time t_1 is the same person as person P_2 at time t_2 if and only if P_1 and P_2 have the same first-person perspective'. However, this is both uninformative and empty. Baker admits that she can give no non-circular account of sameness of first-person perspective, and my criticisms above show why: being a first-person perspective is an impure (circularly described) property and it can be reduced to substantial, personal souls. In this case, sameness of person just is sameness of soul.

Finally, I believe that neither Baker nor other contemporary advocates have made clear how a composed mereological aggregate can avoid mereological essentialism. In my view, the problem lies in the way analytic ontology is too often done today, namely, that truth conditions are given for some analysandum with no ontological analysis of that analysandum to show how the truth conditions could, in fact, obtain. Thus, it is typical to say that vases vs. the atomic simples that compose them, or organisms vs. the atomic simples that compose them have different modal properties and, thus, are not identical. While true enough, such claims fail to provide an ontological analysis of vases or organisms such that we can see how it is that their modal properties are different and whether the relevant ontological factors are sufficient for the vase/organism to survive part replacement. For anyone who says that constitution is not identity, it would seem that he or she must give an ontological analysis of the constituted thing to clarify its ontological constituents that go beyond and prevent it from being identical to the constituting thing. And whatever these extra constituents are, they must be adequate to clarify how the constituted thing has a sufficient unity to avoid a mereological essentialist treatment.

In light of this, let's take another look at David and Piece and grant that there are atomic simples. Let 'the ps' denote all and only Piece's atomic simples. I take a plurality theory of masses according to which terms like 'the ps' do not denote an individual material object; rather, it refers to a plurality of objects each of which is individuated by being a separable part of Piece. Others would take the term to refer to an individual object.

Second we have Piece, the lump of marble. What, exactly, is Piece? Minimally, Piece would seem to be identical to the ps plus all and only the relational instances between and among the various n-tuples of the ps. It would seem that Piece could not be identical to the ps and the relational structure involving them because that relational structure is a universal, not a particular. It cannot help individuate Piece since it could be in several objects at once. So Piece must be identical to the ps plus the relation-instance of that structure. And given that the ps are atomic simples and separable parts, the relation-instances are external relation-instances. Additionally, Piece may have a surface boundary as a simple, dependent part.

Third, we have an Aristotelianly shaped chunk of marble. Whenever a particular x has a property P, the-having-of-P-by-x is a mode of and stands in a modal distinction with x. If two entities stand in a modal distinction with each other, then one can exist without the other but not conversely. One of the two is a dependent entity. Moreover, modes are particulars, albeit dependent ones. Thus, the entity in view is a chunk of marble with a mode that is constituted by the exemplification of the relevant shape by the chunk.

Finally, we have the statue which is the Aristotelianly shaped chunk of marble taken to be a statue. For what it's worth, I do not take intentional properties to be relations; instead, I think they are monadic properties. Thus, the various purposes, intentions, valuations, goals, and so forth directed towards our shaped chunk are constituents of the statue. The statue is identical to the chunk plus the relevant intentional states. There is no property of being a statue that Piece or the shaped chunk of marble exemplifies; there is just a community of intentional entities whose mental states are directed upon the chunk. In general, an artefact is an object upon which the relevant mental states are directed. We may say that these states take the object to be a representation of such and such or to function thus and so. Some objects like our chunk actually resemble the represented object. And in this case, while the resemblance is what qualifies the chunk to be a statue of Aristotle, it is not what constitutes it as a statue. It has often been said that there is no physics of money, and this saying is true. No God's eye view of the constituents of an artefact such as money or a statue will tell one that it is such. The intentional states that are constitutive of artefacts involve properties of the people in the relevant community, not properties of or relations to the relevant object.

Thus, we have four different entities, with the ps either being an object or just a number of individual atomic simples. Our ontological analysis shows why they are non-identical and why they have different modal properties: they are composed of different constituents. Focusing on Piece, could it sustain identity through part replacement? It is hard to see how. If a part is replaced, the ps change to a new collection. And even if only one of the ps is replaced by a qualitatively identical simple that stands in the same relation, one would still have a different relational structure because that structure is itself a mereological compound of relation-instances, and the new set of relation-instances is different from the set involving the original simple. The relational structure (and life itself is a flux of myriads of changing living activities) is in constant flux as parts come and go, or as those parts simply change relations relative to each other. Given that the entire relation-instance is a mereological collection just like the ps (and life is such a collection of the relevant set of living activities), and given that these both seem to be like mere heaps or collections of entities, it is hard to avoid mereological essentialism with respect to them. And adding a boundary doesn't help. If a collection of marbles inside a balloon changes members (or changes in relations with respect to each other) then you no longer have the same structured collection of marbles in a balloon. The presence or absence of the balloon doesn't affect the situation.

To the degree that living organisms or persons are constituted entities, then they are to be analysed according to mereological essentialism, too. They are not unified continuants. But why, then, do we have such strong intuitions that living organisms are continuants? It is because either we are attributing a self, an I, a spiritual substance to the living organism, or we are taking it (along with chunks of marble, and things like tables) as it presents itself to our senses, namely as an ontological blob of goo that is not composed of micro-parts (we still take tables to have legs and a top, but not as composed of atoms and molecules). Our senses present us with smoothly continuous, unchanging blobs of being; they do not present us with the mereological compounds science describes. Our intuitions are 'pumped', as it were, by one of these two sources.

It is only if organisms or persons are simple spiritual substances that they can be continuants. Consider the category of property for a moment and distinguish a structural supervenient property which is a relational structure composed of parts, relations and properties at the subvenient level (e.g. H_2O) from an emergent supervenient property which is a simple *sui generis* property. It seems clear that a structural property cannot remain the same if it gains or loses constituents because it just is a relational entity constituted by those constituents and their relation-instances. But as long as the subvenient base sustains the emergent property in existence, a change in subvenient entities does not cause the emergent property to lose its identity. Why? Because it is an uncomposed simple. The same seems to be true of entities in the category of substance, and to my knowledge, Baker has not provided a sufficient case that qua composed mereological compound, an organism or a person can be a continuant. Since we are, in fact, continuants, I conclude that Baker has not provided a sufficient case for thinking that we are

1 composed mereological compounds, and
2 personal spiritual substances.

Timothy O'Connor and emergent agents

Timothy O'Connor has developed his view of libertarian agent and advances the idea that persons are material substances in a qualified sense.[38] Working within a framework of immanent universals, O'Connor uses these descriptors for the person-as-agent: a biological organism with emergent properties (in his three senses, viz. *sui generis* relative to lower subvenient levels, including top-down active power) that are as basic as the negative charge of an electron; a 3-D continuant with a mental life grounded in its physical nature; a cluster of immanent universals with its own unique particularity not reducible to that of the mereological aggregate from which it arises; an emergent biological organism with a new thisness; a new composite that exhibits an objective substantial unity. These descriptors express O'Connor's desire to steer a via media between a mere ordered mereological aggregate on the one hand and a view such as William Hasker's according to which a brand new emergent mental whole exists and is in no way composed of subvenient entities.[39]

To elaborate, O'Connor claims that a standard mereological aggregate is inadequate to ground a genuine enduring continuant, a continuant that is needed to satisfy the requirements for a responsible libertarian causal agent. He also rejects a Haskerian view on the grounds that only a theistic solution along the lines of AC could account for how a complex physical system could give rise all in one go to a brand new emergent mental entity.[40] O'Connor wants to avoid universalism regarding composite objects, so he attempts to specify conditions under which a new emergent individual arises and he tries to give an ontological account of how such an individual could arise in the first place. Regarding the former, emergent properties are the best candidates for emergent individuals (and the only clear evidence we have for such properties is consciousness). All other candidates are merely mereological aggregates. So in the category of individual, O'Connor's ontology includes atomic simples, mereological aggregates, emergent biological organisms (and as a Christian theist, at least one purely spiritual substance – God).

When it comes to offering an account of all this, O'Connor is not clear about his task, and it is sometimes hard to tell which of these two questions he is answering:

1 How are we to explain ontologically how emergent individuals could come about?
2 When should we judge that an emergent individual has come about?

Questions 1 and 2 are ontological and epistemological, respectively, and I shall take 1 to be O'Connor's focus. So understood, he claims that subvenient entities are always trying to bring about the emergent individual, but it is only when a certain threshold level of complexity is reached that conditions are right for that base to cause the emergent individual to come into being. When emergent mental properties appear, they constitute holistic mental states – perhaps enduring baseline mental states – and these, in turn, confer on persons their substantial unity as thinking biological substances, presumably by bringing about through top-down causation a new particularity over and above that of the series of subvenient mereological aggregates that are in a constant state of flux. This 'composition-conferred-by-holism' view produces an emergent individual that is somehow composed by its composite parts yet has a new thisness all its own.

Why should we believe any of this? There seem to be two reasons. First, first-person direct awareness justifies the view that consciousness is emergent in O'Connor's three senses and this justification overrides any a posteriori ascriptions of micro-structure to conscious states. All empirical knowledge, he tells us, presupposes this knowledge. Second, we should limit our account to the constraints provided by the naturalist mereological hierarchy and the grounds we have for accepting it, we should avoid a theistic explanation of emergent individuals, and on the basis of theoretical simplicity, we should adopt a view of the emergent individual that does two things: grounds endurance and agency beyond the flux of change in a mere ordered aggregate and is as close to the mereological aggregate as possible in order to fit the naturalist viewpoint.

What should we make of O'Connor's modified view? For one thing, it is far from clear how a particular with basic mental potentialities is a physical object. It is not clear how he can hold that the agent self is a physical substance necessarily characterized by emergent mental properties. If the agent self is essentially mental, and if we recognize that a particular's actual and potential properties are both relevant for characterizing the kind of entity the particular is, then the agent self would seem to be essentially a mental/physical particular, and not simply a physical particular with emergent mental properties attached to it. When John Locke argued that thinking matter was possible, some of his critics (Edward Stillingfleet, S. G. Gerdil, Malcolm Flemyng) responded by pointing out that a 'material' substance whose essence was constituted in part by mental potentialities was no longer simply a 'material' substance.[41] I believe O'Connor's agent is subject to the same criticism. To his credit, O'Connor seems to recognize this and, thus, he calls persons material substances 'in a qualified form'. Unfortunately, this 'qualified form' goes beyond the ontological resources of naturalism.

Moreover, O'Connor's new view is more clearly a version of panpsychism, and most philosophers have seen that this is not a legitimate specification of naturalism. For example, when he claims that consciousness is just as basic as negative charge, this claim is closer to theism than to naturalism and it will be a hard pill for naturalists to swallow. This view also renders impossible a strict naturalist explanation of emergence. Instead, mental potentialities and their causal interaction with physical conditions are required, and this is a long way from naturalism.

Third, there are deep metaphysical problems with O'Connor's emergent individuals. For one thing, the framework of immanent universals renders unintelligible the claim that the emergent individual has its own thisness while at the same time being constituted by the relevant mereological complex. The framework of immanent universals depicts property-instances as states of affairs (the so-called thick particular) – in the case of O'Connor's persons, states of affairs that are substantial continuants – with three constituents: the universal, the nexus of exemplification, and an individuator (the thin particular, in my view, a bare particular). Whatever conditions ground the exemplification of the universal are external to the instance itself. And since the person can endure even though the mereological aggregate is in constant flux, it would seem that the aggregate is accidental and external to the continuant. To the degree that his emergent individuals provide what is needed (e.g., being enduring continuants), they look strangely like William Hasker's emergent mental ego rather than some via media.

Further, there just is no baseline conscious state that is constant throughout a person's life and apt for grounding endurance. The property of being conscious cannot provide such a baseline because it is a second-order property of mental properties (being a sensation, a thought) that comes-to-be and ceases-to-be exemplified when first-order states come and go. Our mental lives team with flux just as does the 'underlying' aggregate. There seems to be no metaphysical account of the individual that grounds its endurance unless, of course, we treat the individual as a state of affairs constituted by a mental essence, exemplification, and particularity with the aggregate its cause but outside the being of its effect. But, again, this is Hasker's view not O'Connor's. Finally, in criticizing Hasker's view, he claims that unless one appeals to a theistic explanation, one cannot explain how a complex physical system could give rise, all in one go, to a brand new emergent whole. But this very same argument has been repeatedly raised against emergent properties themselves.

Fourth, I find O'Connor's composition-conferred-by-holism to be deeply troubling. He apparently accepts the dictum that 'thought implies a thinker', or more generally, that consciousness requires a particular to possess it. So far so good. But it seems to me that this is so because the bearer of consciousness is more basic ontologically than the mental properties it exemplifies or the mental states that obtain within it. But O'Connor's view has this backwards. If I understand him correctly, when the mereological aggregate reaches the proper threshold, emergent consciousness arises and this, in turn, causes the conscious individual to come into existence via top-down conferral (by generating a new thisness). Thus, thinkings cause thinkers, but it seems to me that the converse is true.

Moreover, O'Connor claims that emergence is dynamic and causal, not static and formal, that emergent states are caused by temporally prior subvenient states, and, thus, emergence is diachronic and not synchronic.[42] Thus, the following senario seems to arise: at t_1 subvenient conditions cause emergent conscious state C_1 to obtain at t_2 which, in turn, brings about emergent individual I_1 at t_3. Two things seem to follow. First, the very first mental state in one's life (C_1) seems clearly ownerless since at t_2 there is no individual to possess it. Second, beyond the very first conscious state, the following would seem to hold: for all C_{N+1} (for N greater than zero) at t_{N+2}, the individual I_{N+1} conferred by and, thus, ontologically tied to C_{N+1} exists at t_{N+2}. I see no further relevant ontological relationship between a conscious state and an emergent individual other than the conferral relation. If this is correct, then it is hard to see how a continuing 'self' can exist since there just is no single, ongoing 'baseline mental state' throughout one's life (e.g., in sleep or surgery). Since conscious states are in flux, so are the instantaneous individuals upon whom they confer existence. In this case, for any time t greater than one, there may be an emergent individual that exists while a particular conscious state obtains, but it is the wrong one. In general, each emergent individual at a time is ontologically associated with a mental state that obtained instantaneously earlier and, thus, is ownerless.

I may have misunderstood O'Connor and he may have already presented materials for an adequate reply to my objections. Fortunately, for my purposes, it is not the implausibility of his view of the agent that is my main concern. Rather, it is that his modified view is even less compatible with naturalism than his earlier view. In light of the ontology-constraining factors surfaced in Chapter 1, there is a burden of proof on any ontology that goes beyond these factors. O'Connor has clearly done so (e.g., the mental is as basic as negative charge, the emergence of both active power and a new individual, the fact that neither emergent entity is entailed by the Grand Story, top-down causation, epistemic authority given to first-person introspection that trumps a posteriori scientific knowledge), and he has failed to meet the burden of proof required to claim that his position is a plausible version of naturalism.

6

Naturalism, Objective Morality, Intrinsic Value and Human Persons

According to biblical theism, the fundamental being exemplifies virtue properties and other intrinsically valuable attributes. He created the world and imposed upon human persons an objective moral law grounded in his own good nature, along with the intrinsic goodness and properly functioning natures of the things he created. He created human persons with the powers necessary to engage in moral actions as part of an overall life of flourishing, and he gave all human persons his own image which serves as the ontological ground for high, equal human value and rights simply as such.

These three features of the moral order

1 objective, intrinsic value and an objective moral law;
2 the reality of human moral action;
3 intrinsic human value and rights

are very much at home in a biblical theistic worldview to say the least. But things aren't so good for a naturalist worldview, and thoughtful naturalists have concluded that naturalism has its work cut out for it in accommodating these features. And many thinkers – naturalists and non-naturalists – have concluded that naturalism cannot, in fact, provide the epistemic and ontological resources for them. Indeed, for these thinkers, naturalism actually provides defeaters for these features.

For example, regarding an objective moral order, evolutionary naturalist Michael Ruse notes,

> Morality is a biological adaptation no less than are hands and feet and teeth. Considered as a rationally justifiable set of claims

> about an objective something, ethics is illusory. I appreciate that when somebody says 'Love thy neighbor as thyself,' they think they are referring above and beyond themselves. Nevertheless, such reference is truly without foundation. Morality is just an aid to survival and reproduction . . . and any deeper meaning is illusory.[1]

Regarding moral action, naturalist John Bishop frankly admits that

> the idea of a responsible agent, with the 'originative' ability to initiate events in the natural world, does not sit easily with the idea of [an agent as] a natural organism . . . Our scientific understanding of human behavior seems to be in tension with a presupposition of the ethical stance we adopt toward it.[2]

Regarding high, equal human value and rights simply as such, naturalist Peter Singer and Helga Kuhse acknowledge that the best, perhaps only way to justify the belief that all humans have equal and unique value simply as such is in light of the metaphysical grounding of the Judaeo-Christian doctrine of the image of God.[3] This claim by Singer and Kuhse has been acknowledged by a wide number of thinkers for some time. For example, in the early 1960s, Joel Feinberg, arguably the leading legal, political philosopher of that time, advanced the following argument.[4] According to Feinberg, a natural right is a human right held unalterably, unconditionally, and possessing certain epistemological properties (e.g., perceivable by direct, rational intuition) and metaphysical groundings. If human rights are natural rights that apply to all human persons equally, then they presuppose equal human worth but not equal merit. Human merit (e.g., talents, skills, character, personality, various abilities) is graded, but human worth is not. Equal rights accrue to individuals quite apart from their graded merit.

Feinberg believed that the following sceptical question has never been adequately answered: Why should we treat all people equally in any respect in the face of manifest inequalities of merit among them? The simple response 'Because we just have such worth' does not answer the sceptics' query. If 'human worth' is real and generic, said Feinberg, then it must supervene on some subvenient base that

1 we all have equally in common, and
2 is non-trivial and of supreme moral worth.

Operating within a naturalist framework, Feinberg considers several attempts to delineate that base, and he judges them all to be a failure because they

1 require an entity such as 'pricelessness' for which we have no naturalistic answer as to where it came from and with respect to which one must postulate a problematic, mysterious, intuitive faculty of direct awareness of such an entity;
2 are grounded in a degreed property such as rationality (and Feinberg took the potential for rationality to be degreed) which, therefore, cannot do the job of founding equal worth for all;
3 simply name the problem to be solved and do not provide an explanation of the problem itself.[5]

At the end of the day, Feinberg acknowledges that the notion of equal worth and equal rights for all human persons is groundless and may simply express a non-cognitivist, unjustifiable pro-attitude of respect towards the humanity in each man's person. My point in mentioning Feinberg is not to evaluate his claims, but to illustrate just how difficult it is to justify equal value/rights for all human persons if one has taken the naturalistic turn.

I agree with these thinkers, and I believe that some form of ethical naturalism or non-cognitivism is the best way for a naturalist to go in metaethics. And a commonsense view of moral actions and equal value/rights are hard to sustain in a naturalist worldview. In this chapter, I shall do two things. First, I will provide a brief overview of why naturalism has difficulty sustaining objective intrinsic value and moral law, and a robust view of moral action. Second, I shall present two arguments for why the conjunction of naturalism and evolutionary theory fails to have the resources for sustaining high, equal value and rights for all human persons simply as such.

Naturalism, Intrinsic Value and Objective Moral Law

My purpose in this section is to list briefly seven features of morally relevant intrinsic value and objective moral law as we human persons commonsensically know them to be, and explain why these features are defeaters for a naturalist worldview. Space considerations forbid me to engage in consideration of naturalist responses in any detail. The reader should keep in mind that many naturalists agree that these seven features are problems and opt for a reductive or eliminative strategy, for example, ethical naturalism or non-cognitivism, as a response, and other naturalists have tried to sustain these features with a naturalist framework, for example by opting for emergentism. I think it is valuable to have listed in one place these seven features, and I believe that even those naturalists who have formulated various responses to them would agree that these are at least prima facie defeaters for a naturalist worldview.

The existence of objective value

Richard Dawkins gets the naturalist ontology right when he says that 'The universe we observe has precisely the properties we should expect if there is, at bottom, no design, no purpose, no evil and no good, nothing but blind, pitiless indifference.'[6] The sheer existence of intrinsic value and prescriptive 'oughts' is unintelligible on a naturalist framework. Why? If you start with the Big Bang and other facts whose characterization requires a mere descriptive 'is', and the history of the universe is the arrangement of microphysical entities into larger and larger structural compounds, from whence cometh value? The theist begins with a Being who is intrinsically good, but the naturalist begins with the sort of stuff characterized by Dawkins. Given this, it's hard to see how a naturalist can embrace non-natural, intrinsic goodness and objectively true prescriptions.

The nature of the moral law

The objective moral order presents itself to us in the form of commands with imperatival force, and as obligations, duties and prohibitions imposed on us. Moreover, we sense that we are genuinely accountable for these impositions, and perhaps the most widespread, cross-cultural human phenomenon is the ubiquitous shame and guilt we all experience towards the moral law. It is hard to see how there can be imperatival force if there is not a good God with a will who stands behind the moral law. And what imposes obligations and so on if it is not God? To what or whom would we be accountable in a godless universe, and why do we experience a sense of shame and guilt that goes far beyond what we owe each other or what is culturally inbred? One cannot sense shame and guilt towards a Platonic form. These features of the moral order make sense if a good God exists, but they are hard to retain and explain if God does not exist.

The instantiation of morally relevant value properties

Compare the following quotes. The first is by J. L. Mackie:

> Moral properties constitute so odd a cluster of properties and relations that they are most unlikely to have arisen in the ordinary course of events without an all-powerful god to create them.[7]

The second is by Paul Churchland:

> the important point about the standard evolutionary story is that the human species and all of its features are the wholly physical outcome of a purely physical process . . . If this is the correct account of our origins, then there seems neither need, nor room, to fit any nonphysical substances or properties into our theoretical account of ourselves. We are creatures of matter. And we should learn to live with that fact.[8]

Mackie is making the same point about moral properties/relations that Churchland makes about mental properties/substances. We examined the problem of mental properties in Chapter 2, and the same issues surfaced there apply with equal force to moral properties. Put briefly, even if one opts for a sort of moral Platonism such that various value properties are universals and, as such, simply a part of the furniture of the world, the naturalist still has no explanation whatever as to why these properties were ever exemplified.

How or why did the nexus of exemplification reach into Plato's heaven, as it were, and cause these entities to be instantiated in the physical universe? Note Mackie's careful language. Interpreting them plausibly, moral properties/relations are odd in the sense that they are utterly unlike all other entities that are knowable by scientific means, that constitute the Grand Story, and that populate the ontologies of an ideal chemistry and physics. And by 'the ordinary course of events', he means that given the typical activities and processes described by the hard sciences, and given that these constitute the history of the cosmos, the instantiation of intrinsic value properties is so unlikely that their exemplification provides evidence for theism.

The intersection of intrinsic value and human persons

Given that somehow or other, morally relevant intrinsic values became instantiated, it is hard to see why they would have anything to do with human beings. As Mark Linville observes, given evolutionary naturalism, 'What a fortuitous chain of events that resulted in the actual existence of the kinds of creatures to whom eternally and necessarily true, but causally impotent, principles apply.'[9] We have very strong intuitions that human beings instantiate very high, intrinsic, equal value. But why? Why is it a good thing that our species survives? How did the mere relational, structural complexity of human DNA cause this sort of intrinsic value to be instantiated by human beings? As Stewart Goetz and Charles Taliaferro remind us, 'Strict naturalists often get rid of the necessary conditions of morality and value by denying the existence of freedom, consciousness, and a substantial self.'[10] And the claim that somehow these and intrinsic value properties supervene upon human biology is just an assertion that names the problem to be solved, it is not a solution that represents what Bertrand Russell called honest toil. Moreover, it is hard to see why moral action would be within the sphere of human action and flourishing. Why would human beings be able to obey the moral law and why would such obedience contribute towards human flourishing? Christian theism has an obvious answer to these questions, but it is far from obvious that naturalism does.

But not only does naturalism fail to have adequate answers to these questions, it contains a defeater for the claim that humans have high, instrinsic value and should never be used as a mere means to an end. As Charles Darwin noted in his *Autobiography*:

> [Consider] . . . the view now held by most physicists, namely that the sun with all the planets will in time grow too cold for life, unless indeed some great body dashes into the sun and thus give it fresh life . . . Believing as I do that man in the distant future will be a far more perfect creature than he now is, it is an intolerable thought that he and all other sentient beings are doomed to complete annihilation after such long-continued slow progress.[11]

It is just not clear how, on a naturalist view, humans have *any* intrinsic value at all qua human beings. If Darwin's point above is correct, then we current humans have less value than future humans and, in fact, may be properly treated as means to the end of evolving greater creatures. We stand to future products of evolution as amoebas stand to us. Indeed, scientists John Barrow and Frank Tipler draw precisely this conclusion.[12] They argue that humans are just one fleeting stage in evolutionary development that is moving towards higher and higher life forms. All intermediate stages from amoebas to humans have only instrumental value as they contribute to later stages. Earlier stages do *not* have intrinsic value. In fact, Barrow and Tipler claim that it is only the DNA program *in* humans that has intrinsic value, and we exist to perfect that program to bring about future life.

Knowledge of intrinsic value and the moral law

Whatever else one says about value properties, as Hume taught us, they are not empirically detectable nor are they the sorts of properties whose instances can stand in physical causal relations with the brain. However, it would seem that under the demands of evolutionary struggle, humans would evolve faculties apt for sensory interaction with their environments, but that's about it. Any other faculties would seem to go beyond what evolution can explain. And moral knowledge is normative in two senses: it is knowledge of intrinsic value and normative action, and it is itself something that is intrinsically valuable and a normative duty of human knowers. As beings created in the image of God who were placed here to live in light of moral knowledge and knowledge of other intrinsic values (e.g., aesthetic, epistemic ones), these abilities of human faculties are hardly surprising. But given naturalism, they are utterly without precedent in the long history of evolutionary adaptation, their appearance is without explanation, and their veracity as truth gatherers is a paradigm case of queerness.

The nature of moral action

According to folk ontology (the ontology that underlies commonsense), moral actions involve exercises of libertarian freedom in which an enduring self acts teleologically for duty's sake in such a way that the act is autonomous and not heteronomous in Kant's sense. For our purposes, an act is autonomous just in case

1 the intent of the act is to do what is intrinsically right, to do one's moral duty simply as such, and
2 it is universalizable.

Typically, a moral act has three constituent parts: an intent (an exercise of active power which answers the question 'What kind of act is this?' or 'What is the end for the sake of which the agent is endeavouring?'), a motive (why the person acted for the sake of the intended end), and a means (the ordered series of sub-actions done for the sake of the teleological end).

As we have already seen, naturalists have difficulties with an enduring self, active power, and teleology. It follows that the notion of an intent will be a difficult one for a naturalist to sustain. One of the leading naturalist ethicists in the last few decades is James Rachels, and he saw clearly the naturalist implication of the problematic nature of intent for characterizing an act.[13] Accordingly, Rachels makes the difference between acting and not acting (e.g., killing and letting die) turn on the presence or absence of overt body movements while totally ignoring the constitutive role of intent in defining a moral action. For Rachels, two acts can be the same with different intents, and thus intentions are not essential parts of an act. According to Rachels, a moral act involves a motive which, I should say, can be assimilated to the satisfaction of a desire and construed along biological, adaptive, Darwinian lines, a body movement taken as a means, and a result. Indeed, Rachels emphasizes the centrality of results as an expression of his utilitarianism.

Our discussion of the problematic nature of intentions, along with the metaphysical machinery within which they are intelligible – active power, a unified, conscious continuant, teleological action – in Rachels' naturalistic ethics provides a fitting occasion to make a second, general point: It would seem that naturalism most naturally implies a consequentialist evolutionary ethical understanding of moral action; specifically, a view of moral action as a means to reproductive success. We have seen above (pages 143–4) how evolutionary naturalist Michael Ruse deduced that morality had no deeper meaning than 'an aid to survival and reproduction'.[14] Thus, evolutionary naturalism would seem to predict that human moral agents would not be interested in or preoccupied with the illusory intrinsic rightness or wrongness of intents, motives, virtues/vices, moral rules and moral acts. Rather, those agents should be interested in and preoccupied with the reproductively advantageous consequences of intents, motives, and so forth. It could be responded that it may well be the case that, although illusory, objectivist deontological and virtue theory ethical beliefs on the part of moral agents would have more reproductive advantage than would accrue if those agents held to an evolutionary, consequentialist theory. Thus, evolutionary processes may select those mechanisms that tend to produce (illusory) objectivist deontological and virtue ethical beliefs in moral agents.

However, such a claim would be difficult to prove and, in any case, it would have a disastrous implication for evolutionary ethics considered as a moral theory; namely, it would seem to suffer from what is called the publicity objection. To be adequate, a moral theory must provide moral principles that can serve as action guides that inform moral situations. Most moral situations involve more than one person and, in this sense, are public situations. Thus, moral action guides must be teachable to others so they can be publicly used principles that help us in our interpersonal moral interactions. According to the evolutionary consequentialist argument under consideration it may be immoral to teach others to embrace evolutionary ethics because that would not promote reproductive advantage. It would promote reproductive advantage for people to believe (falsely) in objectivist deontological or virtue ethical theory. Thus, it could be immoral for one to go public and teach evolutionary, consequentialist ethics to others and, if so, this would violate one of the necessary conditions for a moral theory; namely, that it be teachable to others. It may be that advocates of evolutionary naturalism are unconcerned about the ethical implications of their view, but to the extent that they are concerned, the publicity objection would seem to present a serious problem for those proponents.

There is another problem with the claim that evolutionary processes may select those mechanisms that tend to produce (illusory) objectivist deontological and virtue ethical beliefs in moral agents because those beliefs would be reproductively advantageous. Richard Swinburne has argued that if beliefs, and the mechanisms needed to form and sustain them, are the result of mere evolutionary processes, then organisms, including humans, would not be able to distinguish these two sorts of propositions:

(P) All crocodiles are dangerous.
(Q) Normally crocodiles are dangerous.[15]

This is because P (a genuine universal proposition) and Q (an approximate generalization) have the same behavioural implications regarding reproducing, fleeing, fighting, and feeding. Evolutionary processes would not be able to select mechanisms for distinguishing P-type from Q-type propositions (the distinction is invisible to processes that select discriminatory mechanisms solely with respect to reproductively advantageous behaviours). Moreover, since Q-type propositions contain less empirical content and do not apply as far beyond sensory stimuli as do P-type propositions, Q-type propositions are simpler and all that would be required for reproductive advantage. Thus, given evolutionary naturalism, one would expect organisms to employ Q-type and not P-type propositions.

Now, argues Swinburne, a deontological moral belief is one that is universalizable, that is, it is a P-type proposition that applies to all relevantly similar cases. For example, all people in this circumstance should keep their promises. Only if an organism can form such universal judgements can it possess a deontological sense of moral duty and only then can it experience a conflict between moral duties or between a moral duty and a desire of some sort. By contrast, Swinburne uses the term 'wanton' for an organism that has no sense of duty at all, but only acts to satisfy his own desires, and thus is capable only of heteronomous actions. The only conflict the wanton knows is that between two or more desires he cannot simultaneously satisfy (e.g., to eat more and lose weight). He knows nothing about duty.

If Swinburne's arguments are correct, then evolutionary naturalism would seem to predict a world of wantons. Since genuine moral agents understand moral duty and conflicts involving moral duty, wantons cannot be depicted as such. What is at issue is whether evolutionary naturalism has the intellectual resources to avoid implying a wanton world. In my view, evolutionary naturalism does not have those resources.

Naturalist philosopher Daniel Dennett has proffered another reason why a naturalist should be a utilitarian, and it follows from Dennett's acknowledgement that all human actions on a naturalist view are determined by factors outside the agent's control. Dennett tries to preserve a remnant of retributive punishment on a naturalist view, but his solution may fairly be taken as a reductio ad absurdum against naturalism.[16] Dennett acknowledges that both alcoholics and child abusers are equally determined to act as they do by forces outside their control. If we wished, we could continue to peel back the layers of people engaged in each action and find the genetic or other determining factors producing the behaviour. Still, we draw a metaphysically arbitrary line between the two, and we hold child abusers and not alcoholics responsible for their behaviour, preferring to treat the latter as a disease. What justifies us in drawing the line where we do? Dennett explicitly appeals to a utilitarian justification, claiming that it maximizes the greatest amount of good for the greatest number of people (e.g., it serves to deter other acts of child abuse) if we act *as if* child abusers are responsible but the same cannot be said for alcoholics.

I cannot enter into a discussion of the relative merits of utilitarianism vs. deontological and virtue ethics. Suffice it to say that naturalists have various problems accounting for moral action and they have tried to adjust their moral views accordingly. I leave to the reader to decide whether those adjustments are adequate.

An adequate answer to the question 'Why should I be moral?'

An adequate philosophy of life should include an answer to the question of why one should be moral. But the question 'Why should I be moral?' needs clarification. Three points should help to clarify the question.

First, one can distinguish specific moral acts (an act of kindness, an act of self-sacrifice) from what philosophers call the moral point of view. The question 'Why should I be moral?' is really asking 'Why should I adopt the moral point of view?' so it is important to understand what the moral point of view is. If one adopts the moral point of view, then one does the following: one subscribes to normative judgements (judgements about what is right and wrong, about what one should and should not do) about actions, things (persons, the environment), and motives; one is willing to universalize one's judgements (if something is right or wrong for me, then it is right or wrong for everyone in a morally relevant situation); one seeks to form moral views in a free, unbiased, enlightened way; one seeks to promote the good. In other words, if one adopts the moral point of view, one submits to and seeks to promote the dictates of normative, universalizable morality in a mature, unbiased, impartial way. One embraces the dictates of morality and seeks to live in light of the moral point of view. Such a viewpoint governs one's life and priorities. So understood, the question 'Why should I be moral?' becomes the question 'Why should I adopt the moral point of view as a guiding force over my life?'

Second, one can distinguish between motives and reasons for adopting the moral point of view. Regarding the former, the question is asking what motivates one to adopt the moral point of view. Motives do not need to be rational factors. For example, one could say that one was motivated to adopt the moral point of view because it brought approval from one's parents and from society, or simply because of a certain urge or feeling to do so. Regarding reasons, the question is asking what rational justification can be given for adopting the moral point of view. The question is usually framed in terms of reasons, but both reasons and motives are relevant to a full discussion of why one adopts the moral point of view.

Third, it is not clear what kind of justification the question is seeking. What kind of 'should' is involved in 'Why should I be moral?' If it is a *moral* 'should', then the question is asking for a moral justification for adopting the moral point of view. If a moral 'should' is used in the question, then some philosophers think that the question involves a pointless self-contradiction. For one is then asking for a moral reason for accepting moral reasons. In other words, if one is using a moral 'should' in the question, then one is already reasoning from *within* the moral point of view, since one is already willing to acknowledge a moral answer to a moral question. But if one has already adopted the moral point of view, then there is not much point in asking for a moral reason for doing so. About the only answer one could give to the question would be that it is just morally right to adopt the moral point of view. But if one is willing to adopt the moral point of view because such an act is morally right, then one has already adopted the moral point of view without knowing it. So the question 'Why should I be moral?' is not really using a moral sense of 'should', and if it is, the only answer is that such an act is just the morally right thing to do.

But there is a different notion of 'should' which is better suited as a part of the question. This is a *rational* sense of 'should'. According to this sense of 'should', one is not asking the question 'Why should I be moral?' from within the moral point of view, but from outside the moral point of view altogether. In other words, one is asking the question:

> What rational justification can be given to me as to why it would be reasonable for me to adopt the moral point of view rather than some other point of view, say, an egoistic self-interested point of view where I govern my life for my own best interests without regard for the moral point of view at all?

As one seeks to formulate a *rational life plan* for oneself, a well thought-out, reasonable approach to the way one will live one's life so as to be a rational person, why should the moral point of view be a part of that rational life plan? In sum, the question 'Why should I be moral?' is asking for the motives, but more importantly, the reasons why someone should adopt the moral point of view as a part of a rational plan of life.

Part of the rational assessment of an ethical theory or, more generally, an entire worldview is the evaluation of the answer that theory or worldview provides to the question 'Why should I be moral?' Different answers have been given to the question, but the two most prominent have been the egoistic and theistic replies. Naturalism cannot give a satisfying answer to the question, and the most fitting naturalist response is the egoistic one. Roughly, the egoistic response says that one ought to be moral just in case it is in one's best interests to be so. But this answer is inadequate because it really says that one should fake caring about morality as long as such faking pays off; otherwise, one should just set morality aside when that pays off.

In one way or another, theistic responses incorporate reference to the existence of God. For example, one ought to be moral because the moral law is true and is constituted by the non-arbitrary commands of a good, just, wise, loving God, or because the moral law is grounded in the way we were designed by such a God to function properly. For the Christian, we should be moral for the same reason that a car should be driven on the road and not on the bottom of the ocean: that is the proper, true, flourishing way we were made to function and by so functioning we get in touch with reality and bring honour to our wonderful Creator.

Human Value, Rights, and Evolutionary Naturalism

In this section, I want to present two arguments to the effect that, given evolutionary naturalism, we have defeaters for the belief that human persons have high, equal, intrinsic value and rights simply as such. The first argument strikes at the very existence of an objective moral order that can be known, while the second focuses on the nature of human persons in an evolutionary naturalist framework.

Thomas Nagel on evolutionary naturalism and objective morality

As Mark Linville notes, '[T]he naturalist's commitment to a Darwinian explanation of certain salient features of human psychology presents an undercutting defeater for our moral beliefs as a whole.'[17] According to Michael Ruse and E. O. Wilson, 'Ethical premises are the peculiar products of genetic history, and they can be understood solely as mechanisms that are adaptive for the species which possess them . . . No abstract principles exist outside the particular nature of individual species.'[18] This statement may be taken as canonical for evolutionary naturalists, and, in my view, Thomas Nagel has presented the most persuasive case for what follows from it.[19] The central problem is that, given evolutionary naturalism, the fact that people have certain moral dispositions/beliefs and the reason they have them are epistemically independent from whatever would make the beliefs true. Our moral dispositions are survival-conducive, not truth-conducive. If Darwinian processes had turned out such that we had evolved with different survival-enhancing dispositions, our beliefs would have tracked in that. The fact that those beliefs do or do not correspond to a non-natural, non-causal, non-empirical moral realm has nothing to do with the moral beliefs/dispositions we develop. Thus, evolutionary naturalism generates an argument for moral scepticism and, lacking any warrant whatsoever for belief in moral facts, for the denial of irreducible moral facts. Given evolutionary naturalism, we have no reason at all to believe the world has anything other than natural facts and subjective reactions to them.

According to Nagel, it is quite plausible to give an evolutionary account of moral and practical reason and action, in which case we have two competing rivals: rationalism (a sort of Kantian, quasi-religious view) and evolutionary naturalism. While the two are not logically inconsistent, we should still consider them as rivals since the latter provides serious defeaters for the former. On a rationalist, Kantian view, there is an objective, true moral order and our moral faculties were designed to grasp and act according to that order. The theistic overtones of the view are obvious.

In this sense, we are justified in relying on moral reasoning and moral content in itself, quite independently of its biological function or evolutionary aetiology. For example, even if we are biologically disposed to be racists, on the rationalist view, we can still ask if racism itself is justified. But, asks Nagel, what if the central Kantian moral principles (e.g., impartiality) are themselves explainable via evolutionary survival. Surely this would count against those principles unless

1 somehow they were also independently true, and
2 as a brute, psychological fact (which itself evolved) these factors just weigh more to us than the appropriateness of racism.

However, apart from some quasi-religious view, it is hard to know what it means to say that our practical reasonings are efforts to get the objectively correct moral answer, rather that viewing those efforts as mere expressions of our contingent, biologically evolved dispositions. One can't appeal to a harmony between thought and reality, says Nagel, because realism regarding practical, moral reason is not a thesis about the natural order; it is a normative thesis about how things ought to be. Evolutionary naturalism cannot, therefore, support practical reasoning since it is a thesis about what is the case, not about what ought to be the case.

Not only is it impossible for evolutionary naturalism to support practical reasoning, it can and does undercut practical reason according to Nagel. Why? Because we would form our moral judgements whether or not they were right. Those judgements are expressions of a contingent set of dispositions that evolved with no regard to their correspondence to an independently existing moral order (whatever that would mean on a non-theistic view); they are not genuine insights into a non-contingent realm of objective, universalizable duty. E. O. Wilson chides 'ethical philosophers who wish to intuit the standards of good and evil', but who do not realize that their moral sentiments really spring from the hypothalamus and the limbic system, not from veridical intuition into an independently existing, objective moral realm.[20]

Human value/rights and the nature of human persons in evolutionary naturalist perspective

Mark Linville points out the following principle: S has moral standing means S is the appropriate object of direct moral duties. He then lays out the following principle:[21]

> (ID) A's harming B is wrong solely because A's harming B affects C.

Arguably, ethical egoism and utilitarianism are normative ethical theories that satisfy (ID), since, for example, A's punishing an innocent man B is wrong solely because that act is not in the agent's best interests or does not maximize utility for an appropriate number of people, respectively. The problem with (ID) is, among other things, that it does not recognize the moral standing of B. Such a recognition treats B as an end in itself with intrinsic dignity and value.

The best, perhaps only way to justify the belief that all humans have equal, direct moral standing, equal and unique, high, intrinsic value simply as such is in light of the metaphysical grounding of the Judaeo-Christian doctrine of the image of God. Such a view depicts humans as substances with a human nature – the genus/species being a human person – and, for at least two reasons, that framework must be abandoned. For one thing, the progress of science has been reductionistic in one way or another in that it has regularly shifted entities (e.g. heat) from the category of substance to the category of quality (warmth), and then to relation and quantity (mean kinetic energy). Thus, there most likely is no such thing as a human nature, and talk of such should be understood solely within the categories of biology, chemistry, and physics and with a view of humans as mereological compounds. Thus, human beings taken collectively would amount to a set of entities constituted by an amount of a certain kind of stuff standing in various relations to each other (DNA) and that bear various degrees of similarity with a selected paradigm case. Varying degrees of relational quantity would be the defining characteristic of the set of human beings.

Second, Darwin's theory of evolution has made belief in human nature, though logically possible, nevertheless, quite implausible. As E. Mayr has said:

> The concepts of unchanging essences and of complete discontinuities between every eidos (type) and all others make genuine evolutionary thinking impossible. I agree with those who claim that the essentialist philosophies of Aristotle and Plato are incompatible with evolutionary thinking.[22]

This belief has, in turn, led thinkers like David Hull to make the following observation:

> The implications of moving species from the metaphysical category that can appropriately be characterized in terms of 'natures' to a category for which such characterizations are inappropriate are extensive and fundamental. If species evolve in anything like the way that Darwin thought they did, then they cannot possibly have the sort of natures that traditional philosophers claimed they did. If species in general lack natures, then so does *Homo sapiens* as a biological species. If *Homo sapiens* lacks a nature, then no reference to biology can be made to support one's claims about 'human nature.' Perhaps all people are 'persons,' share the same 'personhood,' etc., but such claims must be explicated and defended *with no reference to biology*. Because so many moral, ethical, and political theories depend on some notion or other of human nature, Darwin's theory brought into question all these theories. The implications are not entailments. One can always dissociate '*Homo sapiens*' from 'human being,' but the result is a much less plausible position.[23]

Finally, James Rachels claims that a Darwinian approach to the origin of human beings, while not entailing the falsity of these notions, nevertheless provides an undercutting defeater for the idea that humans are made in the image of God and that humans have intrinsic dignity and worth as such. Indeed, according to Rachels, Darwinism is the universal solvent that dissolves any attempt to defend the notion of intrinsic human dignity:

> [T]he traditional supports for the idea of human dignity are gone. They have not survived the colossal shift of perspective brought about by Darwin's theory. It might be thought that this result need not be devastating for the idea of human dignity,

> because even if the traditional supports are gone, the idea might still be defended on some *other* grounds. Once again, though, an evolutionary perspective is bound to make one skeptical. The doctrine of human dignity says that humans merit a level of moral concern wholly different from that accorded to mere animals; for this to be true, there would have to be some big, morally significant difference between them. Therefore, any adequate defence of human dignity would require some conception of human beings as radically different from other animals. But that is precisely what evolutionary theory calls into question. It makes us suspicious of any doctrine that sees large gaps of any sort between humans and all other creatures. This being so, a Darwinian may conclude that a successful defence of human dignity is most unlikely.[24]

This observation has led a number of thinkers to claim that the traditional sanctity of life view of human beings is guilty of speciesism and to settle on personhood and not simply on being human, as constituting our locus of value.

It is important to note that taken together, the statements by Mayr, Hull, and Rachels make three important claims. First, naturalistic Darwinism does not entail the falsity of human dignity, but it does provide an adequate undercutting defeater for human dignity, I would add, in the same way that naturalistic Darwinism provides an undercutting defeater for the existence and knowledge of moral facts that we saw in our discussion of Nagel's argument above. Second, if human dignity is to be believed, there must be some ontological grounding for it. Among other things, these two points imply that, in responding to the problem of moral facts, knowledge, or human dignity, it will not do simply to point out that ethics has its own inner logic that is independent of the grammar of biology and other merely factual disciplines. Even if this is so, the effect of Darwinism is to reduce this autonomous moral grammar to that of a mere fabricated, constructed language game that has no correspondence with reality. Third, Darwinism makes it highly unlikely that there is any such thing as a human essence or any other morally relevant factor that is identical throughout the human species. On a Darwinist view, both species and individual organisms all differ from each other, not in kind, but in degree.

Evolutionary processes are slow and gradual, and where one draws the line that groups members of a species together is somewhat arbitrary. Species turn out to be sets whose members resemble each other to some degree or other. And even if there is a 'universal' that runs throughout the members of a species, it will be characterizable solely in terms of the category of physical quantity and relation, categories that are irrelevant to the presence or absence of intrinsic dignity.

Given that Darwinian naturalism undercuts being human as the appropriate ground for high, intrinsic, equal value and rights, what should we say about the move to personhood? Is it an adequate ground? Recall from our earlier discussion of Joel Feinberg that two things must be present if there is to be an adequate ground for these features of human persons:

(1) we all have the grounding entity equally in common, and
(2) the grounding entity is non-trivial and of supreme moral worth.

As we have seen, Darwinian naturalism undercuts (1) by its depiction of the processes involved in the origin of 'species', and it undermines (2) by its reductive trivialization of being a *Homo sapiens*. We still have a number of plausible grounds left, for example, being a person, having a meaningful quality of life, possessing a biographical life. What these amount to is typically stated in terms of satisfying a list of criteria: having a self-concept, being able to formulate goals and plans in a way that is meaningful to the planner, being able to satisfy subjectively certified preferences, being able to use language, possessing a certain degree of intelligence, self-motivated activity, possessing unified memories, agency and awareness of existing through time. In fact, there have been between 15 and 20 criteria mentioned in this regard.

The idea is that personhood supervenes on a properly functioning human being when some set from this list is satisfied. In this case, a person with intrinsic value is present. But for two reasons, I believe this appeal to personhood fails. For one thing, in a naturalist world, the choice of these criteria seems to be utterly speciesist. According to James Rachels,

> As Darwin clearly recognized, we are not entitled – not on evolutionary grounds, at any rate – to regard our own adaptive

> behavior as 'better' or 'higher' that that of a cockroach, who, after all, is adapted equally well to life in its own environmental niche.[25]

After all, adaptive behaviour is adaptive behaviour, and numerous species have features that contribute equally or, perhaps, even better to their survival than do the criteria of personhood. It is hard to see why, in a Darwinian naturalist world, the criteria of personhood should be given pride of place.

Second, all the criteria of personhood are degreed properties that can be possessed to one degree or another. If such properties are constitutive of being a person, and if being a person is what gives one his/her intrinsic value, it follows that we are not equally persons, nor do we have equal value. This is a problem for those of us who believe that equal value and rights is both a desired item to secure and also the way the world really is.

It could be responded that the attributes described in the list of criteria above are all threshold properties. Like a rheostat that is either on or off, but once it is on, its intensity can vary to different degrees, so the properties of personhood are either exemplified or not by an organism, even though once exemplified, they are so to one degree or another. And, the claim continues, it is possession of the attribute that confers value, not the degree it is realized.

Unfortunately, this response seems contrived and ad hoc. If we are thinking of these properties of personhood (quality of life, etc.) as value-conferring properties, as we must in the view under consideration, then it is not the presence or absence of these attributes that matters. Indeed, they increase in their value precisely to the degree they are realized. For example, if intelligence or the ability to use language are value-conferring, it is clear that the more one has of these the more value is conferred.

In this chapter, I have tried to present the outline of a case that various features of morality, including equal value and rights for all human persons as such, are entailments of Christian theism but are undercut by evolutionary naturalism and not at home in that worldview. It may well be that one could respond without logical inconsistency by opting for moral anti-realism in some form or another. Indeed, that has been a major aspect of moral thinking since the 1930s. In my view, such a stance should be met with therapy, not an argument, but in any case, if one is to adopt the sort of full-blooded, non-natural moral stance referred to in this chapter, then the resources of Christian theism seem required to make sense of that adoption. And the resources of evolutionary naturalism undermine it.

Appendix: Dismissive Naturalism: Responding to Nagel's Last Stand

It is always interesting to follow trends in philosophy, and it is especially significant if one can discern historical patterns of ideas that run parallel in different branches of the discipline. Such patterns invite questions as to whether there is a common driving force underlying them, and if so, what that force is and why it has unfolded as it has.

I think just such a pattern has been unfolding for the last 80 years or so, and if this is correct, it raises some interesting possibilities.[1] Specifically, I think that insights into one pattern to be mentioned shortly allow us to focus our attention on a particular dialectical move whose prevalence and, more importantly, significance across philosophical disciplines thereby becomes apparent. In turn, it becomes clear that natural theologians have a greater duty to rebut or refute this move than may be noticed without locating it as part of that broader pattern and the paradigm crisis it signals.

But I am talking in abstractions. In what follows I shall identify the pattern in question, provide an examination of a dialectical move that is part of a particular incarnation of the pattern in a recent work published by Thomas Nagel, and respond to Nagel's employment of that move.[2]

Naturalism and Emergent Properties

In the first half of the twentieth century, emergent properties were defined epistemologically:[3] Property P is an emergent property of some particular x at level l_n just in case P is a property of x at l_n, and no amount of knowledge of (or descriptive statements about) entities at subvenient levels below l_n would justify a prediction of (or logically entails a descriptive statement about) P at l_n. In this sense an emergent property (or a statement about it) is surprising and unexpected relative to knowledge of (or statements about) lower levels.

Since the late 1950s they have been characterized ontologically: Property P is an emergent property of some particular x at level l_n just in case P is a property of x at l_n, and there are no determinates P′ of the same determinable D as P such that some particular at a level below l_n exemplifies P or P′. In this sense an emergent property is *sui generis*.

The problem I have in mind may be put quite simply. If naturalism is characterized in empiricist terms, for example according to logical positivism, then one must eschew most, or at least a relevant range of emergent properties, specifically, normative properties in epistemology, aesthetics and ethics, and various features of consciousness and the self, such as a Cartesian ego, or various mental states. If naturalism is characterized ontologically in strict physicalist terms, the same result follows except that mind-independent secondary qualities may now be added to the list of forbidden entities. The list of eschewed entities is constituted by those whose appearance cannot be adequately explained by mechanical processes and combinatorial modes of explanation.

My purpose here is not to argue for the fact that each version of naturalism does, in fact, require rejection of the relevant emergent entities, though I believe that (or a somewhat weaker claim) to be the case. I merely note that the evidence for the ubiquitous acceptance of this notion lies in the pervasive pattern of philosophical moves underwritten by that acceptance. To illustrate this pattern, consider treatments of consciousness and mental properties/events. In the first three decades of the twentieth century, experimental psychology (allegedly) finished making a clean break with philosophy, though, during this period, the philosophical and, indeed, *scientific* conception of the ego and consciousness were clearly Cartesian.[4] Admittedly, during this time, the corrosive effects of empiricism were beginning to undermine belief in classic substances in favour of bundle theories with the result that the Cartesian ego was beginning to go the way of the dodo. Still, consciousness was clearly conceived in Cartesian terms. But during the 1930s through the 1950s empiricism morphed into that universal solvent, logical positivism, and the positivist infatuation with operational definitions gave rise to philosophical behaviourism and the analytic reduction of consciousness to body movements or their associated tendencies.

By the beginning of the 1960s, ontological naturalism replaced epistemically motivated positivist naturalism and, accordingly, type identity physicalism came to replace behaviourism as the appropriate naturalist account of consciousness.[5] Certain problems, such as multiple realization,[6] caused many to despair of type physicalism, and various attempts to repair it and a wild variety of physicalist versions of functionalism have been in a horse race ever since. And the eliminativists have seen the whole mess as so much wasted time, preferring to replace consciousness (or at least propositional attitudes) rather than trying to reduce it. Unfortunately, there was one small problem with all this: pains hurt and necessarily so. Setting aside thoughts, beliefs, and other propositional attitudes, phenomenal consciousness was a recalcitrant fact for all versions of strict physicalism. So since around 1990, a growing number of naturalists have opted for some version of emergentism (at least) for qualia: Searle, Chalmers, Nagel, McGinn, and most recently, Kim.[7]

Though I have neither the skill nor the space to justify my belief, I think that the same sort of pattern has occurred in other areas of philosophical investigation: secondary qualities, indexical facts – at least temporal and first-person ones – normative properties in aesthetics, ethics and epistemology, action theory, and universals construed as abstract objects which can exist without being instantiated.[8]

Consider aesthetics and ethics.[9] Cognitivist realism in both areas was eliminated under positivist pressure and replaced by emotivism (late 1930s to 1940s) or prescriptivism (early 1950s to early 1960s). These moves were later replaced with various descriptivist versions of cognitivism (mid-1950s to late 1980s, though still held to the present). When these were found wanting (they left out the intrinsic normativity of aesthetic and ethical properties), at least some naturalists returned to cognitivist non-naturalist aesthetic and moral realism and made peace with them through different versions of emergentism.

Parallels with naturalized epistemology come readily to mind. In action theory, hard determinism was embraced as an important implication of naturalism, only to be replaced with different versions of compatibilism. And very recently, Timothy O'Connor has initiated what I predict is the beginning of a phase discernibly similar to the process of development in the other areas in which important features of agent causation – such as active power, an emergent individual suitably unified to be an enduring continuant – are cashed out in emergent terms that, allegedly, are consistent with a naturalist ontology.[10]

Finally, a similar pattern has occurred regarding universals construed as abstract objects that may exist uninstantiated.[11] Operating within empiricist constraints, in the 1960s naturalist Wilfred Sellars employed a linguistic strategy to eliminate Platonic universals in favour of certain word-tokens he invented. These word-tokens replaced allegedly abstract singular terms (e.g., 'red') with concrete general terms (e.g., his unique dot-quote treatment of 'red things' as the term ·red-things·) that require quantification only over concrete particulars. Dissatisfied with purely linguistic treatments of properties, naturalists in the mid-70s to late 80s, most importantly, Keith Campbell, tried to restore properties to a naturalist ontology by treating them as abstract particulars and not universals. Around the same time, D. M. Armstrong claimed that a naturalist could quantify over universals as long as such universals

1 are not taken to exist uninstantiated, and
2 are pulled back into space and time as multiply-located entities.

Dissatisfied with these solutions, many naturalists, among them Colin McGinn, claim that properties may be construed as abstract objects as long as the only properties that are instantiated are those that characterize straightforward physical facts. As long as abstract objects are well behaved from a naturalist perspective, a naturalist can just add them to her ontology.

I have two comments to make about this pervasive pattern. First, in my view it was inevitable that philosophers would sooner or later reinstate the entities that went through various attempts to reduce or eliminate them, because the pre-pattern view of them is correct and the various reductive or eliminativist depictions are not plausible. Second, the return of these entities means that naturalism is taking on water as it adds to its ontology what I believe are naturalistically inexplicable *sui generis* after *sui generis* entities. I agree with naturalist Terence Horgan when he acknowledges, 'in any metaphysical framework that deserves labels like "materialism", "naturalism", or "physicalism", supervenient facts must be explainable rather than being *sui generis*'.[12]

For present purposes, let's assume I am right about this second observation. I am entitled to this assumption because I am interested in analysing naturalist strategies that acknowledge it. More specifically, I am interested in criticizing a naturalist pattern of treating such inexplicable entities so that they do not provide evidence against naturalism and, in turn, offer fodder for a theistic explanation. If this latter were allowed, then these recalcitrant entities could be taken as evidence for the existence of God.

Elsewhere, I have criticized such naturalist moves in various areas of philosophical investigation, and I shall limit my focus to an especially important naturalist account, namely, Thomas Nagel's treatment of objective reason.[13] Nagel's account is important not only for its ingenuity, but also because it is an essential component of a naturalist way out. If a naturalist is going to admit into his/her ontology an entity whose existence cannot be explained naturalistically, then he or she must adopt a dismissive strategy that in some way or other shows why it is no big deal that we do not have such an explanation. By minimizing the importance of the absence of such an explanation, the naturalist can block the negative impact of not having that explanation. And if the naturalist can also argue that for some reason or other we *cannot* have such an explanation, then the recalcitrant entity can be taken as a brute fact and avoid being fodder for a theistic argument.

Nagel's Dismissive Strategy

In contradistinction to what Nagel claims to be the self-refuting constructivist, relativist treatment of reason by postmodernists, Nagel takes reason to be absolutely authoritative, universal, objective, necessarily presupposed in all thinking and such that 'there is a natural sympathy between the deepest truths of nature and the deepest layers of the human mind'.[14]

So characterized, reason raises a problem: 'there is a real problem about how such a thing as reason is possible. How is it possible that creatures like ourselves, supplied with the contingent capacities of a biological species whose very existence appears to be radically accidental, should have access to universally valid methods of objective thought?'[15] And Nagel claims that the main answers to the question are Subjectivism (deny we do have such access), Evolutionary Naturalism and Theism.[16] Having set aside Subjectivism on the grounds that, among other things, it is self-defeating,[17] Nagel seems to be stuck with Evolutionary Naturalism and Theism.

To make matters worse, for various reasons that are not of major concern for present purposes, Nagel admits that it is virtually impossible,[18] even in principle,[19] for naturalism to provide an answer to this question. Briefly, he mentions three difficulties for any such naturalistic project. The first is hinted at above, namely, that the naturalist creation story is so radically contingent (e.g., wind the clock back, play it again, and it is extremely unlikely that we would appear again) that it is unsuited to justify something that is universally and necessarily valid. Second, besides being contingent, those evolutionary processes are irrational, brute, non-teleological ones that reward organisms whose faculties serve the interests of reproductive advantage. And being a truth-gathering faculty is not particularly relevant to these processes. Thus, the evolutionary story not only fails to justify the rationality of our faculties, it actually provides a defeater for such rationality.[20] Finally, the nature of intentionality and the mental–world connection is both too odd to fit easily into a naturalist ontology and, in fact, it is too Platonistic, quasi-religious or, indeed, theistic for a naturalist to embrace without a great deal of discomfort.[21]

As noted, Nagel acknowledges that there is an obvious theistic explanation for the existence and appearance of reason. The fundamental being, God, is himself rational, and God created us with cognitive capacities so that there would be a natural harmony between them and their noetic environment apt for gathering truth and gaining knowledge.[22]

By admitting the reality of an entity that cannot be reduced to or eliminated in favour of physical entities – reason and all that constitutes it – and by acknowledging the inadequacy, indeed, impossibility of naturalist attempts to justify its trustworthiness in human organisms or to explain its origin, Nagel provided the resources for a theistic argument for the existence of God. And he knows it. So Nagel must undermine the theistic alternative, and while he uses different arguments to do so (e.g., theistic explanation is merely a placeholder for and not really an example of explanation),[23] the dismissive strategy is his trump card. This provides grounds for dismissing a theistic (and, if successful, any other) attempt to answer the question, and thereby greases the skids for taking the objectivity of our finite rational capacities as a brute fact.

What, exactly, is Nagel's version of the dismissive strategy? It is surprisingly simple: Nagel's solution as to how there could be such a thing as universal, normative, objective reason, along with a fundamental mind–world connection, is simply to dismiss the question by saying that it is self-defeating to seek a justification beyond reason for reason itself. All subjectivist attempts to criticize reason from the outside assume what they deny, and are self-defeating. Similarly, all attempts to use something more basic than reason to justify reason assume what they justify, and such attempts are either self-defeating or vacuous.[24] Rather, reason is its own authority and its validity is universal, so reason is its own justification. To seek further justification for it evidences a serious confusion. Any attempt to explain or justify reason will have to use reason and, thus, it will be pointless. So a naturalistic or theistic attempt at such a justification is attempting what neither is needed nor can be done. Reason just is and that's the end of the story. One must trust his/her cognitively relevant faculties themselves, believing in what reason tells him/her in virtue of the content of the arguments reason delivers. In this way, reason is self-justifying.

Defeaters for Nagel's Way Out

There is nothing wrong with a dismissive strategy *per se*. Given two rivals sometimes one will consider a phenomenon basic and not in need of a solution, empirical or otherwise. It may, therefore, disallow questions about how or why that phenomenon occurs and, thus, can hardly be faulted for not providing such an account. As Nicholas Rescher has pointed out:

> One way in which a body of knowledge S can deal with a question is, of course, by *answering* it. Yet another, importantly different, way in which S can deal with a question is by disallowing it. S *disallows* [Q] when there is some presupposition of Q that S does not countenance: given S, we are simply not in a position to raise Q.[25]

Unfortunately, Nagel's specific version of a dismissive strategy is a complete failure. To show this, we need to look at two things: a set of important distinctions Nagel fails to make and an application of these distinctions to Nagel's strategy. First, let's look at some distinctions.

Self-refuting statements (sentences, propositions) exhibit at least three characteristics.[26] First, they are indicative assertions that refer to a group of entities we may call 'a domain of discourse'. Second, they express conditions of acceptability (truth/falsehood, epistemic justification, real/non-existent) that each member in the domain fails to satisfy. Third, the statement itself is a member of the domain.

With this in mind, two distinctions are important. The first is between a first-order statement of a domain and a second-order statement about that domain. Sometimes a statement about a domain is not a member of the domain. For example, the statement 'there are no moral absolutes' is a statement about the domain of moral rules and it is not itself a moral rule, so it is not a statement of but merely one about moral rules. Again, if one asserts in German that there are no English statements, then the assertion is not self-refuting because it is not itself a member of its domain of discourse. If the assertion were made in English, then it would be self-refuting. If the second-order statement is not within the first-order domain of discourse, this is sufficient for the statement to be self-referentially consistent.

In the context of self-refutation, another distinction gets at pretty much the same thing, namely, the difference between use and mention. You may use something (language, English, a specific word such as 'red', reason, one's own existence, truth) without mentioning it. When that occurs, then we have another case in which the item being used is not a member of the domain of discourse. Only in this case, the surface appearance seems to imply that the item is, in fact, a member of the domain, and by showing that this is not the case, the use/mention distinction has solved a number of philosophical problems.

For example, it used to be argued that the characterization of a universal, such as redness, as an entity that all concrete particulars in the relevant natural class (e.g., the class of red things) have in common is circular. The argument went this way:

(1) What do all members of the class of red things have in common? Answer: Redness.
(2) What is redness? Answer: What all members of the class of red things have in common.

The argument allegedly showed that this definition of a universal is circular. The solution involved claiming that redness is mentioned in the answer to (1) and used in the answer to (2). The result is this: the term 'redness' is the name for what is (ostensively) defined by the class of red things, and the entity it names is what all those members have in common, viz., the property of redness.[27]

Applied to our discussion of self-refutation, we may say that a second-order claim about a domain uses a particular statement. And if a second-order claim is also a member of the first-order domain of mentioned entities (e.g., statements) then the statement is used to mention itself precisely because it is itself a member of the domain of mentioned entities.

In sum, in the relevant contexts and domains, a second-order claim is used to mention the members of a first-order domain. If the second-order claim is not a member of that domain, then it is used and not mentioned. If it is, it is used to mention itself, and it is also self-refuting if it fails to satisfy its own standards of acceptability.

Is it sufficient for a statement to be self-refuting that it be within its domain of discourse? The answer is 'no'. The statement 'All sentences of English are less than 15 words' is not self-refuting. Is it sufficient for a statement to be self-refuting that it be within its domain of discourse in which each member fails to satisfy the appropriate conditions of acceptability? The answer is pretty clearly 'yes', but this admission is not enough to justify Nagel's dismissive strategy as he seems to assume. *The reason is that we can index to a possible world the relevant referring term in the used second-order statement to prevent that statement from being mentioned.* Consider a possible world w in which there are no English sentences longer than three words. This may be because no one speaks English in that world or because they are just short-winded. Now consider the statement:

(3) No English sentences-in-w are longer than three words.

We have used (3) to talk about a domain of discourse that includes all and only English sentences-in-w. In this case, (3) is used but not mentioned; (3) is not in the domain of discourse; (3) remains a second-order statement about a domain in which it fails to appear as a member; and (3) is not self-refuting.

Unfortunately, sometimes Nagel fails to distinguish the second-order question when asked in the context of scepticism and subjectivism:

(1) 'Is reason objective?'

from the second-order question(s):

(2a) 'Could reason have failed to be objective?'

or

(2b) 'How could there be such a thing as objective reason?'[28]

On other occasions, he seems to think that because his dismissive strategy works with the first question, it may be applied with equal success to the second question(s). Thus, he says regarding it,

> some things can't be explained because they have to enter into every explanation. The question 'How can human beings add?' is not like the question 'How can electronic calculators add?' In ascribing that capacity to a person, I interpret what he does in terms of my own capacity. And since I can't get outside of *it*, how

> can I hope to get outside of and explain the corresponding thing in anyone else? . . . Perhaps there is something wrong with the hope of arriving at a complete understanding of the world that includes an understanding of ourselves as beings within it possessing the capacity for that very understanding. I think something of this kind must be true. There are inevitably going to be limits on the closure achievable by turning our procedures of understanding on themselves.[29]

What shall we say in response to Nagel? As a starter, note that (1) (Is reason objective?) uses reason to mention itself, that is, it is about all cases of reason, including itself. *Prima facie*, Nagel's dismissive solution works for the first-question case because reason is both used and mentioned. But his strategy does not work for the second question(s) (2a) and (2b) because they implicitly contain indexing and, thus, use reason but don't mention it, that is, they use reason to describe a situation in which reason is not objective or fails to obtain. It is easy to conceive of possible worlds in which there is no such thing as objective reason. Thus, 'Could reason have failed to be objective?' becomes 'Is there a possible world w in which there is no objective reason?' or 'Given that there are possible worlds in which reason is not objective and ones in which it is, the existence of objective reason is a contingent fact and we may ask why there is such a thing as objective reason in the actual world.'

But, you may wonder, how could reason itself fail to be objective? As Nagel points out, the fundamental principles of reason – the laws of logic – are necessary such that there is no possible world in which they are not valid. The answer depends on what one means by 'reason'. If 'reason' means the truth of the fundamental laws of logic, such as non-contradiction, *modus ponens*, then the second-order question(s) is, indeed, pointless as Nagel points out, whether the modal term is understood as ontological or epistemic.

But if 'reason' is understood to refer to contingent aspects of a wider notion of reason or to the faculties of specific organisms in some possible world, then the second-order question(s) is perfectly appropriate. After all, we can easily think of worlds in which, say, induction fails, sensory faculties do not represent the external world accurately, or the 'universal and necessary' principles of objective reason are not exemplified. In such cases, we are using reason (in our second-order question(s)) but not mentioning it (in the envisioned possible world). We are using reason to ask: Could there be some possible world w in which the relevant features of reason are not exemplified by entities in w?

It is this second notion of reason that Nagel must rule out if his dismissive strategy is to be successful, but it is pretty obvious that it cannot be so ruled out. At the very least, Nagel has provided no reasons for thinking that w is not a possible world, and I think it is obvious that it is. But the matter does not need to be left there. There are two analogous areas of philosophical discourse that further illustrate the inadequacy of Nagel's strategy.

First, with respect to the question 'Why should I be moral?' there is a distinction between interpreting the question as a first-order one from within the moral point of view (in which case the 'should' is a moral 'should', the question is pointless, and may be answered only by the vacuous response 'Because it is morally right to act and think morally rightly') vs. a second-order one from outside the moral point of view ('How could there be such a thing as the moral point of view? Why is it rational to accept the moral point of view?'). Admittedly, when one asks the second-order moral question, one is no longer operating from within morality, but when one asks the second-order rational question, one is still operating within rationality. Still, the indexing strategy mentioned above provides the appropriate analogy for the dispute about 'Why should I be moral?' As we have seen, understood according to the indexing strategy, the question 'How could there be such a thing as a rational point of view?' is an intelligible question that cannot be dismissed.

The design argument provides a second analogous area of philosophical debate. Advocates of the design argument sometimes cite as evidence for a Designer the occurrence of various factors necessary for the existence of life (e.g. universal fine-tuning factors such as the various cosmic constants, local fine-tuning factors such as the properties of water, etc.). Critics from Hume to the present have responded in this way: We should not be surprised by these data. If the world had been one in which intelligent life could not have arisen, then we should not be here to discuss the matter. The factors are necessary for people to be around to puzzle over them and, thus, we should not be surprised at their occurrence. It is self-defeating to seek an explanation for why the factors conducive for our existence obtained. If they hadn't, we wouldn't be here to debate the topic. It's hardly surprising that we showed up in a world with the factors required for our existence as opposed to showing up in a world without those factors!

This response is analogous to Nagel's defence of reason. To see what is wrong with it, let us suppose that an advocate of the design argument cites a number of factors, a–g, that are part of the world and are necessary preconditions for the emergence of life. Hume and his followers interpret the design argument as follows: As we have already seen, theists are supposedly saying, 'Isn't it amazing that the factors necessary for life preceded us instead of some other factors that make life impossible preceding us!' In other words, theists are comparing these two different world courses: World Course #1: a through g obtain and human beings appear; World Course #2: alternate factors (say h through n) obtain and human beings appear. Note that worlds one and two differ only in the factors that obtain in them, but the presence of human beings is held constant. Now this is indeed a bad argument, because, again, it is hard to see how humans could emerge in any world other than one in which the factors necessary for their emergence are actualized!

But this is not the correct interpretation of the design argument. Advocates of the design argument are offering the following comparison: World Course #1: a through g obtain and human beings appear; World Course #2: alternate factors (say h through n) obtain and no human life appears. Advocates of the design argument are claiming that the emergence of any life, including human life, was incredibly unlikely and required the actualization of a delicately balanced set of preconditions, and the realization of these preconditions require explanation provided by the existence of a Designer. Even the atheist J. L. Mackie saw the flaw in Hume's criticism:

> There is only one actual universe, with a unique set of basic materials and physical constants, and it is therefore surprising that the elements of this unique set-up are just right for life when they might easily have been wrong. This is not made less surprising by the fact that if it had not been so, no one would have been here to be surprised. We can properly envisage and consider alternative possibilities which do not include our being there to experience them.[30]

Broad Theistic Implications of Nagel's Failed Strategy

Nagel confuses parallel cases of these two interpretations of the design argument by dismissing questions about rationality as though they were like the first interpretation. But according to the (correct) indexing approach, questions about rationality are like the second interpretation and Nagel's 'solution' not only fails to address this question, but by acknowledging the availability of a theistic solution and the inadequacy of a naturalistic solution, it actually provides grounds that strengthen the force of the theistic alternative. Put differently, by admitting the uneliminable, irreducible existence of objective reason, and by acknowledging the existence of a theistic solution along with the inadequacy of a naturalistic one, Nagel puts too much weight on his dismissive strategy as a way of avoiding theism. Given the failure of that strategy, Nagel has actually clarified and inadvertently provided support for the theistic option.

But there's more. So far I have shown that the indexed questions are not in the slightest affected by Nagel's dismissive approach. And these questions are among the ones Nagel himself mentions and about which he worries. Moreover, as Plantinga has shown and as Nagel acknowledges, naturalistic evolutionary answers to the second-order question indexed to naturalistic evolutionary worlds actually provide defeaters for rationality in those worlds for which theism would provide a defeater defeater.[31] Given that the actual world is a rational world, we then have evidence for theism and against naturalism. At the very least, we have an argument for the fact that it is irrational to accept evolutionary naturalism.

Plantinga's argument has been the subject of much debate, and I do not want to enter that dialogue here. My purpose is to draw out an implication for Nagel's first question from my refutation of his dismissive strategy. Nagel takes himself to successfully apply his strategy to the first question, and then to apply it to the second question(s). I plan to go the other way. By showing his strategy fails for the second question(s), I believe I have grounds for undercutting his strategy regarding question (1).

Plantinga wisely focuses his argument about a hypothetical population of creatures for which we have grounds for doubting or should be agnostic about the reliability of their cognitive faculties.[32]

In this way, he follows what I am calling an indexing strategy. Plantinga uses a thought experiment involving a widget factory. A person who sees several red widgets on the assembly line would have a defeater for the belief that they are red if she were told by the shop superintendent that they are being irradiated by a variety of red lights. They may still be red, but she is no longer rational in believing they are red on the basis of the way they appear to her. If the shop vice-president later tells her that the shop superintendent is an unreliable person, she now has a defeater defeater and may properly be agnostic about the widgets. It is easy to conceive of cases in which this second defeater was later defeated, the third was defeated later still, and so on.

Continuing with the indexing strategy, naturalistic evolution provides a defeater for taking the rational faculties of creatures in such a world w to be reliable. But what if we apply the problem to us in the actual world? Does Nagel's dismissive strategy block such a move? I don't think so. Clearly, if I myself were in the widget factory, I would go through various epistemic situations as defeaters, defeater defeaters, and so forth came my way. In such a case, it would not be rational for me to trust my senses. But what about reason itself, especially as it is employed at the level of abstract thought characteristic of Nagel's book and those who disagree with him? Can reason be used to undercut reason?

By getting a beachhead established regarding question(s) (2), I believe we can use reason to undercut reason as it is used and mentioned in question (1). In such a context (in which we grant the legitimacy of problems with rationality surfaced by question(s) (2) and subsequently ask about (1)), we have what Plantinga calls a pragmatically circular situation involving a sceptical dialectical loop:[33] the naturalistic evolutionist uses reason to argue for this view, but he then comes to have a defeater for the reliability of his rational faculties (in Nagel's terms, the objectivity of our reasoning). This provides him with a defeater of naturalistic evolution. But given that this defeater for naturalistic evolution relies on his reasoning and beliefs, he has a defeater for this defeater of naturalistic evolution. He now has no defeater for believing both that his rational faculties are reliable and that naturalistic evolution is true. But he is now in his original position, namely, that of believing naturalistic evolution which provides a defeater for the reliability of his rational faculties. Plantinga concludes: 'So goes the paralyzing dialectic. After a few trips around this loop, we may be excused for throwing up our hands in despair, or disgust, and joining Hume in a game of backgammon.'[34]

I do not need this stronger claim (viz., that my rebuttal of Nagel's dismissive strategy with respect to question(s) (2) provides a defeater for an affirmative answer to question (1)) for my main task in this chapter to be a success. That task was to defeat Nagel's dismissive strategy regarding question(s) (2). I have not attempted to evaluate all of Nagel's case against a theistic explanation for human rationality. I have simply tried to surface and respond to Nagel's dismissive strategy, a strategy that, in the nature of the case, must bear a lot of weight in Nagel's project.

Such dialectic moves are on the increase and it is important for theists to take note of them and show, where appropriate, exactly why they fail. I have attempted to do that regarding Nagel's discussion of reason. By refusing to accept reductive or other naturalized treatments of reason and rationality, and by admitting both that naturalism is incapable by itself of explaining the existence of reason and that many argue that theism does provide the best explanation, the dismissive strategy is called upon to carry more dialectical weight than it can bear.

And while I have not been able to argue for it here, I believe the same point applies to the other atheistic naturalist dismissive strategies referred to earlier in this chapter. If I am correct about this, then the future of intellectual atheism (if such there be) is not bright. They must return to the failed reductive or eliminative strategy, a strategy that requires one to deny some fairly obvious facts about the world, or they must try to dismiss theistic attempts to employ these facts – facts that in principle are incapable of naturalistic explanation – as part of a cumulative case for the existence of God. In this latter case, they must dismiss what seem to many of us to be a fairly obvious explanation of these facts. I, for one, would not like to be on the horns of that dilemma.[35]

Notes

Chapter 1

1 Francis Schaeffer, *Escape from Reason* (Downers Grove, IL: InterVarsity Press, 1968).

2 John Paul II, *Veritatis Splendor* (Boston: Pauline Books & Media, 2003).

3 John Searle, *Freedom and Neurobiology* (New York: Columbia University Press, 2007), pp. 4 and 5.

4 Anthony T. Kronman, *Education's End: Why Our Colleges and Universities Have Given Up on the Meaning of Life* (New Haven: Yale University Press, 2007).

5 Christopher Lasch, *The Culture of Narcissism* (New York: Warner Books, 1979), p. 88; cf. pp. 88–103.

6 Lasch, *The Culture of Narcissism*, p. 103.

7 John Calvin, *Institutes of the Christian Religion* (1536; Grand Rapids: Associated Publishers and authors, n.d.), 1.1.1.

8 See C. John Collins, *Genesis 1–4* (Phillipsburg, NJ: P&R Publishing, 2006), pp. 61–8, especially pp. 62–3.

9 David Papineau, *Philosophical Naturalism* (Oxford: Blackwell, 1993), p. 3.

10 Wilfrid Sellars, *Science, Perception, and Reality* (London: Routledge & Kegan Paul, 1963), p. 173.

11 I am assuming here a realist construal of explanation.

12 Collin McGinn, *The Mysterious Flame* (New York: Basic Books, 1999), pp. 55–6; cf. pp. 54–62, 90, 95.

13 John Searle, *The Rediscovery of the Mind* (Cambridge, MA: MIT Press, 1992), pp. 83–93.

14 Frank Jackson, *From Metaphysics to Ethics* (Oxford: Clarendon Press, 1998), pp. 1–5.

15 See John Haldane, 'The Mystery of Emergence', *Proceedings of the Aristotelian Society* 96 (1996): 261–7.

16 Crispin Wright, 'The Conceivability of Naturalism', in *Conceivability and Possibility*, ed. by Tamar Szabo Gendler and John

Hawthorne (Oxford: Clarendon Press, 2002), p. 401 (the article is at pp. 401–39).

17 Philip Cushman, 'Why the Self is Empty: Toward a Historically Situated Psychology', *American Psychologist* 45 (1990): 599.

18 For more on the self and the soul, see J. P. Moreland and Scott Rae, *Body and Soul* (Downers Grove, IL: InterVarsity Press, 2000); J. P. Moreland, 'Restoring the Substance to the Soul of Psychology', *Journal of Psychology and Theology* 26 (March 1998): 29–43.

19 Terry Eagleton, *The Illusions of Postmodernism* (Oxford: Blackwell, 1996), pp. 27–8.

20 Thomas V. Morris, 'Introduction', in *Divine and Human Action* (Ithaca, NY: Cornell University Press, 1988), p. 3.

21 Roderick Chisholm, *Theory of Knowledge*, 3rd edn (Englewood Cliffs, NJ: Prentice Hall, 1989), p. 16.

22 Timothy O'Connor, *Persons and Causes* (New York: Oxford University Press, 2000), p. 112.

23 O'Connor, *Persons and Causes*, pp. 70–1, note 8.

24 Chisholm, *Theory of Knowledge*, pp. 10–17.

Chapter 2

1 Phillip Johnson, *The Right Questions* (Downers Grove, IL, InterVarsity Press, 2002), pp. 62–3.

2 Robert Boyle, 'Essay IV: An Essay Containing a Requisite Digression, Concerning those that would exclude the Deity from Intermingling with Matter', in *Selected Philosophical Papers of Robert Boyle*, ed. by M. A. Stewart (Indianapolis: Hackett, 1991; originally published in 1663), p. 173.

3 Geoffrey Madell, *Mind and Materialism* (Edinburgh: Edinburgh University Press, 1988), p. 141.

4 Colin McGinn, *The Mysterious Flame* (New York: Basic Books, 1999), pp. 13–14. See G. K. Chesterton's claim that the regular correlation between diverse entities in the world is magic that requires a Magician to explain it. See *Orthodoxy* (John Lane Company, 1908; repr., San Francisco: Ignatius Press, 1950), ch. 5.

5 William Lyons, 'Introduction', in *Modern Philosophy of Mind*, ed. by William Lyons (London: Everyman, 1995), p. lv. In context, Lyons's remark is specifically about the identity thesis, but he clearly intends it to cover physicalism in general. Similarly, while he explicitly mentions an entity in the category of individual – the soul – the context of his remark makes clear that he includes mental properties and events among the entities out of step with scientific materialism.

6 See Robert Adams, 'Flavors, Colors, and God', reprinted in

Contemporary Perspectives on Religious Epistemology, ed. by R. Douglas Geivett and Brendan Sweetman (New York: Oxford University Press, 1992), pp. 225–40.

7 See Richard Swinburne, *The Existence of God* (Oxford: Clarendon Press, 1979), ch. 9; *The Evolution of the Soul*, rev. edn (Oxford: Clarendon Press, 1993), pp. 183–96; *Is There a God?* (Oxford: Oxford University Press, 1996), pp. 69–94; 'The Origin of Consciousness', in *Cosmic Beginnings and Human Ends*, ed. by Clifford N. Matthews and Roy Abraham Varghese (Chicago and La Salle, IL: Open Court, 1995), pp. 355–78.

8 For a more detailed defence of this premise, see J. P. Moreland, 'Searle's Biological Naturalism and the Argument from Consciousness', *Faith and Philosophy* 15 (January 1998): 68–91.

9 Terence Horgan, 'Nonreductive Materialism and the Explanatory Autonomy of Psychology', in *Naturalism*, ed. by Steven J. Wagner and Richard Warner (Notre Dame: University of Notre Dame Press, 1993), pp. 313–14.

10 D. M. Armstrong, 'Naturalism: Materialism and First Philosophy', *Philosophia* 8 (1978): 262.

11 Howard E. Gruber, *Darwin on Man: A Psychological Study of Scientific Creativity* (Chicago: University of Chicago Press, 1974), p. 211.

12 Paul Churchland, *Matter and Consciousness* (Cambridge, MA: MIT Press, 1984), p. 21.

13 Frank Jackson, *From Metaphysics to Ethics* (Oxford: Clarendon Press, 1998), p. 13.

14 Jackson, *From Metaphysics to Ethics*, p. 25.

15 See John Searle, *The Rediscovery of the Mind* (Cambridge, MA: MIT Press, 1992).

16 J. L. Mackie, *The Miracle of Theism* (Oxford: Clarendon Press, 1982), p. 115.

17 Jaegwon Kim, *Philosophy of Mind* (Boulder, CO: Westview, 1996), p. 8.

18 Colin McGinn, *The Mysterious Flame* (New York: Basic Books, 1999).

19 Thomas Nagel, *The View From Nowhere* (New York: Oxford University Press, 1986), pp. 49–53. David J. Chalmers, *The Conscious Mind* (New York: Oxford University Press, 1996), pp. 293–301.

20 For a critique of panpsychism in the process of defending AC, see Stephen R. L. Clark, *From Athens to Jerusalem* (Oxford: Clarendon Press, 1984), pp. 121–57.

21 Madell, *Mind and Materialism*, p. 3.

22 David Papineau, *Philosopical Naturalism* (Oxford: Blackwell, 1993), p. 119.

23 Papineau, *Philosopical Naturalism*, pp. 106, 114–18, 120, 121, 126.

24 Jaegwon Kim, *Mind in a Physical World* (Cambridge, MA: MIT Press, 1998), p. 96.

25 Kim, *Mind in a Physical World*, ch. 4, esp. pp. 118–20.

Chapter 3

1 John Searle, *Freedom and Neurobiology* (New York: Columbia University Press, 2007).

2 See John Bishop, *Natural Agency* (Cambridge: Cambridge University Press, 1989).

3 See J. P. Moreland and Scott Rae, *Body and Soul* (Downers Grove, IL: InterVarsity Press, 2000), ch. 4.

4 Roderick Chisholm, 'Human Freedom and the Self', reprinted in *On Metaphysics* (Minneapolis: University of Minnesota Press, 1989), p. 14.

5 John Searle, *Minds, Brains, and Science* (Cambridge, MA: Harvard University Press, 1984), p. 98.

6 Bishop, *Natural Agency*, p. 1. Bishop's own solution eschews libertarian agency in favour of a version of compatibilism.

7 Bishop, *Natural Agency*, p. 40. An interesting implication of Bishop's view is that naturalism cannot allow for there to be a first event in the absolute sense of not being preceded by other events because all events are caused by prior events or else they are simply uncaused. In the latter case, the coming to be of the event cannot be 'natural' since it is just a brute fact. In the former case, this means that if the kalam cosmological argument is correct and there was a beginning to the universe, then the beginning itself was not a natural event nor was its cause if it had one. For more on this, see William Lane Craig and Quentin Smith, *Theism, Atheism, and Big Bang Cosmology* (Oxford: Clarendon Press, 1993).

8 Joshua Hoffman and Gary S. Rosenkrantz, *Substance: Its Nature and Existence* (London: Routledge, 1997), pp. 98–9.

9 Stephen Jay Gould, 'The Meaning of Life', *Life Magazine* (December 1988), p. 84.

10 Searle, *Minds, Brains, and Science*, pp. 86–7.

11 Jaegwon Kim, *Mind in a Physical World* (Cambridge, MA: MIT Press, 1998), pp. 37–56.

12 Leda Cosmides and John Tooby, *Evolutionary Psychology: A Primer* (1998): www.psych.ucsb.edu/research/cep/primer.html (accessed 4 October, 2008).

13 James Rachels, *Created from Animals* (Oxford: Oxford University Press, 1990), pp. 73–4.

14 Kim, *Mind in a Physical World*. This is Kim's solution proffered

at the end of this work. He has subsequently altered his view. He retains a functional reduction for thoughts, beliefs and related propositional attitudes, but he has become an epiphenomenal property dualist regarding phenomenal consciousness. See his *Physicalism, or Something Near Enough* (Princeton, NJ: Princeton University Press, 2005).

15 See Timothy O'Connor, *Persons and Causes* (New York: Oxford University Press, 2000); Timothy O'Connor and Jonathan D. Jacobs, 'Emergent Individuals', *Philosophical Quarterly* 53 (October 2003): 540–55; Timothy O'Connor and Hong Yu Wong, 'The Metaphysics of Emergence', *Nous* 39:4 (2005): 659–79. For a response, see J. P. Moreland, *Consciousness and the Existence of God* (New York: Routledge, 2008), ch. 4.

16 Daniel Dennett, *Elbow Room* (Cambridge, MA: MIT Press, 1984), pp. 156–65.

17 Searle, *Freedom and Neurobiology*, pp. 37–78, esp. pp. 58–78.

18 Searle, *Freedom and Neurobiology*, pp. 33, 56, 73.

19 Searle, *Freedom and Neurobiology*, pp. 53, 57.

20 Searle, *Freedom and Neurobiology*, p. 57.

21 Searle, *Freedom and Neurobiology*, pp. 55–6.

22 Searle, *Freedom and Neurobiology*, pp. 5, 10–11, 17, 38–9, 59, 60.

23 Searle, *Freedom and Neurobiology*, p. 5.

24 Searle, *Freedom and Neurobiology*, p. 10.

25 Searle, *Freedom and Neurobiology*, p. 11.

26 Searle, *Freedom and Neurobiology*, pp. 38–9.

27 Searle, *Freedom and Neurobiology*, p. 45.

28 Searle, *Freedom and Neurobiology*, p. 11.

29 Searle, *Freedom and Neurobiology*, pp. 42–3.

30 Searle, *Freedom and Neurobiology*, p. 59.

31 Searle, *Freedom and Neurobiology*, p. 55.

32 Searle, *Freedom and Neurobiology*, pp. 40, 70.

33 Searle, *Freedom and Neurobiology*, p. 48.

34 Searle, *Freedom and Neurobiology*, pp. 48–9.

35 Searle, *Freedom and Neurobiology*, p. 55.

36 Searle, *Freedom and Neurobiology*, p. 58.

37 Searle, *Freedom and Neurobiology*, pp. 58–9.

38 Searle, *Freedom and Neurobiology*, p. 70.

39 Searle, *Freedom and Neurobiology*, pp. 61–6.

40 Searle, *Freedom and Neurobiology*, p. 77

41 Searle, *Freedom and Neurobiology*, see p. 44, cf. p. 69.

42 See Kim, *Mind in a Physical World*, pp. 29–56; *Physicalism, or Something Near Enough*, pp. 8–22, 32–69; *Philosophy of Mind* (Boulder, CO: Westview Press, 2nd edn, 2006), pp. 173–204.

43 Jaegwon Kim, 'Mental Causation and Two Conceptions of Mental Properties', unpublished paper delivered at the American Philosophical

Association Eastern Division Meeting, Atlanta, Georgia, 27–30 December 1993, p. 21.

44 Kim, 'Mental Causation and Two Conceptions of Mental Properties', p. 23.

45 David Papineau, *Philosophical Naturalism* (Oxford: Blackwell, 1993), pp. 9–32.

Chapter 4

1 Anthony Flew and Roy Abraham Varghese, *There is a God* (New York: HarperCollins, 2007), p. 167.

2 Victor Reppert, *C. S. Lewis's Dangerous Idea* (Downers Grove, IL: InterVarsity Press, 2003), p. 70.

3 Thomas Nagel, *The Last Word* (New York: Oxford University Press, 1997), p. 75.

4 Daniel Dennett, *Elbow Room* (Cambridge, MA: MIT Press, 1984), p. 21.

5 William Hasker, *The Emergent Self* (Ithaca, NY: Cornell University Press, 1999), pp. 122–46.

6 A. C. Ewing, *Value and Reality* (London: George Allen and Unwin, 1973), p. 84.

7 Dennett, *Elbow Room*, p. 11; cf. 10–12, 29, 49, 103.

8 Dennett, *Elbow Room*, pp. 20–49.

9 John Searle, *The Rediscovery of the Mind* (Cambridge, MA: MIT Press, 1992), p. 11.

10 Robert C. Stalnaker, *Inquiry* (Cambridge, MA: MIT Press, 1984), p. 6.

11 John F. Post, *Metaphysics* (New York: Paragon House, 1991), p. 121.

12 See J. P. Moreland, 'Naturalism, Nominalism, and Husserlian Moments', *The Modern Schoolman* 79 (January/March 2002): 199–216.

13 George Bealer, 'Modal Epistemology and the Rationalist Renaissance', in *Conceivability and Possibility*, ed. by Tamar Szabo Gendler and John Hawthorne (Oxford: Clarendon Press, 2002), p. 73.

14 See Richard Swinburne, *Evolution of the Soul*, rev. edn (Oxford: Clarendon Press, 1993), for a defence of incorrigibility.

15 See Laurence Bonjour, *In Defense of Pure Reason* (Cambridge: Cambridge University Press, 1998), pp. 153–86.

16 For more on these points, see Scott R. Sehon, 'Teleology and the Nature of Mental States', *American Philosophical Quarterly* 31 (January 1994): 63–72.

17 Tom L. Beauchamp, *Philosophical Ethics* (New York: McGraw-Hill, 1982), pp. 83–6.

18 See Dallas Willard, 'How Concepts Relate the Mind to its Objects: The "God's Eye View" Vindicated', *Philosophia Christi* 1:2 (1999): 5–20; *Logic and the Objectivity of Knowledge* (Athens, OH: University of Ohio Press, 1984), pp. 180–82.

19 Jaegwon Kim, *Philosophy of Mind* (Boulder, CO: Westview Press, 2nd edn, 2006), pp. 208–10. Paul Churchland goes so far as to argue this same point with respect to mental states like pain that are clearly categorized as states of phenomenal consciousness. See Paul Churchland, *Matter and Consciousness* (Cambridge, MA: MIT Press, 1984), pp. 52–3. Unfortunately, Churchland fails to see that painfulness is a second-order property, not a first-order one, and as such, it characterizes various kinds of pain which differ phenomenologically with respect to their species and not their genus.

20 Churchland, *Matter and Consciousness*, pp. 47–9.

21 It could be argued that on an Aristotelian depiction of organisms, their parts play a role without being constituted by mental states. But this response would not be available to a naturalist because it requires an ontology (e.g., essences, teleology) that is non-natural. Further, it is open to someone to use an Aristotelian account as providing materials for a design argument for God according to which the immanent constituents of organisms that ground the roles of their parts is evidence of a blueprint in the mind of a Designer. For more on this, see Etienne Gilson, *From Aristotle to Darwin and Back Again* (Notre Dame: University of Notre Dame Press, 1984).

22 D. M. Armstrong, 'Can A Naturalist Believe in Universals?' in *Science in Reflection*, ed. by Edna Ullmann-Margalit (Boston: Kluwer Academic, 1988), pp. 111–12; *Universals and Scientific Realism*, vol, II: *A Theory of Universals* (Cambridge: Cambridge University Press, 1978), pp. 84–8.

23 Reppert, *C. S. Lewis's Dangerous Idea*, pp. 74–6.

24 John Searle, *Minds, Brains, and Science* (Cambridge, MA: Harvard University Press, 1984), pp. 32–3. Cf. John Searle, 'Minds, Brains, and Programs', *Behavioral and Brain Sciences* 3 (1980): 417–24.

25 The incident is documented in Peter Shockey, *Reflections of Heaven* (New York: Doubleday, 1999), pp. 147–8. For an interesting story of an atheistic university professor who died, went to hell, came back, left teaching and is now in the ministry, see Howard Storm, *My Descent Into Hell* (New York: Doubleday, 2005). For an authoritative listing and evaluation of the vast literature on NDEs, see Edward Kelly and Emile Kelly, *Irreducible Mind* (Lanham, MD: Rowman & Littlefield, 2007), pp. 367–421.

26 Hilary Putnam, *Reason, Truth and History* (Cambridge: Cambridge University Press, 1981), p. 4.

27 Geoffrey Madell, *Mind and Materialism* (Edinburgh: Edinburgh University Press, 1988), pp. 16–17.

28 Madell, *Mind and Materialism*, p. 17.

29 Alvin Plantinga, *Warrant and Proper Function* (New York: Oxford University Press, 1993), pp. 216–37. See James Beilby, ed., *Naturalism Defeated? Essays on Plantinga's Evolutionary Argument Against Naturalism* (Ithaca, NY: Cornell University Press, 2002).

30 I am indebted to Gary Osmundsen for pointing this out to me and for his insights on Plantinga's argument.

31 Jaegwon Kim, *Mind in a Physical World* (Cambridge, MA: MIT Press, 1998), ch. 2.

32 Plantinga, *Warrant and Proper Function*, p. 235.

Chapter 5

1 Jaegwon Kim, 'Lonely Souls: Causality and Substance Dualism', in *Soul, Body and Survival*, ed. by Kevin Corcoran (Ithaca, NY: Cornell University Press, 2001), p. 30. Cf. J. P. Moreland, 'A Christian Perspective on the Impact of Modern Science on Philosophy of Mind', *Perspectives on Science and Christian Faith* 55 (March 2003): 2–12.

2 Frank Jackson, *From Metaphysics to Ethics* (Oxford: Clarendon Press, 1998), p. 45.

3 Roderick Chisholm, 'On the Simplicity of the Soul', in *Philosophical Perspectives*, vol. V: *Philosophy of Religion, 1991*, ed. by James E. Tomberlin (Atascadero, CA: Ridgeview, 1991), p. 167.

4 For a treatment of and bibliography for Brentano's treatment of parts and wholes, see R. M. Chisholm, *Brentano and Intrinsic Value* (Cambridge: Cambridge University Press, 1986); for a treatment of and bibliography for Husserl's treatment of parts and wholes, see Barry Smith, ed., *Parts and Moments: Studies in Logic and Formal Ontology* (Munich: Philosophia Verlag, 1982); J. P. Moreland, 'Naturalism, Nominalism, and Husserlian Moments', *The Modern Schoolman* 79 (January/March 2002): 199–216.

5 Two helpful treatments of substances and related entities are Joshua Hoffman and Gary S. Rosenkrantz, *Substance: Its Nature and Existence* (London: Routledge, 1997); Christopher M. Brown, *Aquinas and the Ship of Theseus* (London: Continuum, 2005).

6 Jaegwon Kim, *Philosophy of Mind* (Boulder, CO: Westview, 1996), pp. 131–2, 147–8.

7 Steward Goetz and Charles Taliaferro, *Naturalism* (Grand Rapids, MI: Eerdmans, 2008), p. 21.

8 Daniel Dennett, *Breaking the Spell: Religion as a Natural Phenomenon* (New York: Viking Press, 2006), p. 107.

9 Carl Sagan, *Cosmos* (New York: Random House, 1980), p. 105.

10 See Roderick Chisholm, *Theory of Knowledge* (Englewood Cliffs, NJ: Prentice-Hall, 2nd edn, 1977), pp. 116–18.

11 Jaegwon Kim, *Philosophy of Mind* (Boulder, CO: Westview Press, 2nd edn, 2006), p. 233.

12 Alvin Plantinga, 'Materialism and Christian Belief', in *Persons: Human and Divine*, ed. by Peter van Inwagen and Dean Zimmerman (Oxford: Clarendon Press, 2007), pp. 102–5.

13 Peter van Inwagen, 'Plantinga's Replacement Argument', in *Alvin Plantinga*, ed. by Deane-Peter Baker (Cambridge: Cambridge University Press, 2007), pp. 188ff.

14 Alvin Plantinga, 'Reply to Peter', paper presented to the Department of Philosophy, Notre Dame University, Fall 2007. Permission granted by Alvin Plantinga to cite from this unpublished paper.

15 Stewart Goetz, 'Modal Dualism: A Critique', in *Soul, Body and Survival* (Ithaca, NY: Cornell University Press, 2001), pp. 89–104.

16 Goetz, 'Modal Dualism'.

17 David J. Whittaker, *The Essential Orson Pratt* (Salt Lake City: Signature Books, 1991), p. xxiv.

18 Cited in Whittaker, *The Essential Orson Pratt*, p. 2.

19 Cited in Whittaker, *The Essential Orson Pratt*, pp. 2–3, 29.

20 Cited in Whittaker, *The Essential Orson Pratt*, p. 3. See also John Locke, *An Essay Concerning Human Understanding* (Dover, 1959), Book IV, Chapter III, Section 6, p. 195. Cf. John W. Yolton, *Thinking Matter: Materialism in Eighteenth-Century Britain* (Minneapolis: University of Minnesota Press, 1983).

21 Cited in Whittaker, *The Essential Orson Pratt*, pp. 3, 4, 6.

22 Cited in Whittaker, *The Essential Orson Pratt*, p. 7.

23 Cited in Whittaker, *The Essential Orson Pratt*, p. 15.

24 Cited in Whittaker, *The Essential Orson Pratt*, p. 16.

25 Cited in Whittaker, *The Essential Orson Pratt*, p. 8.

26 Cited in Whittaker, *The Essential Orson Pratt*, pp. 5, 12, 15, 23.

27 My analysis of substance is the classic one that stands in the grand tradition of Aristotle and Aquinas. Pratt's notion of substance is Newtonian (i.e., a solid corpuscle with at least primary qualities).

28 Cited in Whittaker, *The Essential Orson Pratt*, p. 7.

29 John Calvin, *Institutes of the Christian Religion* (1536; Grand Rapids: Associated Publishers and Authors, n.d.), 1.1.1.

30 Franz Delitzsch, *A System of Biblical Psychology* (1899; Grand Rapids: Baker, 1977), p. 55.

31 Alvin Plantinga, 'Advice to Christian Philosophers', *Faith and Philosophy* 1 (July 1984): 264–5.

32 Kevin Corcoran, *Rethinking Human Nature* (Grand Rapids, MI: Baker, 2006), p. 63.

33 J. P. Moreland, *Universals* (Montreal and Kingston: McGill-Queen's University Press, 2001).

34 Chisholm, 'On the Simplicity of the Soul', pp. 167–81.

35 Lynne Rudder Baker, *Persons and Bodies: A Constitution View* (Cambridge: Cambridge University Press, 2000), esp. part I.

36 Charles Taliaferro and Stewart Goetz, 'The Prospect of Christian Materialism', *Christian Scholar's Review* 37:3 (Spring 2008): 317–18.

37 Rudder Baker, *Persons and Bodies*, p. 132.

38 Timothy O'Connor and Jonathan D. Jacobs, 'Emergent Individuals', *Philosophical Quarterly* 53 (October 2003): 540–55; Timothy O'Connor and Hong Yu Wong, 'The Metaphysics of Emergence', *Nous* 39:4 (2005): 659–79.

39 See William Hasker, *The Emergent Self* (Ithaca, NY: Cornell University Press, 1999).

40 O'Connor rejects this move because, among other things, it suffers from the causal pairing problem and the most plausible solution to that problem – singular causation – is bogus. O'Connor seems quite unfamiliar with Thomistic dualist solutions to this problem. See J. P. Moreland and Stanley Wallace, 'Aquinas vs. Descartes and Locke on the Human Person and End-of-Life Ethics', *International Philosophical Quarterly* 35 (September 1995): 319–30.

41 See John W. Yolton, *Thinking Matter: Materialism in Eighteenth-Century Britain* (Minneapolis: University of Minnesota Press, 1983). For more in this in the context of Locke's claims about thinking matter, see Clifford Williams, 'Christian Materialism and the Parity Thesis', *International Journal for Philosophy of Religion* 39 (February 1996): 1–14; J. P. Moreland, 'Locke's Parity Thesis about Thinking Matter: A Response to Williams', *Religious Studies* 34 (September 1998): 253–9; Clifford Williams, 'Topic Neutrality and the Mind–Body Problem', *Religious Studies* 36 (2000): 203–7; J. P. Moreland, 'Christian Materialism and the Parity Thesis Revisited', *International Philosophical Quarterly* 40 (December 2000): 423–40; and *idem*, 'Topic Neutrality and the Parity Thesis: A Surrejoinder to Williams', *Religious Studies* 37 (March 2001): 93–101.

42 See O'Connor and Wong, 'The Metaphysics of Emergence', pp. 665–9.

Chapter 6

1 Michael Ruse, 'Evolutionary Theory and Christian Ethics', in *The Darwinian Paradigm* (London: Routledge, 1989), pp. 262–9.

2 John Bishop, *Natural Agency* (Cambridge: Cambridge University Press, 1989), p. 1. Bishop's own solution eschews libertarian agency in favour of a version of the causal theory of action.

3 Helga Kuhse and Peter Singer, *Should the Baby Live?* (Oxford: Oxford University Press, 1985), pp. 118–39.

4 Joel Feinberg, *Social Philosophy* (Englewood Cliffs, NJ: Prentice-Hall, 1973), pp. 84–97.

5 Nowhere does Feinberg consider the image of God as an answer to the question, but as an example of 3 he considers 'sacredness', which is close to the employment of God's image. Feinberg's difficulty with this solution fails for two reasons: he conflates the question 'What grounds equal human worth?' vs 'How could there be such a thing as a ground for equal human worth?' and his epistemic limits do not allow a proper answer to the first question. Regarding the latter point, whether 'intrinsic, equal worth' is taken as a transcendental, intrinsic value property that is simply exemplified by human persons or as such a property that supervenes on other kinds of properties, in order to avoid a vicious regress, one must stop with a ground for such value that is ostensively defined via direct, intuitive perception. But Feinberg's naturalistic epistemology takes such a capacity to be too mystical. Regarding the former, advocates of the image of God employ this notion to answer both questions, and Feinberg fails to consider this employment as a way of responding to the sceptics' question.

6 Richard Dawkins, *River out of Eden: A Darwinian View of Life* (London: Phoenix, 1995), p. 133.

7 J. L. Mackie, *The Miracle of Theism* (Oxford: Clarendon Press, 1982), p. 115. Cf. J. P. Moreland and Kai Nielsen, *Does God Exist?* (Buffalo, NY: Prometheus, 1993), chs 8–10.

8 Paul Churchland, *Matter and Consciousness* (Cambridge, MA: MIT Press, 1984), p. 21.

9 Mark D. Linville, 'The Moral Argument', in *A Companion to Natural Theology*, ed. by William Lane Craig and J. P. Moreland (Oxford: Blackwell, forthcoming, 2009), p. 47 (typescript).

10 Steward Goetz and Charles Taliaferro, *Naturalism* (Grand Rapids, MI: Eerdmans, 2008), p. 85.

11 Cited in *The Autobiography of Charles Darwin*, ed. by N. Barlow (New York: Harcourt Brace, 1959), p. 92.

12 John Barrow and Frank Tipler, *The Anthropic Cosmological Principle* (Oxford: Clarendon Press, 1986), pp. 658–77.

13 James Rachels, *The End of Life* (Oxford: Oxford University Press, 1986), pp. 92–6, 111–18.

14 Michael Ruse, *The Darwinian Paradigm* (London: Routledge, 1989), pp. 262–9.

15 Richard Swinburne, *Evolution of the Soul* (Oxford: Clarendon Press, rev. edn, 1993), p. 208; cf. chs 11 and 12.

16 Daniel Dennett, *Elbow Room* (Cambridge, MA: MIT Press, 1984), pp. 156–65.

17 Linville, 'The Moral Argument', pp. 3–4 (typescript).

18 Michael Ruse and E. O. Wilson, 'Moral Philosophy as Applied Science', *Philosophy* 61 (1986): 186.

19 Thomas Nagel, *The Last Word* (New York: Oxford University Press, 1997), pp. 140–3.

20 Cited in James Rachels, *Created from Animals* (Oxford: Oxford University Press, 1990), p. 76.

21 Linville, 'The Moral Argumemt', p. 58 (typescript).

22 E. Mayr, *Populations, Species, and Evolution* (Cambridge, MA: Harvard University Press, 1970), p. 4.

23 David Hull, *The Metaphysics of Evolution* (Albany, NY: State University of New York Press, 1989), pp. 74–5.

24 Rachels, *Created From Animals*, pp. 171–2; cf. 93, 97, 171.

25 Rachels, *Created from Animals*, p. 70.

Appendix

1 I believe the pattern began in the United States around 1870 or so. For a defence of this claim and a detailed treatment of the pattern's development from 1870 to 1930, see Julie Reuben, *The Making of the Modern University* (Chicago: University of Chicago Press, 1996).

2 Thomas Nagel, *The Last Word* (New York: Oxford University Press, 1997).

3 For a classic comparison of the epistemic and ontological characterizations, see Ernest Nagel, *The Structure of Science* (Indianapolis: Hackett, 1979), pp. 366–80.

4 For a good treatment of this period, see William Lyons, *Matters of the Mind* (New York: Routledge, 2001), pp. 1–78.

5 Note the dates of the articles in parts two and three of David M. Rosenthal, ed., *Materialism and the Mind–Body Problem* (Englewood Cliffs, NJ: Prentice-Hall, 1971). Cf. Steven J. Wagner and Richard Warner, eds, *Naturalism: A Critical Appraisal* (Notre Dame: University of Notre Dame Press, 1993).

6 I think it is wrong to call the problem 'multiple realization'. Instead, I prefer 'multiple exemplification'. See J. P. Moreland, 'The Knowledge Argument Revisited', *International Philosophical Quarterly* 43 (June 2003): 219–28.

7 John Searle, *The Rediscovery of the Mind* (Cambridge, MA: MIT Press, 1992); *The Mystery of Consciousness* (New York: The New York Review of Books, 1997); *Mind: A Brief Introduction* (Oxford: Oxford University Press, 2004); David Chalmers, *The Conscious Mind* (New York: Oxford University Press, 1996); Colin McGinn, *The Mysterious Flame* (New York: Basic Books, 1999); Jaegwon Kim, *Mind in a Physical World* (Cambridge, MA: MIT Press, 1998); *Physicalism, or Something Near Enough* (Princeton, NJ: Princeton University Press, 2005), pp. 8–22, 32–69; *Philosophy of Mind* (Boulder, CO: Westview Press, 1st

edn, 1996; 2nd edn, 2006). Kim's journey is especially interesting. His 2006 edition of *Philosophy of Mind* contains a fair and respectful treatment of several arguments for substance dualism, while the 1996 edition hardly considers the view worth taking seriously. Especially revealing is the shift from *Mind in a Physical World*, where Kim leaves the problem of consciousness up in the air while suggesting that type identity theory may be needed for a naturalist treatment of phenomenal consciousness, to *Physicalism, or Something Near Enough*, in which Kim embraces a narrow, nuanced version of epiphenomenalist emergent dualism. Cf. J. P. Moreland, 'If You Can't Reduce, You Must Eliminate: Why Kim's Version of Physicalism Isn't Close Enough', *Philosophia Christi* 7 (Spring 2005): 463–73.

8 For a naturalist treatment of secondary qualities, see Frank Jackson, *From Metaphysics to Ethics* (Oxford: Clarendon Press, 1998), ch. 4. For the role of indexicals in debates about naturalism, see Jackson, *From Metaphysics to Ethics*, pp. 18–21; Geoffrey Madell, *The Identity of the Self* (Edinburgh: University of Edinburgh Press, 1981).

9 On aesthetics, see Frank Sibley, 'Aesthetic and Nonaesthetic', *Philosophical Review* 74 (April 1965): 135–59; on ethics, see Panayot Butchvarov, *Skepticism in Ethics* (Bloomington: Indiana University Press, 1989), pp. 1–10; John Rist, *Real Ethics: Rethinking the Foundations of Morality* (Cambridge: Cambridge University Press, 2003); Paul Copan, 'The Moral Argument', in *The Rationality of Faith*, ed. by Paul Copan and Paul K. Moser (London: Routledge, 2003), pp. 149–74; Jackson, *From Metaphysics to Ethics*, ch. 5; Wilfred Sellars and John Hospers, eds, *Readings in Ethical Theory* (Englewood Cliffs, NJ: Prentice-Hall, 1970), part II. While clear parallels exist in twentieth-century Anglo-American philosophical treatments of ethics and aesthetics, the recent history of aesthetics is not as clean-cut relative to my pattern as is ethics. See Paul Guyer, 'History of Aesthetics [Addendum]', in *Encyclopedia of Philosophy*, with Donald M. Borchert, editor-in-chief (Detroit: Thomas Gale, 2nd edn, 2006), vol. I, pp. 63–72.

10 Timothy O'Connor, *Persons and Causes* (New York: Oxford University Press, 2000); Timothy O'Connor and Jonathan D. Jacobs, 'Emergent Individuals', *Philosophical Quarterly* 53 (October 2003): 540–55.

11 For a discussion of the issues mentioned in the paragraph to follow, see J. P. Moreland, *Universals* (Montreal and Kingston: McGill-Queen's University Press, 2001).

12 Terence Horgan, 'Nonreductive Materialism and the Explanatory Autonomy of Psychology', in *Naturalism*, ed. by Steven J. Wagner and Richard Warner (Notre Dame: University of Notre Dame Press, 1993), pp. 313–14.

13 J. P. Moreland, 'The Argument from Consciousness', in *Rationality*

of Theism, ed. by Paul Copan and Paul Moser (London: Routledge, 2003), pp. 204–20; 'Should a Naturalist Be a Supervenient Physicalist?' *Metaphilosophy* 29 (January/April 1998): 35–57; 'Naturalism and Libertarian Agency', *Philosophy and Theology* 10 (1997): 351–81; 'Naturalism, Nominalism, and Husserlian Moments', *The Modern Schoolman* 79 (January/March 2002): 199–216; 'Timothy O'Connor and the Harmony Thesis: A Critique', *Metaphysica* 3:2 (2002): 5–40.

14 Nagel, *The Last Word*, p. 130.

15 Nagel, *The Last Word*, p. 4.

16 Nagel, *The Last Word*, p. 76.

17 Nagel, *The Last Word*, pp. 3–35.

18 Nagel, *The Last Word*, cf. p. 138.

19 Nagel, *The Last Word*, p. 143.

20 Nagel, *The Last Word*, p. 135.

21 Nagel, *The Last Word*, pp. 128–33.

22 Nagel, *The Last Word*, pp. 127–30.

23 Nagel, *The Last Word*, pp. 132–3.

24 Nagel, *The Last Word*, pp. 13–35.

25 Nicholas Rescher, *The Limits of Science* (Berkeley: University of California Press, 1984), p. 22.

26 I shall not bother to distinguish among statements, sentences or propositions, though there are interesting differences in the way each figures into self-refutation. See Joseph M. Boyle, Jr, Germain Grisez and Olaf Tollefsen, *Free Choice: A Self-Referential Argument* (Notre Dame: University of Notre Dame Press, 1976), pp. 122–152.

27 See Michael J. Loux, *Substance and Attribute* (Dordrecht: D. Reidel, 1978), pp. 17–18, 21–2.

28 Cf. Nagel, *The Last Word*, p. 4. On page 3 Nagel clearly has in mind the question of the objectivity of reason to which he plans to give a rationalist answer. But on page 4 he moves without warning into the two second-order questions and, in context, he seems to equate them.

29 Nagel, *The Last Word*, p. 76.

30 See J. L. Mackie, *The Miracle of Theism* (Oxford: Clarendon Press, 1982), p. 141.

31 Alvin Plantinga, *Warrant and Proper Function* (New York: Oxford University Press, 1993), pp. 194–237.

32 Plantinga, *Warrant and Proper Function*, pp. 222–3.

33 Plantinga, *Warrant and Proper Function*, pp. 234–7.

34 Nagel, *The Last Word*, p. 235.

35 A particularly egregious instantiation of this atheist dilemma and the employment of a dismissive strategy to split its horns is Anthony O'Hear, *Beyond Evolution: Human Nature and the Limits of Evolutionary Explanation* (New York: Oxford University Press, 1997). O'Hear explicitly argues that there are numerous aspects of human beings (the norma-

tivity and universality of our faculties, judgements, and search for (and discovery of) knowledge and truth in epistemology, ethics, aesthetics; consciousness, self-consciousness; veridical perception of mind-independent, irreducible, objective secondary qualities; agency and freedom) that lie beyond the limits of scientific naturalist, particularly Darwinian, explanation. O'Hear also acknowledges that his argument can be employed by theists as an argument for God's existence (cf. *Beyond Evolution*, p. 214). But in the space of one small paragraph, O'Hear dismisses such theistic employment out of hand on the grounds that

1 it has been refuted by Kant's critique of the arguments for God, and
2 such employments invariably generate a vicious infinite regress of explanation that theists stop by utilizing the incoherent notion of God as a logically necessary being.

In a way analogous to Nagel, the failure of this dismissive strategy has the result that by acknowledging the inadequacy of naturalistic evolutionary theory to account for a wide range of admittedly irreducible, uneliminable non-natural facts, O'Hear has provided materials for strengthening the case for theism.

References

Adams, Robert, 'Flavors, Colors, and God', reprinted in *Contemporary Perspectives on Religious Epistemology*, Geivett, R. Douglas and Sweetman, Brendan (eds), New York: Oxford University Press, 1992, pp. 225–40.

Armstrong, D. M., 'Can a Naturalist Believe in Universals?', in *Science in Reflection*, Ullmann-Margalit, Edna (ed.), Boston: Kluwer Academic, 1988, pp. 103–15.

Armstrong, D. M., 'Naturalism: Materialism and First Philosophy', *Philosophia*, Vol. 8 (1978), pp. 261–76.

Armstrong, D. M., *Universals and Scientific Realism*, vol. II: *A Theory of Universals*, Cambridge: Cambridge University Press, 1978.

Barrow, John and Tipler, Frank, *The Anthropic Cosmological Principle*, Oxford: Clarendon Press, 1986.

Bealer, George, 'Modal Epistemology and the Rationalist Renaissance', in *Conceivability and Possibility*, Gendler, Tamar Szabo and Hawthorne, John (eds), Oxford: Clarendon Press, 2002.

Beauchamp, Tom L., *Philosophical Ethics*, New York: McGraw-Hill, 1982.

Beilby, James (ed.), *Naturalism Defeated? Essays on Plantinga's Evolutionary Argument Against Naturalism*, Ithaca, NY: Cornell University Press, 2002.

Bishop, John, *Natural Agency*, Cambridge: Cambridge University Press, 1989.

Bonjour, Laurence, *In Defense of Pure Reason*, Cambridge: Cambridge University Press, 1998.

Boyle Jr, Joseph M., Grisez, Germain and Tollefsen, Olaf, *Free Choice: A Self-Referential Argument*, Notre Dame: University of Notre Dame Press, 1976.

Boyle, Robert, 1663, 'Essay IV: An Essay Containing a Requisite Digression, Concerning those that would exclude the Deity from Intermingling with Matter', in *Selected Philosophical Papers of Robert Boyle*, Stewart, M. A. (ed.), Indianapolis: Hackett, 1991.

References

Brown, Christopher M., *Aquinas and the Ship of Theseus*, London: Continuum, 2005.

Butchvarov, Panayot, *Skepticism in Ethics*, Bloomington: Indiana University Press, 1989.

Calvin, John, 1536, *Institutes of the Christian Religion*, Grand Rapids: Associated Publishers and authors, n.d..

Chalmers, David J., *The Conscious Mind*, New York: Oxford University Press, 1996.

Chesterton, G. K., 1908, *Orthodoxy*, John Lane Company, repr., San Francisco: Ignatius Press, 1950.

Chisholm, R. M., *Brentano and Intrinsic Value*, Cambridge: Cambridge University Press, 1986.

Chisholm, Roderick, 'On the Simplicity of the Soul', in *Philosophical Perspectives*, vol. V: *Philosophy of Religion*, Tomberlin, James E. (ed.), Atascadero, CA: Ridgeview, 1991, pp. 167–81.

Chisholm, Roderick, 'Human Freedom and the Self', reprinted in *On Metaphysics*, Minneapolis: University of Minnesota Press, 1989.

Chisholm, Roderick, *Theory of Knowledge*, 3rd edn, Englewood Cliffs, NJ: Prentice-Hall, 1989.

Chisholm, Roderick, *Theory of Knowledge*, 2nd edn, Englewood Cliffs, NJ: Prentice-Hall, 1977.

Churchland, Paul, *Matter and Consciousness*, Cambridge, MA: MIT Press, 1984.

Clark, Stephen R. L., *From Athens to Jerusalem*, Oxford: Clarendon Press, 1984.

Collins, C. John, *Genesis 1–4*, Phillipsburg, NJ: P&R Publishing, 2006.

Copan, Paul, 'The Moral Argument', in *The Rationality of Faith*, Copan, Paul and Moser, Paul K. (eds), London: Routledge, 2003.

Corcoran, Kevin, *Rethinking Human Nature*, Grand Rapids, MI: Baker Books, 2006.

Cosmides, Leda and Tooby, John, *Evolutionary Psychology: A Primer*, 1998, www.psych.ucsb.edu/research/cep/primer.html, accessed 4 October 2008.

Craig, William Lane and Smith, Quentin, *Theism, Atheism, and Big Bang Cosmology*, Oxford: Clarendon Press, 1993.

Cushman, Philip, 'Why the Self is Empty: Toward a Historically Situated Psychology', *American Psychologist*, Vol. 45 (1990), pp. 599–611.

Darwin, Charles, *The Autobiography of Charles Darwin*, N. Barlow (ed.), New York: Harcourt Brace, 1959.

Dawkins, Richard, *River out of Eden: A Darwinian View of Life*, London: Phoenix, 1995.

Delitzsch, Franz, 1899, *A System of Biblical Psychology*, Grand Rapids: Baker, 1977.
Dennett, Daniel, *Breaking the Spell: Religion as a Natural Phenomenon*, New York: Viking Press, 2006.
Dennett, Daniel, *Elbow Room*, Cambridge, MA: MIT Press,1984.

Eagleton, Terry, *The Illusions of Postmodernism*, Oxford: Blackwell, 1996.
Ewing, A. C., *Value and Reality*, London: George Allen and Unwin, 1973.

Feinberg, Joel, *Social Philosophy*, Englewood Cliffs, NJ: Prentice-Hall, 1973.
Flew, Antony and Varghese, Roy Abraham, *There is a God*, New York: HarperCollins, 2007.

Gilson, Etienne, *From Aristotle to Darwin and Back Again*, Notre Dame: University of Notre Dame Press, 1984.
Goetz, Stewart, 'Modal Dualism: A Critique', in *Soul, Body and Survival*, Ithaca, NY: Cornell University Press, 2001, pp. 89–104.
Goetz, Stewart and Taliaferro, Charles, *Naturalism*, Grand Rapids, MI: Eerdmans, 2008.
Gould, Stephen Jay, 'The Meaning of Life', *Life Magazine* (December 1988), p. 84.
Gruber, Howard E., *Darwin on Man: A Psychological Study of Scientific Creativity*, Chicago: University of Chicago Press, 1974.
Guyer, Paul, 'History of Aesthetics [Addendum]', in *Encyclopedia of Philosophy*, 2nd edn, with Borchert, Donald M., editor-in-chief, Detroit: Thomas Gale, 2006, vol. I, pp. 63–72.

Haldane, John, 'The Mystery of Emergence', *Proceedings of the Aristotelian Society*, Vol. 96 (1996), pp. 261–7.
Hasker, William, *The Emergent Self*, Ithaca, NY: Cornell University Press, 1999.
Hoffman, Joshua and Rosenkrantz, Gary S., *Substance: Its Nature and Existence*, London: Routledge, 1997.
Horgan, Terence, 'Nonreductive Materialism and the Explanatory Autonomy of Psychology', in *Naturalism*, Wagner, Steven J. and Warner, Richard (eds), Notre Dame: University of Notre Dame Press, 1993, pp. 313–14.
Hull, David, *The Metaphysics of Evolution*, Albany, NY: State University of New York Press, 1989.

Jackson, Frank, *From Metaphysics to Ethics*, Oxford: Clarendon Press, 1998.

John Paul II, *Veritatis Splendor*, Boston: Pauline Books & Media, 2003.
Johnson, Phillip E., *The Right Questions*, Downers Grove, IL: InterVarsity Press, 2002.

Kelly, Edward and Kelly, Emile, *Irreducible Mind*, Lanham, MD: Rowman & Littlefield, 2007.
Kim, Jaegwon, *Philosophy of Mind*, 2nd edn, Boulder, CO: Westview Press, 2006.
Kim, Jaegwon, *Physicalism, or Something Near Enough*, Princeton, NJ: Princeton University Press, 2005.
Kim, Jaegwon, 'Lonely Souls: Causality and Substance Dualism', in *Soul, Body and Survival*, Kevin Corcoran (ed.), Ithaca, NY: Cornell University Press, 2001, pp. 30–43.
Kim, Jaegwon, *Mind in a Physical World*, Cambridge, MA: MIT Press, 1998.
Kim, Jaegwon, *Philosophy of Mind*, Boulder, CO: Westview Press, 1996.
Kim, Jaegwon, 'Mental Causation and Two Conceptions of Mental Properties', unpublished paper delivered at the American Philosophical Association Eastern Division Meeting, Atlanta, GA, 1993.
Kronman, Anthony T., *Education's End: Why Our Colleges and Universities Have Given Up on the Meaning of Life*, New Haven: Yale University Press, 2007.
Kuhse, Helga and Singer, Peter, *Should the Baby Live?* Oxford: Oxford University Press, 1985.

Lasch, Christopher, *The Culture of Narcissism*, New York: Warner Books,1979.
Linville, Mark D., 'The Moral Argument', in *A Companion to Natural Theology*, Lane Craig, William and Moreland, J. P. (eds), Oxford: Blackwell, 2009.
Locke, John, *An Essay Concerning Human Understanding*, New York: Courier Dover Publications, 1959.
Loux, Michael J., *Substance and Attribute*, Dordrecht: D. Reidel, 1978.
Lyons, William, *Matters of the Mind*, New York: Routledge, 2001.
Lyons, William, 'Introduction', in *Modern Philosophy of Mind*, Lyons, William (ed.), London: Everyman, 1995.

Mackie, J. L., *The Miracle of Theism*, Oxford: Clarendon Press, 1982.
Madell, Geoffrey, *Mind and Materialism*, Edinburgh: Edinburgh University Press, 1988.
Madell, Geoffrey, *The Identity of the Self*, Edinburgh: Edinburgh University Press, 1981.
Mayr, E., *Populations, Species, and Evolution*, Cambridge, MA: Harvard University Press, 1970.

McGinn, Colin, *The Mysterious Flame*, New York: Basic Books, 1999.

Moreland, J. P., *Consciousness and the Existence of God*, New York: Routledge, 2008.

Moreland, J. P., 'If You Can't Reduce, You Must Eliminate: Why Kim's Version of Physicalism Isn't Close Enough', *Philosophia Christi*, Vol. 7 (Spring 2005), pp. 463–73.

Moreland, J. P., 'The Argument from Consciousness', in *Rationality of Theism*, Copan, Paul and Moser, Paul (eds), London: Routledge, 2003, pp. 204–20.

Moreland, J. P., 'The Knowledge Argument Revisited', *International Philosophical Quarterly*, Vol. 43 (June 2003), pp. 219–28.

Moreland, J. P., 'A Christian Perspective on the Impact of Modern Science on Philosophy of Mind', *Perspectives on Science and Christian Faith*, Vol. 55 (March 2003), pp. 2–12.

Moreland, J. P., 'Timothy O'Connor and the Harmony Thesis: A Critique', *Metaphysica*, Vol. 3:2 (2002), pp. 5–40.

Moreland, J. P., 'Naturalism, Nominalism, and Husserlian Moments', *The Modern Schoolman*, Vol. 79 (January/March 2002), pp. 199–216.

Moreland, J. P., *Universals*, Montreal and Kingston: McGill-Queen's University Press, 2001.

Moreland, J. P., 'Topic Neutrality and the Parity Thesis: A Surrejoinder to Williams', *Religious Studies*, Vol. 37 (March 2001), pp. 93–101.

Moreland, J. P, 'Christian Materialism and the Parity Thesis Revisited', *International Philosophical Quarterly*, Vol. 40 (December 2000), pp. 423–40.

Moreland, J. P., 'Locke's Parity Thesis about Thinking Matter: A Response to Williams', *Religious Studies*, Vol. 34 (September 1998), pp. 253–9.

Moreland, J. P., 'Restoring the Substance to the Soul of Psychology', *Journal of Psychology and Theology*, Vol. 26 (March 1998), pp. 29–43.

Moreland, J. P., 'Searle's Biological Naturalism and the Argument from Consciousness', *Faith and Philosophy*, Vol. 15 (January 1998), pp. 68–91.

Moreland, J. P., 'Should a Naturalist Be a Supervenient Physicalist?', *Metaphilosophy*, Vol. 29 (January/April 1998), pp. 35–57.

Moreland, J. P., 'Naturalism and Libertarian Agency', *Philosophy and Theology*, Vol. 10 (1997), pp. 351–81.

Moreland, J. P. and Nielsen, Kai, *Does God Exist?* Buffalo, NY: Prometheus, 1993.

Moreland, J. P. and Rac, Scott, *Body and Soul*, Downers Grove, IL: InterVarsity Press, 2000.

Moreland, J. P. and Wallace, Stanley, 'Aquinas vs. Descartes and Locke on the Human Person and End-of-Life Ethics', *International Philosophical Quarterly*, Vol. 35 (September 1995), pp. 319–30.

Morris, Thomas V., *Divine and Human Action*, Ithaca, NY: Cornell University Press, 1988.

Nagel, Ernest, *The Structure of Science*, Indianapolis: Hackett, 1979.

Nagel, Thomas, *The Last Word*, New York: Oxford University Press, 1997.

Nagel, Thomas, *The View From Nowhere*, New York: Oxford University Press, 1986.

O'Connor, Timothy, *Persons and Causes*, New York: Oxford University Press, 2000.

O'Connor, Timothy and Jacobs, Jonathan D., 'Emergent Individuals', *Philosophical Quarterly*, Vol. 53 (October 2003), pp. 540–55.

O'Connor, Timothy and Wong, Hong Yu, 'The Metaphysics of Emergence', *Nous*, Vol. 39:4 (2005), pp. 659–79.

O'Hear, Anthony, *Beyond Evolution: Human Nature and the Limits of Evolutionary Explanation*, New York: Oxford University Press, 1997.

Papineau, David, *Philosophical Naturalism*, Oxford: Blackwell, 1993.

Plantinga, Alvin, 'Materialism and Christian Belief', in van Inwagen, Peter and Zimmerman, Dean (eds), *Persons: Human and Divine*, Oxford: Clarendon Press, 2007, pp. 99–141.

Plantinga, Alvin, 'Reply to Peter', paper presented to the Department of Philosophy, Notre Dame University, Fall 2007.

Plantinga, Alvin, *Warrant and Proper Function*, New York: Oxford University Press, 1993.

Plantinga, Alvin, 'Advice to Christian Philosophers', *Faith and Philosophy: Journal of the Society of Christian Philosophers*, Vol. 1:3 (July 1984), pp. 253–71.

Post, John F., *Metaphysics*, New York: Paragon House, 1991.

Putnam, Hilary, *Reason, Truth and History*, Cambridge: Cambridge University Press, 1981.

Rachels, James, *Created from Animals*, Oxford: Oxford University Press, 1990.

Rachels, James, *The End of Life*, Oxford: Oxford University Press, 1986.

Reppert, Victor, *C. S. Lewis's Dangerous Idea*, Downer Groves, IL: InterVarsity Press, 2003.

Rescher, Nicholas, *The Limits of Science*, Berkeley: University of California Press, 1984.

Reuben, Julie, *The Making of the Modern University*, Chicago: University of Chicago Press, 1996.

Rist, John, *Real Ethics: Rethinking the Foundations of Morality*, Cambridge: Cambridge University Press, 2003.
Rosenthal, David M. (ed.), *Materialism and the Mind–Body Problem*, Englewood Cliffs, NJ: Prentice-Hall, 1971.
Rudder Baker, Lynne, *Persons and Bodies: A Constitution View*, Cambridge: Cambridge University Press, 2000.
Ruse, Michael, *The Darwinian Paradigm*, London: Routledge, 1989.
Ruse, Michael, 'Evolutionary Theory and Christian Ethics', in *The Darwinian Paradigm*, London: Routledge, 1989, pp. 262–9.
Ruse, Michael, and Wilson, E. O., 'Moral Philosophy as Applied Science', *Philosophy*, Vol. 61 (1986), pp. 173–92.

Sagan, Carl, *Cosmos*, New York: Random House, 1980.
Schaeffer, Francis, *Escape from Reason*, Downers Grove, IL: InterVarsity Press, 1968.
Searle, John, *Freedom and Neurobiology*, New York: Columbia University Press, 2007.
Searle, John, *Mind: A Brief Introduction*, Oxford: Oxford University Press, 2004.
Searle, John, *The Mystery of Consciousness*, New York: New York Review of Books, 1997.
Searle, John, *The Rediscovery of the Mind*, Cambridge, MA: MIT Press, 1992.
Searle, John, *Minds, Brains, and Science*, Cambridge, MA: Harvard University Press, 1984.
Searle, John, 'Minds, Brains, and Programs', *Behavioral and Brain Sciences*, Vol. 3 (1980), pp. 417–24.
Sehon, Scott R., 'Teleology and the Nature of Mental States', *American Philosophical Quarterly*, Vol. 31 (January 1994), pp. 63–72.
Sellars, Wilfred, *Science, Perception, and Reality*, London: Routledge & Kegan Paul, 1963.
Sellars, Wilfred and Hospers, John (eds), *Readings in Ethical Theory*, Englewood Cliffs, NJ: Prentice-Hall, 1970.
Shockey, Peter, *Reflections of Heaven*, New York: Doubleday, 1999.
Sibley, Frank, 'Aesthetic and Nonaesthetic', *Philosophical Review*, Vol. 74 (April 1965), pp. 135–59.
Smith, Barry (ed.), *Parts and Moments: Studies in Logic and Formal Ontology*, Munich: Philosophia Verlag, 1982.
Stalnaker, Robert C., *Inquiry*, Cambridge, MA: MIT Press, 1984.
Storm, Howard, *My Descent Into Hell*, New York: Doubleday, 2005.
Swinburne, Richard, *Is there a God?*, Oxford: Oxford University Press, 1996.
Swinburne, Richard, 'The Origin of Consciousness', in *Cosmic Beginnings*

and Human Ends, Matthews, Clifford N., and Varghese, Roy Abraham (eds), Chicago and La Salle, IL: Open Court, 1995, pp. 355–78.

Swinburne, Richard, *Evolution of the Soul*, rev. edn, Oxford: Clarendon Press, 1993.

Swinburne, Richard, *The Existence of God*, Oxford: Clarendon Press, 1979.

Taliaferro, Charles and Goetz, Stewart, 'The Prospect of Christian Materialism', *Christian Scholar's Review*, Vol. 37:3 (Spring 2008), pp. 303–21.

van Inwagen, Peter, 'Plantinga's Replacement Argument', in *Alvin Plantinga*, Baker, Deane-Peter (ed.), Cambridge: Cambridge University Press, 2007, pp. 188–200.

Wagner, Steven J., and Warner, Richard (eds), *Naturalism: A Critical Appraisal*, Notre Dame: University of Notre Dame Press, 1993.

Whittaker, David J., *The Essential Orson Pratt*, Salt Lake City: Signature Books, 1991.

Willard, Dallas, 'How Concepts Relate the Mind to its Objects: The "God's Eye View" Vindicated', *Philosophia Christi*, Vol. 1:2 (1999), pp. 5–20.

Willard, Dallas, *Logic and the Objectivity of Knowledge*, Athens, OH: University of Ohio Press, 1984.

Williams, Clifford, 'Topic Neutrality and the Mind–Body Problem', *Religious Studies*, Vol. 36 (2000), pp. 203–7.

Williams, Clifford, 'Christian Materialism and the Parity Thesis', *International Journal for Philosophy of Religion*, Vol. 39 (February 1996), pp. 1–14.

Wright, Crispin, 'The Conceivability of Naturalism', in *Conceivability and Possibility*, Gendler, Tamar Szabo and Hawthorne, John (eds), Oxford: Clarendon Press, 2002, pp. 401–39.

Yolton, John W., *Thinking Matter: Materialism in Eighteenth-Century Britain*, Minneapolis: University of Minnesota Press, 1983.

Name and Subject Index